PRAISE FOR *MEDITATION FOR THE LOVE OF IT*

"This is classic wisdom of the East, cast in a very personal and accessible form. It is authoritative and inspiring and will make you want to meditate for the highest reasons and in the most effective ways."

ANDREW WEIL, MD, author of *Spontaneous Healing* and
Meditation for Optimum Health

"This is an inspired, beautiful, and thoroughly sage-like book! Sally Kempton writes about meditation as very few can—combining the perspectives of scientist, devoted seeker, authoritative spokesperson of the ancient tradition, and, I venture to say, one who dearly loves and seeks to know the highest truths. *Meditation for the Love of It* offers both practical teachings on 'how to' meditate and an inspired survey of what meditation ultimately is meant to lead us to, the recognition and capacity to live knowing that life is indeed sacred. I encourage anyone seeking more happiness, clarity, and love in their life to drink of its curative wisdom—better yet apply any of the practices that Sally, so expertly, lays out. You and our world will, no doubt, be made better for it."

ROD STRYKER, founder of ParaYoga, author of *The Four Desires*

"Love this book! Sally Kempton is a modern communicator of a traditional practice, and in this book she generously shares her forty-plus years as a committed explorer of the soul. With great compassion and depth of experience, she affirms the challenges of quieting the mind while opening you to those realms of consciousness where you are able to exist wondrously within the pulse and flow of your own being. Her poetic prose invites you into the vast landscape of the mind, where all are welcome, all are divine. I'm grateful to Sally for this how-to guide for the soul, and I am excited to deepen my own experience of meditation through her inspiration and guidance."

SEANE CORN, international yoga teacher and activist,
co-founder of *Off the Mat, Into the World*

"A thoughtful, intuitive, and uncommonly well-written book, which can only be welcomed by all who follow the way of meditation."

PETER MATTHIESSEN, author of *The Snow Leopard*

"Sally Kempton is one of the great realized teachers on the meditation path, whose Integral understanding of life merges seamlessly with her mastery of meditation. She is a guide for our time."

KEN WILBER, author of *A Brief History of Everything*

"One of the most practical, clear, and fascinating guides on meditation that has ever been written. This book can totally revolutionize your meditation practice and quite possibly your life!"

JOHN FRIEND, founder of *Anusara Yoga*

"Sally Kempton is a true gift to the yoga world, for she is able to communicate the living wisdom of meditation through her engaging, natural, and practical writing style, which vibrates with flowing consciousness. Sally awakens meditation from within, and her teachings in this book will resonate with people at all levels of experience on the spiritual path."

SHIVA REA, yogini, martial artist, and creator of *Yoga Shakti, Inner Flow Yoga,* and *Solar Flow Yoga* DVDs

"Deep thanks for *Meditation for the Love of It.* It is a warm, gentle, immediately relevant book that will help many people and touch many hearts."

ROBERT A. JOHNSON, author of *We, Inner Work,* and *Balancing Heaven and Earth*

"Sally Kempton is well equipped to guide on how to love our way to the divine life and the joyous oneness it epitomizes. I often recommend Sally Kempton to my own meditation students as a realized guide on the path of awakening. The chapter on her three-week meditation program alone is worth the price of this book, but I would say that the true delight here begins with getting to know this extraordinary yogi Sally Kempton. We are all blessed to have her and her genuine tantric lineage and teaching transmission in our lifetime."

LAMA SURYA DAS, author of *Natural Radiance* and
Awakening the Buddha Within

"*Meditation for the Love of It* is a gift to the world; a kiss to the inner life."

MARIANA CAPLAN, PHD, author of *Halfway up the Mountain*
and *Eyes Wide Open*

"Sally Kempton can awaken your heart and still your mind in a way that will radically amaze and delight you. If you are going use just one guide to meditation, this book should be it."

MARC GAFNI, PHD, author of *Soul Prints,* co-founder of iEvolve,
Integral Spiritual Experience, Center for World Spirituality

"Don't meditate because you think it is good for you—that can be a waste of time—do it because your soul craves the love it was meant for. Let sitting down on your cushion be a rendezvous with your beloved. Meditation can be the most fulfilling love relationship you will ever have in your life—a love that lasts more than one night, a love that is true, eternal, boundless, delight. With this book to show you how, begin now to meditate for the love of it."

SHARON GANNON, author of *Jivamukti Yoga:
Practices for Liberating Body and Soul*

MEDITATION
FOR THE
LOVE
OF IT

MEDITATION
FOR THE
LOVE
OF IT

enjoying your own deepest experience

SALLY KEMPTON

sounds true
Boulder, Colorado

Sounds True, Inc.
Boulder, CO 80306

Cover and book design by Jennifer Miles
Printed in Canada
Permissions credits listed on page 355
Every effort has been made to contact the license holders for quoted content in
this book. All questions about permissions should be directed to the permis-
sions department at Sounds True: 413 S. Arthur Ave., Louisville, CO 80027.

Library of Congress Cataloging-in-Publication Data
Kempton, Sally.
    Meditation for the love of it : enjoying your own deepest experience /
Sally Kempton.
        p. cm.
    Rev. ed. of: The heart of meditation.
    Includes bibliographical references and index.
    ISBN 978-1-60407-081-1
    1. Siddha yoga (Service mark) I. Kempton, Sally. Heart of meditation.
II. Title.
    BL1283.755.K46 2010
    294.5'435—dc22

                                            2010026782

E-book ISBN 978-1-60407-329-4

10 9 8 7 6 5 4 3 2 1

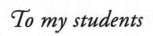

To my students

Set fire to the self within by the practice of meditation.

—SHVETASHVATARA UPANISHAD

CONTENTS

ix ACKNOWLEDGMENTS

xi FOREWORD
by Elizabeth Gilbert

xv PREFACE

1 INTRODUCTION
Awakening to Meditation

9 CHAPTER ONE
The Lure of Meditation

25 CHAPTER TWO
How Do We Experience the Inner Self?

49 CHAPTER THREE
Preparing for Practice

71 CHAPTER FOUR
Choosing the Right Doorway

109 CHAPTER FIVE
Moving Inward: The Practice of Oneness

125 CHAPTER SIX
*Working with the Mind, Part I:
Navigating the Thought-Stream*

141 CHAPTER SEVEN
*Working with the Mind, Part II:
Liberating Your Thoughts*

163 CHAPTER EIGHT
Letting the Shakti Lead

Contents

183   CHAPTER NINE
      Where Do You Find Yourself?
      A Road Map of the Meditation Journey

233   CHAPTER TEN
      Coming Out of Meditation:
      Contemplation, Recollection, and Journal Writing

245   CHAPTER ELEVEN
      The Daily Life of a Meditator:
      Holding Inner Attention

263   CHAPTER TWELVE
      The Three-Week Breakthrough Program

289   CHAPTER THIRTEEN
      The Process of Ripening

297   EPILOGUE
      Let the Inner Dance Unfold

301   APPENDIX ONE
      Kundalini

313   APPENDIX TWO
      Troubleshooting Guide

335   NOTES

345   GLOSSARY

351   SOME FURTHER READING

355   PERMISSIONS CREDITS

357   INDEX

367   ABOUT THE AUTHOR

ACKNOWLEDGMENTS

*M*uch of what I know about meditation I learned from Swami Muktananda and Gurumayi Chidvilasananda, to whom I offer immense gratitude.

My inner life also owes a lot to the inspiration of Ramakrishna Paramahamsa, to the Kashmir Shaivite guru Abhinavagupta and his disciple Kshemaraja, and to the twentieth-century sage Ramana Maharshi.

Thanks to everyone who read this book in both its earlier and later incarnations, and offered valuable suggestions, including Jonathan Shimkin, Margaret Bendet, Swami Ishwarananda, Paul Muller-Ortega, Rudy Wurlitzer, John Friend, Richard Gillett, and at Sounds True, Tami Simon, Jennifer Coffee, and my brilliant editor, Haven Iverson.

Thanks to the students whose questions and insights helped teach me how to communicate subtle truths in words. Deep bows to my friends on the journey, particularly to Ruthie Hunter, whose insightful support has been indispensable in my life as a teacher, and to Marc Gafni for his wisdom and creativity both as a colleague and as a provocateur. Bringing *Meditation for the Love of It* to publication would not have been possible without the help of Michael Zimmerman. Many thanks to him.

Finally, now and forever, I offer salutations to the original guru of gurus, Shiva Mahadeva, the inner guide who lives as

Acknowledgments

Awareness in all of us, and is present wherever the truth is known and expressed. And above all, to the ever-playful Shakti, the pulsing love at the heart of reality, who has become all that is, and by whose grace we are each, in the end, set free.

FOREWORD

*T*he thing about me and meditation is that I do it pretty much all the time. If meditation is devotional, focused, one-pointed concentration on a single thought or notion or feeling . . . well, turns out I'm really fantastic at that. Would you like to know what I was meditating about this morning, as I walked my dog in the lovely summer woods? I'd recently had a quarrel with a friend of mine, and I was meditating on how unfairly he had treated me. With devotional, focused, one-pointed concentration, I got my meditation boiled down to a single word, echoing endlessly throughout my head: *unfair, unfair, unfair, unfair, unfair . . .*

So that was a successful, enlightening way to spend a few focused hours.

But that's not my only accomplishment! Sometimes I also find myself lost in this deep old meditation: *tired, tired, tired, tired, tired . . .*

On other days, it's: *stressed, stressed, stressed, stressed, stressed . . .*

Or: *hungry, hungry, hungry, hungry, hungry . . .*

And although such meditations are, of course, *deeply* uplifting, after a while you do start to wonder if perhaps you could be putting your mind to better use. You start to wonder if this is all you are—a constant singsongy litany of complaint, of want, of indignation, of frustration, of weariness. Is this really how you want to spend your one miracle of a human life? In a clanging mental cage of never-ending blah-blah-blah . . . ?

Yeah, me neither.

This why, over the years, I've made efforts to replace my bouts of *accidental* meditation with a practice of *deliberate* meditation—which is to say, I have been striving to learn the art of replacing the mundane din with a mind full of quiet wonder. What I really want (what we all want, I believe, deep down inside) is the ability to choose my own thoughts, rather than living forever in the sometimes whiny, sometimes angry, sometimes lethargic, always chattering monkey-hut of my unfettered human brain.

My journey began over ten years ago, when I started practicing hatha yoga because of a physical ailment, but found myself strangely transported by the short (but powerful) episodes of guided meditation that followed each practice. My curiosity about that feeling—the absolutely unaccustomed sense of peace and well-being that meditation fleetingly brought upon me—led me to seek out true teachers, who could help me learn how to master this practice. Luckily for me, my search led me to Sally Kempton, whose writings on meditation were beyond helpful to me; they were lifesaving.

The wonderful gift of Sally is her utter lack of pretension. She is not only one of the best meditation teachers in the world; she is also *one of us*. She manages to fearlessly explore the outer reaches of the universe without ever losing the warm voice of your dear friend from just around the block. Most generously of all, Sally is honest about her own shortcomings. She is unafraid to share her own disappointments, her own frustrating episodes where meditation lost all its joy for her and became inaccessible, dry, or a chore. And then she shows us how she got it all back again, how she stubbornly forged her way once more to the source of all enduring sweetness. And then she shows us how we can get there, too.

Sally's groundedness—her supreme approachability—is a gift beyond measure in a field of study that too often turns teachers into imperious, droning despots of obscure esoterica. Simply put, a patronizing perfectionist is not what you need when you're learning the bone-rattlingly difficult practice of meditation. You don't need somebody who will make you feel even *worse* about your very natural human failings. Instead, you need real warmth and compassion, patience and empathy. Sally has all this.

Not to mention, of course, that she is an encyclopedia of utter wisdom. *Meditation for the Love of It* is like a precious road map, generously handed over from a seasoned and experienced pilgrim. Think of this book as the most important travel guide you'll ever encounter, written by a true nomad of the mind—one who has faced down every demon, investigated every trick door, unburied every mystical hidden village that Consciousness has to offer—and who now offers to show you the way.

Take her counsel. Take her comfort. Yes—even take her tips. (You will need every one of them along your journey.) Best of all, though, please take with you a measure of Sally Kempton's spirit—the irresistibly fun part of her who recognizes that meditation should not merely be a lifeline, or a salvation, but should also be an adventure, nothing less than a stupendous exaltation, a thrilling revolution of the self. What else, after all, are we going to do with our short, wondrous lives that could possibly be more important than transforming ourselves, molecule by molecule, into an experience of pure love?

Embrace that teaching, and watch your mind start to change. And then watch your life start to change.

As Sally puts it so beautifully: "Let the inner dance unfold." *Why not start now?*

—Elizabeth Gilbert
August, 2010

PREFACE

I learned meditation from an Indian guru, a master who worshiped reality as divine energy, or shakti. He was a yogi of radical accomplishment and fearsome discipline, and he also used more abstract words like "Consciousness," "Awareness," and "God" to describe the mystery at the heart of life. Yet the great lesson he taught me was how to connect to the pulsing energy that makes life juicy and delicious, while at the same time being aware of an observing, detached Presence that stands aside from all activity. In the years I lived with him and the years since, his example prodded me to do whatever I could to unite the two sides of my nature—the devotional, emotional part that loves the melting sweetness of an opening heart, and the objective Knower that holds all experience in spacious awareness. That fusion of knowing and loving is what I call devotional contemplative *tantra*. It is what inspires me to meditate. It is what I have tried to convey in this book.

This way of meditating is tantric in that it recognizes the world and ourselves as a tapestry woven of one single intelligent energy. It is devotional because it cultivates a loving attentiveness to ourselves and the world. It is contemplative because it asks us to turn into and take rest in the interior spaciousness where we know the self as pure transcendent awareness.

I should also let you know what I mean when I use the word *tantra*. There are many schools of tantra, but the tantric tradition

I follow is at its heart a methodology, a set of yogic practices that aim at yoking us (*yoga* means "yoke") with the numinous energy at the heart of things. One fundamental premise of tantra is that a skillful practitioner can use anything—any moment, any feeling, any type of experience—to unite with the divine.

The core tantric strategy is to harness and channel all our energies, including the apparently distracting or obstructive ones, rather than trying to suppress or eliminate them. When we do that, the energy within thoughts, within emotions, in our moods, and even in intense feelings like anger or terror or desire, can expand and reveal the ground that underlies everything, the pure creative potential of consciousness itself. Tantrikas call that creative potential shakti.

Shakti, the so-called feminine aspect of divine reality (often personified in Hindu tradition as a goddess), is the subtle pulsation of creative potency that permeates all experience. It is normally so subtle and hidden that tuning into shakti can feel as if the veils came off your senses, or like that moment in *The Wizard of Oz* when the landscape goes from black-and-white to Technicolor. In our reflective moments, the felt sense of shakti can be accessed by sensing the life force that pulses in the breath, and that is often experienced as energy currents moving in the body. In the yoga traditions, this internal shakti is called *kundalini*. It is quite literally the power that impels spiritual evolution. Though kundalini has hundreds of facets, one of the simplest ways we experience it is as a subtle energetic pull—sometimes called the "meditation current"—that draws the mind inward when we meditate. Many of the practices in this book help draw your attention to this energetic presence in the mind and body.

You'll also find some devotional practices and invocations in these pages. I offer them for the same reason that I practice them: because they help awaken the heart, and open us to the love that is the true essence of life.

Awakening to *Meditation*

*O*ne summer afternoon during a meditation retreat, I discovered that I contain the entire universe. It happened quite unexpectedly, all in a rush. I was sitting with my eyes closed in a room with several hundred other people, very much aware of the sensations in my body and of the faint rustles, coughs, and other sounds around me. The next thing I knew, there was a kind of implosion. Instead of being around me, the room with all its sensations and sounds was inside me. My awareness started to swell until I could feel the earth, the sky, and even the galaxy inside me. In that moment, I understood, with a surety that was both exhilarating and terrifying, that there is only one thing in the universe—that it is Awareness, and that Awareness is me.

The experience faded after an hour or so, but the understanding it gave me has never gone away.

At the time, I'd been traveling a winding spiritual path for a couple of years. Like so many people, I started meditating not because I longed for enlightenment, but because I was in a moderate life-crisis, and hoped meditation would make me feel better. I was living in New York, writing for *Esquire, New York Magazine,* and the *Village Voice,* leading the life that my left-wing humanist upbringing had laid out for me, priding myself on my hipster creds. On the outside, it was fine. I had an advance from a major publisher, a new boyfriend whom I was sure was the love of my life, a rent-controlled apartment—and a chronic case of restlessness and slight despair that never really went away. I'd already investigated marriage, politics, romance, psychotherapy, and the fruits of money without discovering an antidote to my low-grade emotional pain. Meditation drew me because it seemed like a way of getting to the roots of myself. Even in those days, when meditation was still considered an activity for saints, hippies, and other eccentrics, it was supposed to be a great way to settle the mind.

My new boyfriend happened to be a seasoned tourist on the spiritual circuit. He encouraged me to take a three-month spiritual training being conducted by a Bolivian teacher named Oscar Ichazo. The training promised enlightenment—which didn't happen, at least not for me. It did, however, confront me with some inner demons I'd been doing my best to ignore. It also made me fall in love both with yogic wisdom and with the refining power of spiritual community. Along with getting to know some of the tricks of my own ego, I began to crave interior experience.

So when I arrived at that summer meditation retreat, I was ready to let meditation transform me. It was why I had come: the retreat was being conducted by a celebrated spiritual master from India, famous for being able to unlock meditative depth in others.

After that awareness-expanding meditation, I was in a new relationship to myself and to my own inner world.

I opened my eyes to a world scintillating with love and meaning, and felt sure that I had found the answer to everything I wanted in life. Like my expansion of awareness, ecstasy didn't last; but like the expansion itself, it changed everything. The meditation master in whose presence the experience had arisen became my guru—the teacher whose transmissions and guidance would guide my practice for years to come. And meditation became my path.

KUNDALINI AND MEDITATION

What had happened that afternoon was an awakening of the *kundalini shakti,* the inner energy that nearly every esoteric tradition recognizes as the force behind spiritual transformation. Kundalini (literally, "coiled energy"—so-called because when the energy is inactive it is said to be "coiled") can be awakened in several ways: through yoga postures, through deep meditation, or, as happened that afternoon, through the transmission of energy from a teacher whose own kundalini is active. The awakening of kundalini can be subtle or dramatic, but however it occurs, it brings the energy of Spirit into the foreground of our lives, shifting our priorities and stirring our hidden resources of love, understanding, and insight.

Kundalini's power unfolds as we meditate. The awakened energy draws us into meditative states and begins showing us the tracks of our inner country even as it tunes the body and mind to a new level of subtlety and awareness. Over time, kundalini transforms our vision until we see the world as it really is: not hard and bumpy and irrevocably "other," but filled with a single loving energy that connects us with one another and the world.

The effects of this awakening on my life have been widespread and various. Mainly it has shifted my sense of being. Once I had seen that vastness, no matter how caught up I might get in my thoughts or emotions or agendas, a part of me would always know that I contain a reality beyond all that: that in truth, "I" am expansive Consciousness. Over the years, I have come to measure my spiritual progress by how much I am in alignment with that initial insight—by how firmly I am able to identify myself with Consciousness rather than with the person I sometimes think I am.

It has been a road with many sidetracks and hairpin turns. Yet, little by little, the alignment comes. I've been meditating daily for nearly forty years, and though it didn't happen all at once, I've come to count on entering the space of expanded Awareness for at least a while every day. Over time, meditation has chipped away at my feeling of being only this physical person, defined by my history, my looks, my intelligence, my opinions and emotions. Meditation taught me to identify—precariously at first, then more and more firmly—with that subtler part of myself, with that field of spaciousness behind thoughts, with the tender energy in my heart. With the pulsation of pure spaciousness that arises when thoughts die down. With love.

From the beginning, sitting meditation has been the most reliable way I know to touch the tenderness of pure being. I have treasured it. Of course, my love affair with meditation has been like any other unfolding relationship. It has had its ups and downs, its fertile seasons, and its apparently barren ones. Meditative states, after all, arrive spontaneously and naturally. They come in their own time and their own way, gifts of the unfolding kundalini. I have fallen spontaneously into meditation while walking, writing, or sitting in a meeting. I have also had weeks when I couldn't touch the meditation bandwidth at all. Meditation is often surprising, and certainly cannot be forced.

But neither can it be approached passively—which is the point of this book. The effort required of a meditator is quite subtle, a matter of attunement and awareness. We learn this attunement gradually, and we learn it by meditating. Fortunately, much of what we learn can be shared, and over the years as I've worked with students and taught classes and retreats in meditation, I've found that some of the attitudes and practices that have helped me have also been useful to other people. This book evolved as an offering to other committed meditators. It is a way to share certain principles and attitudes that meditation has taught me, and that seem to work not just for me but for others as well.

The most important principle to understand about meditation is this: we meditate to know ourselves. We usually think of meditation as a practice or a process, yet meditation is also a relationship. If it is a process, then it is the process of coming into loving relationship with our own Consciousness. In the *Bhagavad Gita,* Krishna defines meditation for his disciple Arjuna by saying, *"dhyanen atmani pashyanti"*: "In meditation, the Self [the pure Awareness that is our essential nature] is seen."[1] This sounds like a simple enough statement, but as we meditate, we come to realize that knowing the Self is far from simple. Which "self" do we encounter when we meditate? The greater Self, for sure—the *atman,* as the Indian sages call it, the luminous Consciousness beyond the discursive mind. Yet, we also encounter a lot of other aspects of our selves, including the parts of us that seem to hinder the experience of our essence. One of the boons of meditation, if we allow ourselves to engage in it fully, is that we not only come to see all this; we also learn how to move through it with love. In this daily act of plunging into our inner world, the separated parts of ourselves do come together. The loose ends of our personalities meld with our Awareness, and we become whole.

The spirit is so near that you can't see it! But reach for it . . . Don't be the rider who gallops all night And never sees the horse that is beneath him.

—RUMI [2]

Of course, this level of transformation doesn't happen overnight. That is where we sometimes get confused. Most of us enter into meditation rather naively. We bring along expectations, ideas, assumptions. For instance, we sometimes imagine that successful meditation is a kind of prolonged honeymoon in which we rove through fields of bliss and float along deep lagoons of peace. If our relationship with the inner world becomes troublesome, boring, or more intimate than we bargained for, we feel frustrated, disappointed, or even ashamed. We might decide that we really aren't so good at meditation, and it is often at this point that we give it up.

We would feel a lot better if we realized that meditation is like any other intimate relationship: it requires patience, commitment, and deep tolerance. Just as our encounters with others can be wondrous but also baffling, scary, and even irritating, our encounters with the self have their own moods and flavors. Like any other relationship, this one changes over time. And it is best undertaken with love.

CHAPTER ONE

The Lure of Meditation

Meditation is not something for which you need a special talent, the way you need a talent for mathematics or art. The real key to going deep in meditation is *wanting* to go deep. The more you crave the taste of the inner world, the easier it is to meditate. In Sanskrit that desire is called *mumukshutva,* the wish for the freedom that comes with Self-knowledge. Your desire doesn't have to be huge at first. Even a slight spark of interest is enough, because the inner world is actually yearning to open up to you. Once your meditation energy has been awakened, it keeps pulsing inside, just under the skin. It is constantly sending you signals, whispering, "Here I am! Meet me! I'm your guide! I have so many things to show you about yourself!" That is why the moment you become truly interested in knowing your Self, in entering the field of your own Awareness, the inner world begins to reveal itself. It can't help it. That's what it exists to do.

The problem is that we aren't always interested in our meditation. Many of us, when we meditate at all, do it because we know it is good for us. Perhaps it is part of our ongoing self-improvement project or a strategy we use to keep stress at bay. Shortly after this book began taking shape, a friend complained to me about her meditation practice. It had become flat, she said. It didn't deeply engage her. In fact, she didn't much enjoy meditating. I could tell from her tone that as a serious spiritual practitioner, she felt slightly ashamed about this. So I asked her, "What's the best thing about meditating for you?"

She thought for a minute, and then said, "It's my therapy. When I sit down, I'm usually burning with inner upheaval, worried about something, or just stuffed with negativity. I repeat my mantra for fifteen or twenty minutes, and when I get up, my mind is calm. I feel quiet. I can go on with my day." Then she said, "I know I have to do it every day, or else my mind makes me crazy."

My friend is getting something important from her practice. In fact, she's experiencing one of meditation's major gifts: its power to clear the mind. Yet because that's all she wants, she gets up from meditation just at the moment when the real sweetness inside her could start to reveal itself. It's when the mind calms that we begin to discern the wideness of our own being, the love inside. If, along with appreciating meditation's therapeutic benefits, my friend could meditate for the sake of entering into herself, she might stay in meditation a little longer and go deeper than she is going now.

The people who seem to get the most out of their practice are the ones who simply *enjoy* the act of meditating. This doesn't necessarily mean that they have exotic experiences. Far from it. Many swear that they have never so much as glimpsed a light or seen a vision or felt their thoughts dissolve into spaciousness. Yet if you listen to them talk about their practice, you realize that they are tasting the richness of their entire meditation experience in all its seasons.

When you approach your meditation with interest, that simple time of sitting becomes enjoyable in itself. You listen to the whisper of the breath, you savor the pulsation of a mantra—a meditative word—as it sinks through the layers of your consciousness. You enjoy the rising stillness, the vagrant images flitting through the inner space, and the gradual shift into a quieter mind. Each moment, whether dramatic or seemingly boring, can be full of fascination. You are with yourself. You are with God. Your meditation is an entry into the cave of the heart, the cave of the spirit.

On the other hand, if you look at meditation as a duty, or if you approach it with impatience and rigid expectation, waiting for an *experience* and feeling bored or angry with yourself when your mind doesn't immediately get quiet, you fall out of relationship with your meditation. That is because meditation is anything but a mechanical act. Seeing your inner experience as boring, feeling discouraged when it doesn't unfold as you think it should, telling yourself "I'm not a good meditator anyway"— all this is actually a rejection of your inner energy, your shakti. Just as a friend cools toward you when you hold back from her, the shakti that makes your meditation dynamic becomes elusive when you ignore it. But it will leap up to meet you once you begin attending to it with love.

So one of the secrets of deepening our meditation is to discover how to awaken our love for meditation and to keep it alive—even when our experience is subtle or apparently dull.

Take a few moments to look at your own relationship with meditation. How do you feel about meditation? Do you enjoy it? Do you approach it dutifully or methodically? Does it ever surprise you? If you're new to meditation, are you unsure where to start? Do you wonder whether you're doing it "right"? What does meditation mean to you? You can also ask yourself how you feel about the Self you experience in meditation. What is your relationship with that Self?

MEDITATION AS PLAY

Most of us would like to love our meditation. We want it to be a delight to us, a source of joy. For this to happen, it helps to stop worrying about whether you have "good" meditation. The truth is that there is no such thing as "good" or "bad" meditation. There is only your unfolding inner awareness and your relationship to the Self. You don't need to worry, "Suppose I blow this session? Suppose I do something wrong? Suppose I waste my time?" Instead you can look at meditation as an experiment or, better yet, as a game you are playing with yourself, as an exploration. You can give yourself permission to be creative. For example, when you sit to meditate, you might ask, "What will happen if I breathe with the feeling that I'm being breathed by the universe?" Then you could try this and note the results. You might wonder, "How would it be if I spent this meditation period just witnessing my thoughts?" and try that. You might have an impulse to work with some classical form of self-inquiry, like "Who am I?"—and then spend an hour noticing what happens to your feeling of identity. You might think, "I'd like to have a more devotional feeling in meditation," and then spend a few minutes praying or invoking grace with some imaginative form of inner worship, like offering flowers on the altar of the heart. Or you might decide, "Today I'm just going to ask for grace and see where the meditation current takes me," and then surrender yourself to whatever experience comes. You can allow yourself to be playful in how you approach your meditation sessions.

> *The true practice of [meditation] is to sit as if you were drinking water when you are thirsty.*
>
> —SHUNRYU SUZUKI [1]

Permission to Play

I had been meditating for many years before I fully realized that meditation yielded its greatest riches to me when I gave myself permission to play. It happened at a time when I had let myself fall seriously out of relationship with my meditation practice. Ironically, by then I was a swami, a renunciant monk, and a teacher in an order of Indian monks. But, like many people who live in spiritual communities, I had made work and service—*karma yoga*, as it's traditionally called—my core practices. Though in earlier years I had meditated intensely—and experimentally, trying out different approaches and different techniques—at some point my meditation had become fixed in a certain routine. I had my accustomed ways of sitting, of focusing, and I rarely thought to go beyond them. It didn't occur to me to contemplate my meditation experience or to work with my practice. Instead I took it as it came, enjoying the moments of contact with my deeper Self. When these moments didn't come, I sat my daily hour anyway, hoping that kundalini was somehow moving me along. In truth, meditation had become an almost unconscious act—something I did every day and took for granted, like eating and sleeping.

Then one day I found myself assessing my practice. What I found surprised me. I had been meditating for twenty years. I had experienced many positive changes in my character, and my mind had become calmer, sharper, and smarter. My emotions were less unruly. I felt an equanimity I had never had before. I was happier.

Yet it had been some time since I had moved deep into meditation. Usually my thoughts remained, like a substratum of static underneath everything. Usually my consciousness stayed on the surface of itself. In fact, I spent a lot of time drifting through realms of thought and reverie.

It was clearly time for a reevaluation. So I began asking myself some basic questions:

Why do I meditate?

What is my real goal in meditation?

What do I like about my meditation practice?

What do I feel needs improvement or change?

Would I be willing to live with my current level of inner experience for the next ten years?

The answers I came up with were a little disconcerting. The first thing I realized was that the shallowness of my meditation was a symptom of lost clarity about my goal. If you had asked me what I wanted from meditation, I would have glibly answered, "To realize my true Self," but in reality I was not living as though Self-realization were a real goal. Instead I was using my spiritual practices as Band-Aids or perhaps as tonics—nourishing techniques that I employed to keep myself in good working order.

WHAT DO YOU REALLY WANT FROM MEDITATION?

As I was in the process of discovering, to ask yourself what you really want from meditation is a key first step in building or re-building your practice. For me, the answers came with a surprising power. I wanted freedom, I realized. I wanted an end to the anxiety and craving and fear that have created so much unnecessary suffering in my life. I wanted meditation to take me beyond the neuroses, attachments, beliefs, and fears that still plagued my inner world. And I wanted meditation to be what it was when I first discovered it—dynamic and engaging, a rendezvous I approached with love and excitement no matter what happened.

Set fire to the Self within by the practice of meditation. Be drunk with the wine of divine love. Thus shall you reach perfection.

—SHVETASHVATARA UPANISHAD [2]

At that point, I stopped and reminded myself that meditation can't always be fun. Meditation is also a process of purification, I told myself, so there are bound to be days when sitting is somewhat boring and even painful—aching knees, long stretches of time when I just field my thoughts. If I insisted that meditation be fun all the time, I wouldn't last long as a meditator. I wouldn't be able to sustain the simple daily effort it took to sit every morning and keep my mind from wandering.

But wait a minute! I said to myself. Don't be so puritanical! Even if it's not always fun, surely meditation should engage me, interest me, and create anticipation for the next meditation. Otherwise why would I do it? It's all very well to say that we meditate to become better people, or to give ourselves the inner wherewithal to live compassionately, or to be better parents or writers or bankers. Those are fine reasons to meditate, of course. Yet, I thought, the sages who first drew me to the spiritual path—Ramakrishna, Ramana Maharshi, Kabir, Muktananda—lured me with their joy in the quest, with their wonder at the experience of the inner world. There was a promise, in fact, that meditation would be dynamic, would open up something unseen and unheard, would surprise me, extending my senses to a new level of awareness. That it would be, in fact, joyful. I did truly want joy in my meditation.

The Infinite Goodness has such wide arms that it takes in whatever turns to it.

—DANTE ALIGHIERI [3]

With this in mind, I decided to reenter my meditation practice as a beginner. So I began approaching my daily practice as an experiment. I decided that I would let myself work with my meditation in an open way, not looking for specific results. I wouldn't expect anything when I sat. I would simply regard the time I spent in meditation as a time of learning, as a time to be with my own consciousness and with the basic teachings of my tradition. I would see what was there. I also decided to meditate with a sense of fun. In other words, I would give myself permission to bring an element of lightness and spontaneity into my meditation. I would let myself play. In fact, each time I sat to meditate, I would consciously remind myself, "It's okay to be playful."

These two strategies—seeing meditation as an experiment and giving myself permission to play—turned out to be crucial to the process that followed. First of all, they helped me slip past the voice of my inner critic, the judgmental inner observer who often hovered over my shoulder, pointing out the flaws in my practice. Second, the experimental attitude freed me from a tendency to make meditation into a routine. Fear of meditating in the "wrong" way or of simply wasting my time had sometimes made me turn techniques that were supposed to be helpful guidelines into unbreakable rules, which became hedges around my imagination and intuition. The realization that it was fine to play with meditation uncoiled springs of tension, so that I could begin to see what was actually there when I closed my eyes and turned my attention inward.

The first instruction I began to play with came from Ramana Maharshi, one of my early heroes. His words: "Taking the Self as the target of your attention, you should keenly know it in the heart." The focus on the Self—the underlying Awareness behind all experience—was the crucial part of the equation. But the second part of Ramana's instruction, I'd always found, was just as essential. Of course, I thought I "knew" the inner Self. I even had standard ways to turn toward the heart. But on this particular morning, I decided just to turn my focus inside. Not to work with any particular technique, just to sit with my attention trained inward, on the field of my own inner heart.

Exercise: Exploring the Inner Heart

Perhaps you would like to try this. Close your eyes, and let your attention move gradually down toward the inner center behind the breastbone, a few inches to the right of the physical heart. You can start by focusing on the front of your breastbone, about eight finger-widths below the U-shaped bone at the base of your throat. Then, imagine a plumb line dropping from just behind your nostrils into the middle of the chest, behind this spot on the breastbone. Let the breath flow in and out to that spot. Feel and sense the energy there, in the inner body, behind the breastbone. Without judgment, notice how the energy feels there in the heart-center. It might feel soft or prickly, melting or hard. For now, let the inhalation flow from the nostrils down into the heart center, and flow back up from the heart before it passes out through the nostrils.

THE FIELD OF YOUR CONSCIOUSNESS

When we turn into the energy of the heart center, we may experience it in many different ways. Sometimes, especially at the beginning, emotions come up—love, sadness, even anger. If we focus on the energy in the emotions, rather than the content, the emotions we encounter begin to melt, and their energy takes us deeper. At other times, we may see colors, or simply feel energetic sensations. That day, I focused on the felt sensations of energy in my heart-field. I let my attention move backward, moving "into" the energy-field. I let myself be with it, just as it was. As I sat with this inner field, I noticed that I was observing it as something outside of me. I began to wonder what would happen if instead of keeping myself outside the field of my heart-energy, I were to actively enter into it. Would this bring me more deeply into the inner world?

At that point, I did something that is rather hard to describe: I entered the field. I did it by imagining an opening in the heart-space, and projecting my attention through it, as if I were entering into the energy in the heart. As I did, the heart seemed to expand. I became aware that there was a seemingly endless spaciousness behind the heart. I began to "move" through it—not of course, moving my body, but my attention.

After a few minutes of traveling through this inner field, I found myself in a deep heart-space. I call it a "heart-space" because when I was in it, I felt rooted in myself: still, soothed, and full of loving tenderness—all feelings I associate with the heart. My mind was quite awake, and from time to time would send up a thought or a query. But "I" was sunk deep into this heart-space.

I began to explore it, to feel out its qualities and its subtle attributes. I could feel a pulsation, a subtle ripple of movement, a resonance, and as I focused on that pulsation, it opened further. Each time it did, it moved me deeper into the sensation of love. There was a luminous quality to it as well. It was like being inside a soft crystal—utterly transparent and shining.

From then on, my meditations became explorations of the inner heart-field, that world of subtle sensation, love, and clarity. It grew subtler the more I entered it, and the trick to deepening the experience (for me, at least) was to keep moving further into that field of energy.

Sometimes the field of luminosity would take on colors or turn into a landscape. More often it would remain a kinetic experience, a subtle sensation of being touched from within by a loving energy, a presence that moved and flowed, sometimes very light and subtle, sometimes thrillingly intense.

THE INNER BELOVED

After a few months of this kind of practice, I became aware of an elusive, loving Presence within the field of myself. There was something intensely personal about the Presence, as if I were being introduced to an inner lover, the Beloved that the Sufi saints speak of so enticingly. He (at the time, I related to it as "he," though obviously it has no gender) would seem to call to me from inside at certain times of the day—around noon and in the late afternoon. The call took the form of an intense feeling of pressure in the heart. My attention would be pulled inside, so powerfully that it was painful to resist. If I found

> *There is a Secret One inside us; The planets in all the galaxies pass through his hands like beads.*
>
> —KABIR [4]

myself in a meeting or on a walk when the pull came, I would feel irritable because resisting the inner pull to meditate was as uncomfortable as trying to resist hunger pangs or the need to sleep—it was that intense and that physical. If I was sitting at my desk, I would be almost forced to abandon what I was doing, close my eyes, and hurry down the corridors of consciousness toward the presence.

My afternoon and evening meditations became like successive rendezvous with that inner presence. It was elusive, always slightly out of reach, yet each time it surrounded me with a blanket of love that, on different days, throbbed softly or strongly. On the days when I gave in completely to the call and sat until I came out of meditation spontaneously, the encounter with the Beloved was so entrancing, so ecstatic, and so subtly delicious that its afterglow would pervade my entire day. I'd find myself seeing hidden beauty and sweetness in people whom I'd ignored or found irritating, as though I were seeing through the eyes of my inner lover. There were days when I felt literally intoxicated with tenderness.

For several months, my schedule allowed me to make time to sit in meditation for more than an hour each morning and evening. I found, however, that I had to make meditation a major priority; otherwise a resistance—almost a resistance to the intimacy of the encounter—would tempt me to read or walk or in some way fill those hours with activities. But I discovered that if I kept my practice steady, the deepening process remained steady as well, and that when I didn't honor the inner call, it created a kind of distance from myself, an energy barrier that made it more difficult to step into the heart-space the next time.

The encounter with the inner Beloved is one of the most alluring fruits of meditation. But there are many different ways in which your consciousness can open when you sit. I came to realize through these journeys—as I believe you will also find as you take your own journeys into the subtle field of your own Awareness—that the inner world is filled with loving Presence. One secret of encountering that loving Presence in yourself is to pay persistent, tender attention to the energy that presents itself as you meditate. This kind of attention is soft. It's a relaxed, yet intentional willingness to be fully present with yourself, to attend to the energetic substance of your own mind, rather than its contents. You perceive with tenderness whatever arises—a thought, an image, an emotion (even a hard or painful one)—as you feel your way into meditation. Yet you don't get fixed on its contents, on its "story." Instead, you stay with the felt sense of the energy. Presence is a feeling-state, and it emerges when we approach our inner world with intention to feel and sense our way into its mysteries.

THE FRUITS OF DEEP PRACTICE

The processes I've described—questioning my attitudes toward practice, experimenting playfully with meditation, approaching my practice not as a task but as a way of being present with myself—changed my experience of meditation, as it will change yours. Most mysteriously, it changes your relationship to yourself. After just a few months of this exploration, I had more confidence in myself. I sensed an inner solidity and decisiveness that were quite new. Instead of feeling unclear about my truth and needing validation from others in order to accept my own insights as important and valid, I had begun to trust that my inner experiences, my intuitive feelings and reactions, were reliable guides to action. Friends told me that I had become more spontaneous and more "real" in my relationships. More than that, deep layers of shame and unworthiness fell away. All this was—and continues to be—the result of entering into direct relationship with my own shakti, with the subtle energy inside me. One primary teaching of the Indian yogic traditions is that our fears, doubts, and suffering arise from ignorance of our real nature and are burned away through the knowledge of the Self. Over the years, I've often had the feeling that I was experiencing this directly—experiencing how an hour's immersion in my own wider mind, or a few moments of recognizing the play of my own deeper energy in the movement of thoughts, could shift my behavior and relationships.

Use your own light and return to the source of light. This is called practicing eternity.

—LAO-TZU [5]

Meditation is the basis for all inner work. We might struggle conscientiously to change our limiting qualities; we might saturate ourselves with instructions and help, both concrete and subtle. Yet in the end, it is the direct, naked encounter with our own Awareness that shifts our understanding of who we are and gives us the power to stand firmly in the center of our being. No one else can make this happen for us. Meditation does.

To make use of the principles and practices that follow, you needn't commit yourself to meditating for hours at a time. What you do need is continuity of practice, even if at first it's only fifteen or twenty minutes a day. The act of sitting every day with a clear intention to explore your inner being will begin the process. Then, as you learn to pay attention to the signals from within, you'll know when it is time to begin meditating for longer periods. It is your intention, your sense of the goal, that makes even a brief meditation powerful and allows you to enter your own core.

I suggest that as you read, you try the exercises in the chapters. You can do this in several ways. First, you might like to read through a chapter and then go back and practice the exercises.

The world of qualities becomes green and is dried up, but Kabir meditates on the One who is the essence of the world.

—KABIR [6]

Alternatively, you could stop reading when you come to an exercise and try it for a moment or two. Many of these exercises, especially in the early chapters, are designed to help you assimilate one of the basic principles of meditation. Practicing the exercise can actually bring the concept alive. You might also want to keep a journal or notebook beside you as you read, so you can record any insights or inner shifts that arise when you practice an exercise. In that way, reading this book can become an experiment in meditation and contemplation, and an exploration of your own inner world. It is my hope that this exploration brings you revelation and delight, and that it helps you open more deeply to yourself and to the greatness inside you.

CHAPTER TWO

How Do We Experience the Inner Self?

*F*or many people, the first great breakthrough in meditation practice comes when they begin to contemplate their goal. Until then, it is often a rather haphazard process. We close our eyes, following the instructions that we've been given, and then hope that something happens. We wonder if we're doing it right. Does correct meditation mean sticking like a limpet to the point we're focusing on? Is it the focus that brings results? Or is the desired experience something that is just supposed to "happen," to arise on its own? Some of the most dedicated meditators I know have wasted months, even years, wondering what they should be looking for or doing to allow the meditative state to arise. When we have no real idea where we are going, we often end up in a kind of trance or daydream instead.

> *The one you are looking for is the one who is looking.*
>
> —FRANCIS OF ASSISI [1]

There's a football legend about Roy Riegels, a center/lineman for the University of California, Berkeley's 1929 Rose Bowl team, who carried the ball the wrong way down the field, and had almost reached his own team's end zone when he was tackled. Riegels was a great lineman, the story goes. But, of course, none of his skills were of any use once he started running in the wrong direction.

In the same way, however serious a meditator you are, it won't help you if you're not clear about where you're going. So, even when you're beginning your meditation journey, it's enormously important to understand your goal.

The ultimate goal of meditation, of course, is to experience the full emergence of your own pure Consciousness, the inner state of luminosity, love, and wisdom that the Indian tradition calls the "inner Self" or the "true Self" or the "Heart." (A Buddhist might call it "Buddha nature" or "Big Mind"; a Christian might call it "Spirit.") In fact, we want to do more than just experience that state. We want to realize that we are that—not just a body or a personality, but pure Consciousness, pure Awareness. By this definition, a successful meditation is one in which we enter the Self—even if just for a moment. Our intention to understand and experience the Self gives directionality to our consciousness. It's like aiming an arrow. Yet even as we aim our attention toward the Self, we need to remember that we *are* the Self. As Ramana Maharshi said, "Knowing the Self means being the Self."[2] When we forget this—that the Self is not only the goal of our meditation but also who we really are—we inevitably find ourselves stuck in one of the countless byways in the inner world.

The most common of these side roads is reverie—falling into the mazy realms of thought and image. You sit down to meditate and end up caught on some irrelevant thought train, letting it carry you from association to association: "Who was that blues singer? He was blind, from the Bahamas. I think his first name was John. No, Joseph. Jonathan would know. 'Gonna live that life I sing about in my song.' Jonathan's wife—Rachel? Roberta? How many children?"

Losing yourself in thought is not the only way you can get distracted. I know people who have amazingly dynamic meditations: cascades of light, beautiful visions, and brilliant moments of insight—expansions of the mind into absolute spaciousness. Yet their practice doesn't seem to change their relationship to themselves, nor does it help shift the platform on which they live their lives. This is because they treat their meditation like a light show, an entertainment, or an achievement of some kind. They are not looking for their ground, for the Self, for their own essence amid the movement within their meditation. For this reason, despite the gifts they receive in meditation, they don't feel they have gone deep. They don't feel peace. They don't experience satisfaction.

> *The eye through which I see God is the same eye through which God sees me; my eye and God's eye are one eye, one seeing, one knowing, one love.*
>
> —MEISTER ECKHART [3]

So, to begin your meditation practice, become clear about your goal. Begin to look for, to identify, and to identify *with* your essence.

IDENTIFYING THE SELF

As we just saw, the great secret about the Self, the inner God, is that it is you. Ramana Maharshi used to say, "Be as you are. See who you are and remain as the Self."[4] This is the knowledge that all the enlightened spiritual teachers, from Shankaracharya, to Meister Eckhart, to Bodhidharma, have shared. You don't have to get into an altered state to experience it; all you need to do is to become aware of the part of you that sees and knows. When you touch that inner Knower, even for a second, you touch your essence.

Even when a person says, "I am," "This is mine," and so on, his thought goes to that absolute "I" which does not depend on any support. When he contemplates That, he attains lasting peace.

—VIJNANA BHAIRAVA 131 [5]

The way I most easily understand this is to think of myself as composed of two different aspects: a part that changes, that grows and ages; and a part that doesn't. The changing part of me—the body-mind-personality part—looks very different now than she did when she was a twelve-year-old playing Fox and Geese with the neighborhood kids in Princeton, New Jersey. Her occupations and preoccupations have changed radically since then. Not only has this person played all kinds of different roles through the years—student, journalist, spiritual seeker, disciple, monk, teacher—she also has taken on several dozen inner roles. So this changing part has various outer personalities and as many secret selves. There are aspects of the personality that seem ancient and wise, and parts that seem impulsive, undeveloped, and foolish. They assume different attitudes as well. There is vast detachment, along with a large capacity for emotional turmoil; there is frivolity and depth, compassion and selfishness. There are, in short, any number of inner characteristics inhabiting our consciousness, each with its own set of thought patterns and emotions, and each with its own voice.

Yet amid all these different and often conflicting outer roles and inner characters, one thing remains constant: the awareness that holds them. This is the part of the Self that doesn't change. Your awareness of your own existence is the same at this moment as it was when you were two years old. That awareness of being is utterly impersonal. It has no agenda. It doesn't favor one type of personality over another. It looks through them all as if through different windows, but it is never limited by them. Sometimes we experience that awareness as a detached observer—the witness of our thoughts and actions. Sometimes we simply experience it as our felt sense of being: we exist and we feel we exist. The unknown author of *The Book of Privy Counseling,* a fourteenth-century Christian text, describes it as "the naked, stark, elemental awareness that you are as you are."[7] In Kashmir Shaivism, it is called *purno'ham vimarsha,* the "pure

Who is it who knows when the mind is filled with anger or with love? Who is it that is awake when we are sleeping? Who knows that we slept and reports to us on our dream? We have to meditate on that One who is the witness of everything.

—SWAMI MUKTANANDA[6]

awareness of I-am"—the true "I" that is free of the body and continues to exist even after death.

When you focus in and get to know that awareness, it becomes the doorway to your deeper Awareness, or Consciousness. (To avoid confusion, the initial *c* in "consciousness" is capitalized when the word refers to pure or absolute Awareness. It is written in lowercase when it refers to consciousness in one of its ordinary psychological usages, as the state of being aware of something or as a synonym for the human psyche with its faculties of perception, cognition, sensation, and volition. The word "awareness" also receives this treatment.)

Exercise: Become Aware of Your Awareness

Sit comfortably, with your back upright yet relaxed, and your eyes closed. Spend a moment listening to the sounds in the room. Then bring your awareness into your body. Notice how your body feels sitting in your posture. Become aware of the sensation of your thighs meeting the seat you're sitting on, of how the air feels against your skin, how the clothes feel against your body. Notice whether your body is warm or cool. Now feel the sensations in your inner body. Perhaps you are aware of your stomach rumbling. Perhaps you notice sensations of contraction or relaxation in your muscles.

Become aware of your breath—the sensation of the breath entering the nostrils, the slight coolness as it comes in, the slight warmth as it goes out.

Become aware of what is going on in your mind. Observe the thoughts and images that move across your inner screen. Notice the deeper feelings, the emotions, any mental static that arises. You are not trying to change any of this. Simply hold it in your awareness.

Now turn your attention to Awareness itself. Become aware of your own Awareness, the knowingness that lets you perceive all this, the inner spaciousness that holds together all the sensations, feelings, and thoughts that make up your experience in this moment. Focus your attention on your own Awareness, as if you were paying attention to attention itself. Let yourself be that Awareness.

If you keep exploring Awareness in meditation, it emerges more and more distinctly. Thoughts and other sensations gradually recede, and you begin to experience the still, yet fluid field of bare Consciousness that is the underlying ground of you. Eventually, the Awareness that was at first only perceptible in snatches will reveal itself to be a huge expanse of being. "No words are necessary to see into reality," Rumi wrote. "Just be and It is."[8]

According to most of the great Eastern spiritual traditions, our inner awareness/energy, or consciousness, is actually a limited, contracted form of the great Awareness/energy

There is something beyond our mind, which abides in silence within our mind. It is the supreme mystery beyond thought. Let one's mind and spirit rest upon That, and not anything else.

—KENA UPANISHAD [9]

that underlies, creates, and sustains all things. The Upanishads call it Brahman, the Vastness. The sages of Kashmir Shaivism called it Chiti (universal Consciousness), Paramashiva (supreme Auspiciousness), Parama Chaitanya (supreme Consciousness), or Paramatma (supreme Self). The great Shaivite philosopher Abhinavagupta called it Hridaya, the Heart. Physicists today call it the quantum field. In Buddhism it is called the Dharmakaya, the "body" of Truth. And, of course, it is also called God.

In its original, expanded form, that vast creative intelligence encompasses and underlies everything. In an individual, it is the mind-stuff (in Sanskrit, *chitta*) that forms the background of our thoughts, perceptions, and feelings. Kashmir Shaivism, which elaborately describes the different stages that this creative intelligence passes through in the process of becoming the material world, in the end has a simple formula for it: "Supreme Consciousness *(chiti)*, descending from its state of complete freedom and power, becomes the consciousness of a human being *(chitta)* when it begins contracting into the form of objects of perception." In other words, the moment we begin to focus on objects—including thoughts, perceptions, and ideas—we lose touch with the underlying vastness within us. And because thoughts, feelings, sensations, and perceptions fill our awareness almost every moment of our existence, it is no wonder that we rarely see the ocean of Consciousness inside us.

Some years ago, a friend of mine had an automobile accident. She was thrown clear of the car. As she lay on the ground, she found herself in a subtle state of awareness that was new to her, yet strangely familiar. She felt bodiless, yet very secure, joyful, and free. For what seemed like a long time, she simply rested in

32

a vast expanded space of love. Then, as slowly as an ant crawling across a windowpane, words began to trickle into her mind: "I . . . wonder . . . if . . . they'll . . . think . . . this . . . was . . . my . . . fault."

The moment she perceived that thought clearly, she was back in her body, in her so-called normal state, feeling her bruises. She saw that she had actually experienced how the contents of the mind limit Awareness.

It is not only thoughts that are limiting. The very act of perceiving something as a separate object contracts Awareness, as do the energy patterns created inside us by desires and their attendant emotions, and by the waves set up by dreams and fantasies. In short, everything that coagulates the subtle energy of the mind, or makes it undulate into waves and ripples instead of remaining steady and calm, helps to disguise the luminosity and openness of our inner Consciousness.

The work of meditation is to coax the mind into letting go of the perceptions and ideas that keep it stuck, so it can expand and reveal itself as it really is. As vast creative Awareness. Pure light and ecstasy. An ocean of peace and power. The Self.

WHAT IS THE SELF? OR DESCRIBING THE INDESCRIBABLE

The word "Self" as it is used in most English translations of Indian philosophy refers to the Sanskrit word *atman*, which is sometimes also translated as "itself." This is actually a good word for something that is wordless, formless, and essentially ungraspable—something that doesn't look or feel like anything in the sensory universe and can only be known by direct experience.

Lacking form, it is also without name. So the sages called it *atma* (Itself) or *tat* (That). The forest-dwelling sages of Vedic India—whose teachings, collected in the Upanishads, are the basis of the vast body of Indian spiritual philosophy—tried to describe the indescribable using the language of simile, analogy, and metaphor. Images like these suggested the experience of pure beingness:

> Like oil in sesame seeds, like ghee in butter, the Self lies within the mind.

> The Self is that which makes the mind think, but cannot be thought by the mind.

> That which shines through all the senses, yet is without senses.

Any one of these statements, if you were to ruminate over it, would give you a feeling for the Self, for pure Awareness. Oil and ghee are subtle elements that are extracted from the grosser seed and the thicker butter, just as the pure Awareness that is the Self is a subtle essence that needs to be discovered within the cloudy substance of the mind. The Self gives power to the mind and the senses so that they can think or perceive. Yet because the Self empowers thinking, your ordinary mind can't find a way into it, any more than a puppet can perceive the person pulling the strings. When you look for the Self, what you are looking for is actually that which is doing the looking. Zen teachers delight in describing how impossible it is to see the Self with our ordinary perception. "It is like an eye looking at an eye," one Japanese master wrote.

Even though the Self is indescribable, the sages did find ways of describing its characteristics so that we could begin to recognize them. One of the most important things they clarified is that the Self, atman, is not the same as the empirical, personal ego. It is not the "me" who identifies with the body and personality, who creates boundaries and sets limits, and who is always telling us where "I" ends and the "outside" begins.

One way you know you are experiencing the ego and not the Self is that the ego (*ahamkara* in Sanskrit) always experiences itself in comparison to others. The ego never feels fully equal to others: it sees others as higher or lower, as better or worse, as friendly or potentially hostile. The Self, on the other hand, just is. The Self sees everything and everyone as equal to itself.

No, my soul is not asleep.
It is awake, wide awake.
It neither sleeps nor
dreams, but watches,
its eyes wide open,
far-off things, and listens
at the shores of the
great silence.

—ANTONIO MACHADO [10]

The ego bears the same relationship to the Self as does a light-bulb to the electrical current coursing through it. The bulb looks as if it gives light independently, but in fact it doesn't. It is just a container. The true source of illumination is the electrical current that runs through the bulb.

In the same way, it is the Self that gives energy to the ego and enables the ego to perform its function of making you think that the boundaries it sets are the real you. The ego is a useful instrument. For one thing, if it weren't for the ego, we would have no feeling of being an individual self. The ego tells us who we are in the limited, worldly sense: where the body comes from, how old it is, what we "like" and "don't like." So the ego is not always a bad thing, an enemy to extirpate. It is simply limited—and limiting. To become fully immersed in the Self, to experience Self as it is—pervasive, totally impersonal Consciousness that is both connected to everything and boundless—you need to penetrate beyond the ego's confining messages. Once you let go of the tendency to identify with your body, mind, and emotions, then you'll naturally experience yourself as vastness, as pure being, as joy, as Awareness, as light. As any and all of the many ways that the Self can manifest itself. According to the sages of Vedanta, the Self has three basic qualities: It is *sat*, or ever existent and permanently real. It is *chit*, or aware of itself and everything else. And it is *ananda*, or joyful.

The Self Is Ever-Present

Unlike the ego, which comes and goes, inflating or deflating according to its position in relationship to other egos, the Self never goes anywhere. It is the part of us that never changes. Everything else in your life changes and shifts. Your body grows and then ages. You put on weight and lose it. Your life circumstances change—sometimes alarmingly. Your personality is subject to strange shifts and discontinuities. But through it all, the thread of Self remains constant. It is present when you are asleep and dreaming, as the Awareness that remembers your dreams. It is also present during deep sleep, though this is something most of us aren't conscious of until we've advanced considerably in meditation. When you are awake, of course, the Self is present as the awareness that allows you to experience your life. In fact, this is the great liberating secret about the Self: it provides the context for your entire life experience, the thread on which the beads of your thoughts, experiences, and perceptions are strung.

Even though it is easier to experience the purity of Consciousness when the mind is quiet, the Self doesn't go away when the mind is full of thoughts. In fact, the Self is the source of those thoughts: all your thoughts and emotions arise from and subside into the same Consciousness-stuff. Whether you are happy or sad, agitated or calm, the Self as your inner field of Consciousness, your inner Awareness, underlies and contains all these feelings.

This means that at any moment, even in the midst of thinking, you can drop into the Self. As the fifteenth-century poet-saint Kabir said, "Wherever you are is the entry point." This is one of the secrets that every true spiritual tradition reveals. Though many techniques can help us enter meditation, the final truth is that the Self is so present in our ordinary experience that we can contact it merely by focusing on the gap between one breath and another, or between one thought and another. The fractional pause in the flow of the breath or in the flow of thoughts then opens out into the vastness of Consciousness, into what in Sanskrit is called the *madhya* (midpoint), the center, the inner space where we experience our connection to the whole.

Traditionally, the way to enter the madhya, the space of the heart, is through the instructions and grace of a Self-realized spiritual teacher. Because such a teacher lives in constant contact with that inner space, she not only can point it out to us, but can also open the inner door that reveals it. That is why following the instructions of such a teacher can be so revolutionary: the instructions contain a subtle power that can bring them to fruition.

Once when I was meditating with my guru, he gave an instruction: "Meditate on the space from which your mantra arises and into which it subsides." Intrigued, I began to look for the little gap in the flow of the words I was repeating, the space at the end of the last syllable of the mantra and before the first. Did the mantra really arise out of that space in the mind? As I "looked," focused, and tried to feel the space between repetitions of the mantra, I felt myself dropping, like Alice down the rabbit hole, into a huge space. I could still feel my body, but I didn't feel confined inside it. Instead, "I" surrounded the body and somehow contained it. My thoughts and emotions were also inside my Awareness. It was impossible in that state to take my small, anxious mind seriously. There was no doubt at all that this calm wideness was the real me.

This state lasted for several days. While I was in it, everything felt different, especially being with other people. Normally in social situations, I felt a slight alienation and insecurity, a sort of low-grade discomfort. In this state, that feeling was gone. I felt easy, flexible, tender, and secure in myself in a new way. I literally felt that I rested in my own center.

What had happened? I had entered into the space of pure Consciousness, the baseline experience of Self. The instruction had opened the doorway, and following the instruction had allowed me to slip through it.

The Self Is Aware

The Self permeates our experience in much the same way light permeates the room you are sitting in. If you were asked to

Exercise: Focus on the Space between One Thought and Another

This practice is easier to do with a mantric thought—that is, a positive thought that you repeat over and over again—than with your random thoughts. We'll use the mantric thought "I am." But feel free to substitute a different short, positive thought, or a mantra with which you are used to working.

Close your eyes, and attend to your breathing, following the flow of the breath for a few minutes to let your mind calm down. Begin to repeat to yourself the phrase "I am." (Resist the urge to add something to "I am," such as your name.) After you have said it to yourself a few times, start to focus on the place in the mind where the word "am" fades away. Notice the tiny pause there, the gap. As the words "I am" arise again, see if you can gently stay attentive to that pause. Begin to feel that the words are arising from and subsiding into that space in the mind. Let your focus be on the space rather than on the content of the words. Your mind may stop there, in which case take rest in the pause for as long as it lasts.

describe that room, what would you say? You might mention the furniture, the color of the walls, the objects on the table or desk, even the lamps. But would you mention the light in the room? Would you even notice it? Yet only because the light is present can you see the room and its contents. In the same way, just as the ever-present Self gives us our sense of being, it is the Self that allows us to experience everything. The Self is the screen on which we experience our inner and outer life. It is what makes it possible for us to see, to know, and to experience. The *Kena Upanishad* says that the Self "shines through the mind and senses," which is a poetic way of saying that it is the power of the Self which allows the mind and senses to function. So the eternally conscious Self is what makes us conscious. Essentially, it is light.

That which cannot be expressed in words, but by whom the tongue speaks—know that to be the Absolute. That which is not known by the mind, but by which the mind knows—know that to be Absolute.

—KENA UPANISHAD [11]

At times when our inner vision becomes pure enough to let us see through the layers of psychic debris that thicken our consciousness and make it opaque, we realize that everything is actually made of light. We understand that we are light, that the world is light, and that light is the essence of everything. This is why so many people's experiences of touching the Self are experiences of light—visions, inner luminosity, or profound and crystalline clarity.

However, there are other ways to experience the luminosity of the Self. It also reveals itself as our capacity to know, to be aware, and to experience. You don't have to see the inner light to feel how the Self illuminates experience; you only have to notice what it is that allows you to know things. The "knowing" in your mind is separate from thoughts. In other words, it's not thinking that lets you know what you are experiencing—thoughts are part of what you can see, or know. If you can know something, then it isn't you. It is outside you. You can witness your hand—so you know that you are not your hand. In the same way, you witness your thoughts. So one way to locate the Self is to try to become aware of the part of you that is observing your experience, the part of you that is always witnessing your body, emotions, and thoughts.

One easy, immediate way to do this is to imagine observing your body from all sides, as if you had 360-degree awareness.

Exercise: 360-Degree Awareness

Close your eyes and take three deep, slow breaths. Then place your attention behind your own body, so that you can see your body from every angle—from above, from below, from behind, from in front. Notice the shift in perspective that occurs. See if you can station yourself as that observing witness of your body, seen from all sides.

Now, still holding that perspective, ask yourself, "Who or what is witnessing my body? Who or what is witnessing my thoughts?"

Don't try to answer the question in words. Instead, let your attention turn toward the felt experience that arises in response to the question.

Many people, when they try some version of this exercise, notice a spacious presence that often seems to be located somewhere above and behind the head.

If you focus on that witnessing presence for a while, you might become aware of another witnessing presence just beyond it. You could go on focusing on the witness of the witness of the witness almost indefinitely, without ever completely grasping it. So now, instead of trying to *find* that seer, have the feeling that you *are* the seer. As you keep this up, sooner or later you may notice a shift in your state. Thoughts move to the background. The knowing Awareness moves to the foreground. You may experience a sense of huge clarity and freedom, as if the boxy walls that normally contract your consciousness have dropped away, setting you loose into a spacious state that is potentially infinite and infinitely relaxed, infinitely peaceful, silent, and aware. You will have moved into the experience of what we could call the "absolute knower," the pure Awareness that doesn't change or slip away. The Awareness that not only knows everything else, but also knows itself. You will be meditating on the one who is always meditating on you: consciousness facing Consciousness, awareness reflecting on Awareness, the *aham vimarsha,* or "I experiencing itself."

The Self Is Joyful

The third aspect of the Self is ananda, or joy. The ananda aspect of the Self encompasses many different kinds of experience, including love, bliss, and ecstasy. Ananda is also the source of all true creativity: the impulse to make something—to do anything—actually comes out of our inborn joy, excitement, and delight. The enlightened philosopher of Kashmir Shaivism, Abhinavagupta, explained how the whole world arises out of divine delight, which he called the *ananda chalita shakti,* or the divine energy leaping forth in bliss. The *Taittiriya Upanishad* says, "All things are born out of bliss. They live in bliss and dissolve into bliss."[12]

Who could live, who could breathe, if that blissful Self dwelt not within the heart? It is That which gives joy!

—TAITTIRIYA UPANISHAD [13]

Of course, this is a basic teaching of the Indian wisdom tradition. One of the first things that we read or hear when we start becoming aware of this view of life is that our experiences of happiness are possible only because happiness is already inside us. In short, it is not the other person, the beautiful scene, the film, or the tiramisu that creates joy. These things may *trigger* it, but the joy is intrinsic to us. In fact, the pleasure we experience through the senses is literally a shadow of the joy we have inside.

The deep joy we call "the bliss of the Self" bears the same resemblance to our ordinary states of pleasure as a panther does to a Siamese kitten. It is the same happiness, true, but it is infinitely fuller, more powerful, and more thrilling. Moreover, it gives us a sense of fulfillment. Instead of exciting the mind and creating a craving for more, the experience of ananda feels complete. That's because the ananda of the Self is self-sustaining: it doesn't come and go according to the conditions of our lives. Once we learn how to call forth the pure bliss within us, it often rushes up from inside all by itself, with no sensory trigger at all. Ananda is there when things are going well for us. Ananda is also there when things are falling apart.

His experience of ananda allowed Saint John of the Cross to write sublime poetry while living in a prison cell too small for him to lie down or stand up. It gave the Sufi Mansur al'Hallaj the ability to laugh while he was being executed. Many people discover that pure ananda when kundalini awakens. "Oh, now I understand what they mean when they talk about bliss," people often say to me, describing how they caught their first glimpse of that underlying happiness.

The experience of that deep joy, which deepens through our meditation practice, is one of the ultimate gifts of the spiritual journey. Even though in the West we have an odd tendency to distrust joy as somehow frivolous, the fact remains that for Christian mystics as well as for Islamic seers, and certainly for the sages of the mystical traditions of India, one pinnacle of inner experience is the joy of divine love. Love is itself the highest goal of meditation because the very fabric of the Absolute is love. The love you feel—any love—is, at its core, divine love. If you want to get theistic about it, love is what God feels. It is also the substance of everything, the inner ground of our experience.

Everyone who pursues the path to the ultimate reality discovers this eventually. Though different traditions give it different names and attributes, most agree that the nature of the ultimate reality is love or bliss.

Because joy and love are intrinsic to the Self, the sages tell us that we can enter the experience of the Self's expansive happiness through the doorway of our ordinary feelings of happiness or affection. All of us have moments of spontaneous joy in our lives, and, whether we are aware of it or not, those moments give us profound and significant glimpses of our deeper truth. The key is to separate the experience of happiness from its external trigger. If you think that being with Joan is what makes you happy, then you will seek out Joan in the expectation of feeling good—even though you may be aware that being with Joan doesn't always do that! However, if you can enter the moment of immediate enjoyment or happiness, the moment when you feel love, and *hold on to the feeling without attaching it to the person or sensation that might have triggered it,* the feeling itself can expand and allow you to enter the Self.

The *Vijnana Bhairava,* considered one of the key texts on meditation in the Hindu Tantras, is a compendium of techniques for entering into the pure Self through the avenue of our so-called ordinary experience. The following exercise is based on a verse from this text.

It is my nature that
makes me love you often,
For I am love itself.
It is my longing
that makes me love
you intensely,
For I yearn to be
loved from the heart.
It is my eternity that
makes me love you long,
For I have no end.

—MECHTHILD OF
MAGDEBURG [14]

Exercise: Focus on an Experience of Love

Close your eyes. Focus on your breathing, following the breath for a few moments to let your mind calm down. Then think of someone for whom you feel love or whom you have loved in the past. Imagine that you are with this person. Visualize him or her before you or beside you. To anchor yourself in the memory, you might become aware of the setting or notice what this person is wearing. Let yourself feel love for this person. Open yourself to the feeling. Once you are fully present with that feeling of love, let go of the thought of the person. Focus entirely on the feeling of love. Allow yourself to rest in it. Feel the energy of love within your body and within your heart.

You may need to repeat this exercise a few times before you get the hang of it. Once you have experienced how the felt sensation of love and happiness remains even after you let go of the idea of the person inspiring it, you will begin to realize that your love is actually independent of anything outside yourself. This is one of those insights that can change your relationship to other people, and certainly to yourself.

So, the experience of the Self—any experience of the Self—has the following qualities: It is an experience of pure being. It is an experience of awareness—the Self knows itself. It is witness to its own existence as well as to everything else. And it is an experience of bliss, for the Self is joyful, loving. Sometimes one of these qualities is so dominant that we may not be aware of the others. But when we enter into any experience of our deeper reality and allow its facets to reveal themselves, we will eventually find that all these qualities are there.

The question is, how do we know that we are experiencing the Self? Is it as simple as it sounds when we say that the Self is our own thought-free Awareness? Or is it only really accurate to call the Self the condition of expanded Consciousness, the spaciousness we enter when we shift out of ordinary awareness into a larger, wider, and deeper state? Are we in the Self when we experience pure joy? Or is the joy of the Self the huge, all-encompassing love that can sometimes seem too big for our body to bear? Is the tiny light we see at times in meditation the Self? Is the Self the rush of exaltation we feel when we watch the moon come up over the ocean, or the first snowfall? Or are these moments just glimpses of something much bigger and more extraordinary, something that we can only fully experience in a state of expanded or transpersonal Consciousness?

He who goes to the bottom of his own heart knows his own nature; And knowing his own nature, he knows heaven.

—MENCIUS [15]

Here is one way of looking at it. Our experience of the Self is a continuum. Since the Self is always present, we can experience it in different degrees and in many different ways. The Self is both an extraordinary experience and something very close, simple, and familiar. It is light, bliss, and an Awareness so global that we feel everything is a part of us. It is also the calm that arises when you identify with the watcher of thoughts. You are experiencing the Self when you look into the eyes of someone who annoys you, and realize that the Consciousness peeking out of his or her eyes is the same one you experience in yourself. Or when you look at a flower and sense the creative force manifesting as color, fragrance, and curving petal and leaf. Or when you enter the state of "flow," of perfectly skillful action with no sense that you are acting. Or when you have a moment of utter trust in the process of life. One of the major boons of awakened kundalini coupled with an ongoing daily meditation practice is that such experiences come regularly—and not always in meditation. The experience can arise at any time.

For example, there is this moment, described by one of my students in a letter: "Yesterday I was walking in the woods, watching the leaves fall. I looked up and found myself following a single leaf as it descended. There was a kind of hush. My awareness shifted. There was nothing in existence but the leaf and me. I saw the leaf falling, and it seemed to be falling through a vast space, and my own awareness became the space."

For many of us, the "big" experiences of expansion happen outside of meditation, with our eyes open. Full-blown, dramatic experiences of expanded Awareness, powerful shifts of vision, are gifts. We can't make them happen. They come to us through grace, in their own time—as the *Katha Upanishad* says, the Self reveals itself by its own will.[16] No technique, no practice, and no amount of longing can force the Self to reveal its vastness.

And yet, here is the paradox. Even though we can't make that experience happen, we can invoke the power that brings revelation. This is one reason why the relationship we form with the Self, with our meditation practice, and with the inner shakti makes such a difference. The more we learn how to honor the loving power that inspires our meditation practice, the more we remember it and invoke it; and the more we learn to love it, then the more we experience its presence and its blessings.

CHAPTER THREE

Preparing for *Practice*

Several years ago, a student in one of my workshops told me an interesting story. In the early seventies, he had set out on a spiritual quest, going from India to Japan, from teacher to teacher. Like so many others during those years, he wanted to have a palpable experience of the Truth. He wanted to know unity; he wanted to know God. Finally, after years of unsuccessful practice, he decided to give his inner Self an ultimatum. He sat down one evening on his meditation mat and announced, "I'm going to sit here until dawn. If I don't have an experience by then, I'll get up and never practice meditation again."

Nothing happened. Nothing at all. So he got up and went about his life, determined that he wouldn't turn inside again.

Ten years later, a friend brought him to a meditation center in Los Angeles. He went into the meditation room and sat down in the dark. As he sat there, he felt a sensation of great sacredness. He realized that he was in a place where many, many people had performed spiritual practices. He felt strangely humbled, imagining their sincerity and their effort. His heart turned over with an unaccustomed feeling of reverence.

There is an unseen presence we honor, that gives the gifts.

—RUMI [1]

Suddenly, without warning, a vast feeling of love rose up inside him. Then, as if an inner window had opened up, he was ejected out of his ordinary self and into a huge inner sky. All around him was deep, shimmering light—light in rainbow colors, vibrating with this same awesome love.

Challenging the universe to give him an experience of his inner world hadn't helped at all. Love, gratitude, and reverence opened the door. The *Katha Upanishad* says, "The Self reveals itself by its own will." The inner world can't be forced open. Try as we might, we can't make meditation happen. But our inner attitude can coax it forth. With love you can, as Rumi wrote, "make a way for yourself inside yourself."

It comes back to relationship. The Self, the inner Consciousness, is both an "I" and a "thou," a living, dynamic, love-filled intelligence, which some mystical poets call "the Friend." Like any friend, it reveals its secrets when there is trust and respect. The Self is love, so it responds to love. The Self is subtle, so it is attracted to subtlety. The Self is tender, so of course tenderness calls it forth. We draw close to the Self when we make ourselves like the Self—loving, subtle, tender, and generous.

We draw the Self close to us when we invoke it with honor, and when we ask for its grace by being gentle both with ourselves and with the energy inside us.

In this chapter, we will look at different ways to create this open, loving state, the state that can draw forth the grace of the inner Friend.

HONOR YOUR PRACTICE

The most basic way to invoke meditation is simply to honor your practice, to treat the time you have set aside for meditation as sacred, and to enter into it with respect. It helps to create some simple rituals around your practice—physical acts you do to induce a feeling of respect.

If possible, set aside a place where you'll regularly meditate. The space will collect subtle energy, and eventually just sitting in it will trigger the mind to turn inside. You don't need an entire room (I know people who have turned a closet into a meditation room!). Your meditation place can be a corner. If even that isn't practical, create a portable meditation space—a cushion or mat that you keep only for meditating, and that you can place on the floor or on a chair when it's time to sit.

A simple altar helps enhance remembrance. Your altar will come to represent sacred space to you, and can even trigger feelings of stillness or remembrance when you pass it during the day. Traditionally, an altar is raised. I've sometimes used a cardboard box covered by a beautiful cloth as an altar, or set up my altar on a bookshelf. You can even have a portable altar—a cloth that you keep with your meditation cushion.

On the altar, you might want to place a candle or small lamp (to remind you of the light of Awareness). You can add flowers or leaves, pictures of people or places that create a sense of sacredness in you, and a special object, rock, or crystal.

Before you sit for meditation, take some time to cleanse your body. When you shower or even just wash the face, hands, and feet before meditating, you are performing a basic and time-honored act of physical and mental purification. The sages recited mantras while they bathed. Even if you don't do that, you can have the feeling that the water running over your body is also washing detritus from the mind. You can also wear a set of clothes that you keep for meditation; in time they will become saturated with your meditation energy so that wearing them will make it easier for you to go inside. Before you sit, you can light a candle or incense. And you can bow.

Bowing is the most immediate way we have of honoring the power that can take us beyond egoic fear, pride, and distraction. In the Indian tradition, yogis bow to each of the four directions before meditating, thus acknowledging that the divine source is everywhere. Then they bow to their own meditation seat. When you try this practice, you'll soon discover all kinds of nuances in it. Honoring the seat of meditation is not only a way of honoring the power of meditation that gathers in the cushion you sit on, but also a way of signaling to your inner being that you honor yourself. The great Sufi poet Hafiz wrote:

> The Friend has such exquisite taste
> That every time you bow to Him

Your mind will become lighter and more
Refined;
Your spirit will prepare its voice to laugh
In an outrageous freedom.[2]

Whether you bow at an altar or simply to the universe itself, you can have one of the following thoughts: "Let the shell that separates me from love melt" or "I offer myself just as I am, with humility and love" or "I take refuge in the Self." The idea is to soften the stiffness that clings to your heart and to allow a feeling of inner surrender and tenderness to emerge.

It helps to do all this slowly and consciously; if you enter meditation in a hurry, you'll often bring a sense of restlessness to your entire meditation. In fact, if you notice a feeling of agitation in meditation, you might consider going back and mentally redoing the preliminary ritual—the bow, the waving of the incense—taking it very slowly and noticing that when you do this, it brings your mind into a more balanced state. Ritual practice happens to be a time-honored method for concentrating the mind.

Another very basic way to draw close to the Self at the beginning of meditation is to relax. It sounds so simple and obvious: just relax. Yet sometimes it is the last thing we think to do. So many times I have sat rigidly upright for an hour, doing hard practice and keeping myself mono-focused by a mighty effort. Then, once the hour was over, I would draw my legs up to my chest, and with the feeling of taking off a tight belt, I'd relax. At that very moment, the contraction that had been keeping my consciousness limited and my heart small would release, and I would be in deep meditation.

Rather than waiting until after meditation to relax, it makes sense to relax in the beginning. You relax the body with the breath. You relax the mind by accepting yourself as you are in that moment, in whatever state you happen to be, and by entering into meditation without demands or expectations. An expectation is different from the intention described earlier. Having a strong intention, an awareness of your goal, helps focus you in the right direction. But having an expectation actually blocks your experience, because it superimposes an idea of what is supposed to happen over the spontaneous actuality of the unfolding moment.

It is a good idea to give yourself time at the beginning of meditation to scan the body, noticing where your muscles are holding tension. Then you can breathe into each place of holding—into your tight shoulders and belly and forehead—and breathe out any tension found there. In the same way, you can breathe into the energy held in the mind, into the tightness of your coagulated thoughts, and let the thoughts flow out with the exhalation. As you focus on your practice, keep that sense of relaxation, remembering to keep your attention soft and to release any sense of strain. This form of relaxed attentiveness is sometimes called "effortless effort."

INVOKING GRACE

What allows us to relax into meditation, to make our effort without straining? Essentially, it is trust. First, we trust that the Self, the goal of meditation, is real and can be experienced. Second, we trust that we are connected to a greater power, a power that supports our meditation and brings it to fruition. In nearly every spiritual tradition, that power is called "grace"—the cosmic force that awakens the heart to its own vastness and love. Grace is the energy that connects to the ultimate truth, to the source of our being, to what a friend of mine likes to call the "God-field." The masters of Kashmir Shaivism—an Indian tradition that sees all of life as an expression of divine energy—point out that grace is an ever-present force in the universe, more pervasive than gravity (and infinitely more subtle). That means that we can access it anywhere and at any time—in nature, in the presence of someone we love—by tuning in to the presence that opens up in moments of stillness and in countless other ways. Grace is inside us, after all, never distant. Yet just as you need to tune the radio dial to catch the right station, or connect to a server to get online, you also need to intentionally invoke the particular forms of grace that directly enliven meditation.

There are four basic forms of grace that we can tune in to in meditation:

One is the grace of Spirit itself, the formless, impersonal love-intelligence that flows as the cosmos.

The second is the grace of our own self—our Awareness, but also our own body, mind, heart.

The third is the grace of a personal deity archetype, like Shiva, Laksmi, Kuan Yin.

The fourth—and, for me, always the most immediate and powerful—is the grace of an enlightened master, especially one connected to one of the great spiritual lineages. As you experiment with your practice, you can play with any of these invocations. You might find yourself choosing to work with one in particular, or even making all four of them a part of your routine.

Invoking the Grace of the Universe Itself

We know that there is Presence in the universe. The Native Americans address that universal Presence as Great Spirit. It manifests as the life force, as the intelligence in cells, the power that pushes the child out of the womb, as the felt sense of aliveness that is so much a part of our experience that we tend to take it for granted. The grace of the universe is impersonal, and therefore it is sometimes called "Third Person Spirit"—spirit manifesting as a Suchness that surrounds and pervades everything. This is the form of grace that we most easily experience in nature—how many of us have our first experiences of Spirit in the mountains, or under a starry night sky, or in the ocean?

Exercise: Connecting to Spirit in the Universe

Close your eyes, and focus for a moment on your breath. If you like, you might remember a time when you felt truly open to a benign and loving presence, the presence of Spirit, of the power that flows as this world. You might have been in a redwood grove, on the ocean, looking at an open sky. The connection might have happened during a moment of love with a partner or a friend or a child.

Connect for a moment to the sense of presence. If you don't feel it, don't worry: the invocation will still have power.

Now speak or think these words, or create your own customized prayer:

I invoke the grace of the universe, the grace of God, the grace of Spirit, ever-present in this world. With gratitude, I open myself to the benign grace that guides my meditation and fills me with peace, clarity, and love.

You might want to do a shortened form of the invocation, perhaps saying simply, "I ask grace to fill my meditation" or "May grace enliven my body, mind, and spirit." And of course, you can substitute qualities like awareness, dynamism, enlightenment, and wisdom for the qualities I've mentioned above.

Invoking the Grace of Your Body, Mind, and Heart

Wilhelm Reich was not the first to recognize the wisdom of the body. The practices of hatha yoga are specifically designed to tune us in to the meditative power concealed in our muscles, our bones, and our subtle-energy channels. When the body's rhythm and intentions are in sync with our intention to meditate, the body itself can draw us into deep meditation. In the same way, the mind (more on this later) can be a friend of meditation or a most obstreperous distraction.

Exercise: *Asking Your Body, Mind, and Heart to Help You Turn Inside*

I always like to take a moment to ask my body, my mind, and my heart for their permission to enter meditation—and for their grace. This only takes a moment, but can make a real difference:

Dear Body, please give me permission to sit quietly and turn my awareness inside. Please help me go into meditation.

Dear Mind, I ask you, with love, to support my meditation. Please reveal your stillness and depth to me.

Dear Inner Heart, I honor you. Please open to the sweetness that is your real nature, and allow my meditation to be filled with your grace.

If it feels slightly weird to you to make petitions to your own body and mind, try a statement like this:

My intention now is to meditate, allowing my attention to flow inward, and to rest in the depths of my inner Being. I invoke the grace and help of my body, my mind, and my heart.

Connecting to the Guru Energy

If there is one fundamental tantric secret about meditation, it's that invoking the energy of an enlightened being can set your practice on fire, bring sweetness to a dry meditation, and open you to the subtle, protective, and transforming forces of the cosmos. In Vajrayana Buddhism, the practice of tuning in to the energy of an enlightened master is called "Guru Yoga." It is indeed a yoga, a powerful and transformative esoteric practice. Many mystical traditions have similar methods: Sufism, contemplative Christianity, and Hassidic Judaism all use meditations and prayers meant to invoke the great teacher of the path. And in the Indian and Tibetan tantric traditions, you simply do not start your meditation without invoking the help of the Guru—spelled here with a capital *G*, because invoking the Guru is never about paying obeisance to a human being. A famous tantric commentary describes the Guru as the "grace-bestowing power of the divine." The body and heart of an individual guru is actually the *vehicle*, the container for that power, which is also an energy within your own soul.

The specific teacher you invoke can be someone living on earth, but it is also very powerful (and for many people, preferable) to connect yourself to one of the legendary departed masters. Christ, Buddha, Padmasambhava, Ramakrishna Paramahamsa, Ramana Maharshi, or a Hassidic master like the Baal Shem Tov. Any of these beings can be a link to the secret source that brings meditation alive. Tukaram Maharaj, one of the poet-saints of the Maharashtrian tradition, wrote in the seventeenth century: "God lives with the Guru. So remember the Guru. Bring him into your meditation. When you remember the Guru, you find God both in the forest and in the mind."

O grace of the Guru, one who is supported by your favor becomes like the creator of the whole world of knowledge.

—JNANESHWAR MAHARAJ[3]

I often contemplate what Tukaram meant by "God lives with the Guru." It is one of the great mysteries in this universe: how the universal power of grace, the principle of divine help, roots itself in the person of an enlightened teacher, then flows into anyone who connects to that teacher—centuries or even years after that teacher is no longer present on the earth.

It's no accident that so many mystical traditions insist that when a meditator links him or herself to a spiritual lineage, the meditator specifically links the self to the form of grace that ignites higher states of Awareness within. At every stage of the journey, from the moment of initiation until long after final realization, the guru's grace gives power to our practice and opens the inner world. "My Guru gave me the grace to see that inside and outside are one," wrote the Sikh Guru Nanak, and the *Katha Upanishad* says:

> Unless taught by a teacher, there is no access there,
> For—being more subtle than the subtle—
> That is inconceivable.
> Dearest one! This knowledge is not attained
> through reasoning.
> Truly, for ease of understanding, it must be taught
> by another.[4]

The poet-saint Kabir sang:

> Think this over and understand it.
> The path is very narrow and precarious;
> it is so subtle that you need the Guru's help to discern it.[5]

But the question is, what do we mean by "guru"—especially in an age when the word is popularly applied to any expert as in "fitness guru" or even "hair guru"?

The Sanskrit syllables *gu-ru* mean "darkness-light," so "guru" is sometimes defined as the one who guides us from darkness to light. But here's where it gets confusing. In spiritual life, the same word is used to describe both the archetype of the divine Guide *and* a human teacher—who may or may not be enlightened. In India, your music teacher, your Sanskrit teacher, or even your biology teacher might be addressed as *guruji*, because all teachers are considered worthy of respect. In the same way, in spiritual life, you may first meet the guru-principle through a teacher or mentor who happens to be a fairly ordinary human being with some spiritual knowledge. In Sanskrit, one name for this kind of teacher is *acharya*, meaning "the one who instructs." The therapist who introduces you to deep breathing, the yoga teacher who takes you into your first meditative *shavasana*, and the author of your favorite meditation book are all important for your practice at different stages. (And any of them, in traditional India, might be addressed as "guruji" or "respected teacher.") Different acharyas can provide particular kinds of instruction. If you're a serious student, you'll learn to recognize who can help you at each stage, when to stay with a teacher despite doubts or resistances, and when it might be time to move on.

The acharya of meditation does not have to be fully enlightened, but they should be experienced, well trained, and, especially, versed in the texts and subtle transmissions of the style of meditation you are learning. A teacher who is connected to a lineage of teachers is also likely to carry the energy of that lineage, which can deeply enhance your practice. A skilled teacher can do much more than give meditation instructions—they can help troubleshoot your practice, give experienced guidance at crucial points, and help you enter subtle states in your practice. The guru-energy may flow through such a teacher on occasion. At the same time, they should not be confused with a *sadguru,* or truth-master—an enlightened being who owns the skill of imparting enlightenment to others.

Guru as the Awakening Force

A sadguru is a teacher who fully incarnates the guru-function. Such a truth-master has the capacity to awaken you to your own concealed truth, and then guide you until you've learned to embody the truth within yourself. Not everyone has the good fortune to physically come in contact with such a teacher. Yet, if you understand the principles behind guru yoga, it is still possible to meet the guru, even if you never run across such a teacher in the flesh. We don't need physical contact to experience the awakening power that the tantras call "guru." At the mystical level, what we receive from the guru is a kind of quickening, a subtle and constant transmission of an awakened state. This transmission can happen in any state of consciousness, including in dreams (Tukaram himself received initiation from a departed master, in a dream), in meditation, and even in the states after death. When there is a real inner connection with the guru, their guidance is with us no matter what.

That's why, in both Eastern and Western traditions, it's the *inner* connection with a spiritual lineage that matters most. Like the enlivening sap that brings buds and blossoms to a winter-barren tree, the spiritual force that flows from the subtle connection to the guru and the guru lineage gives life, juice, and potency to practice. It can kindle our desire to meditate, make the hidden Self discernible, and enliven a technique so that the secret landscapes of our inner consciousness open to us. Just remembering the guru can open the door to that transmission, and lift a routine meditation to an entirely different plane.

Here's an example: Many years ago, sitting in meditation in an ashram in India, I found myself in a state of radical upset. I'd had a difficult encounter the day before, and I couldn't get it out of my mind. My emotions were churning, my body felt restless, and at times it actually seemed that I would explode up out of my seat.

Suddenly the face of my guru appeared inwardly, a vivid vision. He brought his face inches before mine, and said, "Your mind is crazy. I'm going to . . ." I never heard the end of the sentence because in the next moment, his face had merged into mine, and my head exploded in light. Cascades of white radiance filled my body, along with a sweet stillness. When I came out of meditation, my mind was still. And although thoughts came back, what didn't come back was the obsessive worrying that had been such a feature of my inner universe.

When we ask a guru, a deity-figure, or awake being to be present in our meditation, what we are actually asking is that this being's inner state of clarity, love, and subtle Awareness come alive in us. In fact, we are opening ourselves to the light inside us, to the meditation-bestowing presence of our inner teacher, the unseen guide whom each of us carries inside.

For lifetimes, this inner guru has lived within us, unseen and unknown yet constantly drawing us along, guiding us through different experiences, and bringing us to the point where we are ready to turn inside and know ourselves. When that moment comes, the inner teacher will bring us to teachers who can help us in the process. Sometimes the inner teacher may bring us to a physical human being destined to be our master, our sadguru. But ultimately, the inner teacher draws us to an external teacher so that the outer teacher can make us conscious of the presence of the teacher inside. Eventually, we come to see the human teacher as a kind of embodied form of the wisdom and love of our own soul, our own Christ consciousness or Buddha nature. As the *Guru Gita,* a Sanskrit poem on the guru, tells us, "The guru is not different from the aware Self."[7]

So when you invoke a guru or a deity-form at the beginning of meditation, you are not doing it for superstitious reasons or to create psychological dependency. You invoke such a being so that their enlightened state can touch your own concealed enlightenment, activate the enlightened teacher inside you, and enliven your meditation.

> *Affix to the bow the sharp arrow of devotional worship; then, with mind absorbed and heart melted in love, draw the arrow and hit the mark—the imperishable Absolute.*
>
> —MUNDAKA UPANISHAD[6]

64

Sometimes we hold back from this kind of practice because we don't feel particularly loving or devotional. Yet, paradoxically, this is often when we most need to do it! One friend of mine, a scientist, has an efficient, cut-to-the-chase attitude about her practice, and a preference for meditating on pure Consciousness rather than on forms of any kind. At one point, her meditation became so dry that she could hardly find the interest to sit. Then she signed up for a meditation retreat in which every session began with a series of elaborate devotional practices: bowing to each of the four directions, saying prayers to the teachers of her lineage, and chanting. Back home, she added this ritual to the beginning of each meditation session.

"I did it very mechanically," she said. "I didn't have much feeling about it. I just did it—doing my bows, remembering my teacher, praying. After a few weeks, my heart started to feel tenderized. Literally tenderized. Now I just start the invocation, and this tender feeling rises up, and my whole meditation practice is full of love."

Her story reminded me of something an acting coach told me years ago. He said that when you have to act the role of being in love with someone, the way to do it is to pay very close attention to the actor you are supposed to love. The audience, he said, will feel your attentiveness as love. In spirituality, paying close attention doesn't just simulate love, it actually evokes it. Practicing prayer, invocation, and surrender will always eventually create

> *I am the same Self in all beings; there is none hateful or dear to me. But those who worship me with devotion, they are in me and I am also in them.*
>
> —BHAGAVAD GITA [8]

feelings of devotion, even if we start out mechanically. That's why we do the practices: because they give rise to love inside us. The Sanskrit word for devotion is *bhakti,* which comes from a root that means "to relish." Prayer, invocation, praise, remembrance, worship, and ritual—the practices that come from the tradition of bhakti—are actually means to relish the different flavors of sweetness inside us. They give rise to very high and subtle feelings of enjoyment, and that enjoyment enlivens our whole practice.

From the blossoming lotus of devotion, at the center of my heart, Rise up, O compassionate master, my only refuge!

—JIKME LINGPA [9]

Invoking the guru can be as simple as taking a moment to invite them to be present, or as elaborate as the tantric practice of imagining that your body is the guru's body. However you do the invocation, it's important to begin by reminding yourself that you are calling upon a universal power, the force of grace itself. In fact, the tantras say that our attitude toward the guru and ourselves determines how much we imbibe from the guru.

An invocation like the one in the next exercise affects us most powerfully when we do it with the feeling that the guru is a form of our own inner teacher—that the form we are invoking is not something separate from the Self.

You can practice this invocation with the spiritual teacher with whom you feel the closest connection, or with the image of a being like Buddha or Christ or the Baal Shem Tov, the sixteenth-century Hassidic master. You might also want to practice with the figure of one of the great transformative deity-forms—like Shiva, Krishna,

Kuan Yin, Tara, or the Indian goddesses Laksmi, Durga, or Kali, who embody the grace-bestowing function of the divine feminine. It can be interesting to experiment with invoking different forms, especially when you are new to devotional practice. However, this practice really begins to blossom when you practice, day after day, with one particular form. In all practice, but especially in devotional

Exercise: Invoking the Guru

Sit in a comfortable, upright meditation posture and close your eyes. Let your attention merge with the breath and follow the breath as it comes in and goes out. Imagine that you are sitting before your guru, or before the great saint or enlightened master with whom you feel most connected. Have the awareness that your guru is not simply an individual being. Understand them to be the embodiment of the entire power of grace that runs through countless lineages of enlightened masters.

It is not necessary to "see" the form of the guru. The most important thing is to feel their presence, to allow that presence to be fully real for you. Feel this presence as a divine awakening force, a power of grace with which you are deeply familiar and deeply connected. Recognize that this is the particular embodiment of the grace-bestowing power that has chosen to draw you close to the state of enlightenment, the state of Truth. The guru is showering blessings on you. And it is happening through the breath.

As the guru breathes out, they breathes into you the entire power of love and all the blessings of a vast lineage of enlightened beings. As you inhale, you breathe the love and blessings into yourself. As you exhale, you breathe these blessings through your whole body, feeling the guru's well-wishing filling you from head to toe.

Now sit with the feeling that the love of the guru and the guru's entire lineage fills your body. Feel the energy of those blessings within yourself. Rest in the blessings you have taken in. Offer your thanks.

practice, repetition ignites the power inside the practice. The more you connect to one particular being, the more you set loose the grace-stream that flows inside the form to which you're connecting.

Give up to grace.
The ocean takes
care of each wave
Till it gets to shore.
You need more help
than you know.

—RUMI [10]

If you don't want to do such an elaborate practice of invocation, simply remember your chosen guru and then ask for their grace. Your invocation can be simple and short, or elaborate and poetic. If you are full of longing, fill the invocation with your longing. If you feel dry and uninterested, confess your dryness and ask for help. If your mind is disturbed by anger, fear, or worry, offer up the mind to be transformed. Your invocation is your dialogue with the power of grace, and the more personal, direct, and heartfelt it is, the more effective it will be. Just as it is important to feel the largeness of the teacher's grace-bestowing power, it is equally crucial to understand how close the guru is to you. Again, the guru is actually present within you, part of the inner fabric of your being. The power of grace you are invoking is not coming from somewhere else. It is manifesting from within you.

Once you have opened yourself like this, once you have touched the power of grace, you are standing at the threshold of meditation. It is time to choose your gateway, the portal you will step through.

CHAPTER FOUR

Choosing the Right Doorway

*I*n my early years of meditation, I wasted countless hours wondering which technique to use. Should I do mindfulness practice? Practice one of the complex visualizations that my first teacher offered? Repeat my mantra? Just follow the breath? Some early mentor had told me to decide on one technique and stick with it, and I reasoned that if I had to choose one practice, it had better be the right one. So I worried. I worried about which mantra to use, about whether to meditate on "the witness" or on "the breath," about when it was permissible to leave the technique behind and just relax into myself. It wasn't until I stopped making techniques into icons that I began to discover how liberating it can be to work with different practices—and how important it is ultimately to move beyond them.

We use techniques in meditation for a very simple reason: most of us, at least when we begin meditation, need support for our mind. A technique provides a place for the mind to rest while it settles back down into its essential nature. That's all a technique is really: a kind of cushion for the mind. No meditation technique is an end in itself, and no matter which meditation technique you use, it will eventually dissolve when your meditation deepens.

The mind is truly fickle. But . . . it frequents places familiar to it. Therefore, show it often the delight of the experience of the Self.

—JNANESHWAR
MAHARAJ[1]

I like to think of meditation techniques as portals, entry points into the spaciousness that underlies the mind. The inner spaciousness is always there, with its clarity, its love, and its innate goodness. It is like the sky that suddenly "appears" over our heads when we step out of the kitchen door and glance upward after a harried morning. The Self, like the sky, is ever-present yet hidden by the ceiling and walls of our minds. In approaching the Self, it helps to have a doorway you can comfortably walk through, rather than having to break through the wall of thoughts separating us from your inner space.

As you practice, the technique becomes a vehicle that connects you to that subtle inner current of meditation, the natural in-drawing power. Then the natural meditation current itself carries the outgoing awareness inside, into a state of meditation. (It's also been my experience, as we'll see in chapter 8, that techniques can arise spontaneously from the awakened meditation energy—the shakti.) Different techniques often seem to lead us into different corners of the inner kingdom. The Self is one, yet it has endless facets. So working with a technique that's new to you can land you in a part of the inner country you may not have known before.

There's another reason why it is good to experiment with techniques: the technique you use currently may be keeping you stuck. That happens to a lot of people. They learn one practice and they stick with it, even if it doesn't help them go deeper. After a while, they feel that they aren't good meditators, or that meditation is just too hard or too boring, or even that it comes so easily they miss a feeling of growth. Often their only problem is that they are trying to enter meditation through the wrong doorway or through a door that once opened easily but is now stiff on its hinges.

The best reason to do any meditation practice is that you like it. This piece of advice comes from no less an authority than Patanjali's *Yoga Sutras,* a text of meditation so fundamental that every yogic tradition in India makes it the basis for meditation practice. After listing a string of practices for focusing the mind, Patanjali ends his chapter on concentration by saying, "Concentrate wherever the mind finds satisfaction."[2] How do you know that the mind is finding satisfaction in a technique? First, you should enjoy it. You should be able to relax within it. It should give you a feeling of peace. Once you've become familiar with it, the practice should feel natural. If you have to work too hard at the practice, it may be a sign that it is the wrong technique for you.

Most people who have meditated for a while have a sense of which modes of meditation feel most natural. Some people have a visual bent and respond well to practices that work with visualizations. Others are more kinesthetic and attuned to sensations of energy. There are auditory people, whose inner world opens in response to sound, or people whose practice is kindled by an insight or a feeling.

Once you become aware of how you respond to different perceptual modes, you can often adjust the way you do a practice so that it works for you. Someone who has a hard time visualizing can bring a visual form to life inside her if she imagines its presence as energy or an inner sensation, rather than trying to see it as a visual image. A highly visual person might get bored with mantra repetition when he focuses on sounding the syllables, but may feel the mantra's impact if he visualizes the letters on his inner screen. One person might experience great love when he repeats a mantra with a devotional feeling, while his friend's meditation only takes off once she lets go of all props and meditates on pure Awareness.

This alone is obligatory, . . . that the mind be firmly applied to the true reality. It matters little how this is achieved.

—MALINI VIJAYA TANTRA [3]

We each have to find our own way. To do this, we need to give ourselves full permission to play with the different practices we are given.

THE POSTURE

The core, the foundation, the basis of all practice is posture. A correct meditation posture is comfortable enough that you can sit in it for a while, steady enough that you feel free to forget the body, yet strong enough that it helps you stay alert. Here is a set of simple posture instructions that you can use when you practice the meditation exercises on the pages that follow. At this moment, as you are reading, you might want to align your body in this posture.

Posture Instructions

- The most important aspect of a meditative posture is that the spine be held naturally erect, so that the energy of meditation can flow freely. For this, it isn't necessary that you sit in a traditional meditation posture, like full lotus or half lotus. There's no question that these postures enhance meditation, since they can redirect the subtle-energy flow in your body so that it starts to turn inside on its own. So, if your body is flexible, I encourage you to learn to sit in one of these postures long enough to get into meditation. (A good way to train yourself in posture is to start with ten minutes, then add one minute a day for a month until you're sitting for forty minutes. At the same time, make sure you're also practicing some hatha yoga to open your hip flexors. Try cobbler's pose, where you put the soles of your feet together and draw your feet in toward the body.

A yogi in a steady posture easily becomes immersed in the heart.

—SHIVA SUTRAS [4]

- That said, when you're first practicing, the most important aspect of posture is simply that you are able to sit comfortably, with your spine erect, long enough to go deep into meditation. So I often recommend to beginners that if their back or knees give them trouble, they can sit on a straight-backed chair or against a wall, supporting their back with pillows to keep it straight.

- If you can sit on the floor, sit in a comfortable cross-legged posture with a firm pillow, yoga wedge, or folded blanket under your hips. Raising the hips helps to keep your back from rounding or slumping, and maintains the natural curve of the lower back. Your knees should be slightly lower than your hips.

- If you would rather sit in a chair, place your feet flat on the floor, hip-width apart. Sit straight on your chair or cushion, so that your upper back doesn't round and slump. You may also support your lower back by placing a small cushion between the small of your back and the back of the chair.

- Place your hands palms down on the thighs with thumb and forefinger touching, or fold them palms up in your lap with the back of one hand resting in the palm of the other.

- Feel that your hips and thighs are heavy and grounded, as if they were sinking into the chair or the floor. Feel your spinal column rise out of this grounded base, straight up through the crown of the head. Let your neck be soft.

- Let your head float freely, rising upward in line with the spine. Soften your face. Let your eyelids and cheeks relax. Let your tongue rest on the floor of the mouth.

- Inhale gently, and on the exhalation allow your chest
  to open and lift, as if you were lifting it from the heart.
  Inhale, and on the exhalation allow the shoulderblades to
  melt down the back.

- Once your body is aligned, let the breath help relax you
  in the posture. On the inhalation, let the breath flow into
  any places in the body that feel tired or tense. On the
  exhalation, allow any tightness or constriction to flow
  out with the breath. This opens the body, softens it, and
  prepares it to hold the energy released in meditation.

- Sit for a moment in the posture. Close your eyes, and let
  the breath come in and out naturally. Listen to the sounds
  in the room. Feel the sensations in your body. Let yourself
  fully experience the sensation of being inside your body, in
  this posture, in this moment. Let yourself be where you are.

It is important to be at ease in your posture; if your body feels
uncomfortable during meditation, feel free to adjust it. However,
let your movements be mindful and slow, so that you don't bring
yourself out of meditation.

BASIC PRACTICES

Every spiritual tradition has its own meditation techniques and
its own language for describing them. For practical purposes,
most techniques fall into three categories. First, there are the
concentrative practices, which ask you to focus on something—
a sound, a visual form, the breath, a center in the body such as

the heart or the central channel in the spine, or a subtle idea or inner experience.

Second, there are practices that integrate your meditative awareness with ordinary experience. Basic mindfulness—being present with sensations, breath, and thoughts as they arise—is an integrative practice. So is "witness awareness," the process of recognizing the knowing Awareness that is present to all your experience.

Third, there are contemplative or analytical meditation practices. In these, you might inquire into the deeper truth behind ordinary experience, or focus on a question or a spiritual idea, letting it sink deeper into your consciousness in order to bring forth an inner shift or insight.

Tantric traditions are known for creative meditation and contemplative techniques. A tantric-practice text like the *Vijnana Bhairava* offers a huge menu of options for sinking into the Self, including such radical practices as contemplating the void inside the armpits, or the taste of your favorite sweet. In this chapter, we'll look at some basic concentrative practices from a tantric perspective: a sound practice (repeating a mantra), a kinesthetic or energy practice (following the breath or focusing on the space between the breaths), and various visual practices. We'll also touch on practices that focus on inner centers, like the *sushumna nadi* (the subtle-energy channel that runs up the spinal column) or the heart center. And we'll spend some time with another basic practice, meditating on the witness or on bare Awareness, which works directly with the formless, with Consciousness itself.

Keep in mind that techniques can often be combined. For example, you might combine a mantra with the breath, or you might observe the breath and allow yourself to gradually become aware of the Awareness that is actually "doing" this observation. I often begin meditation by focusing on the space between the breaths until my attention becomes centered, and then rests in the space of the heart.

Before we examine these practices in depth, we will look at some principles that can help bring a practice to life for us.

THE SUBTLE ESSENCE OF A PRACTICE

The most important key to any practice you do is to keep looking for its subtle essence. Every technique has its own unique feeling-tone. It creates an energy space inside us. For example, when repeating a mantra with the breath, you might feel a specific sensation of air moving between the throat and the heart, as well as a subtle feeling of expansion or pulsation in the heart space

God is at the midpoint of all things.

—JULIAN OF NORWICH [5]

when the mantra syllables "strike" it. Focusing on the space between the breaths, you might begin to feel the breath moving in and out of your heart and notice a subtle expansion of the heart-space until it seems to include everything outside. You might notice that certain parts of the inner body are activated by a particular practice: the space between the eyebrows, for example, might begin to pulsate when you turn your attention to your own Awareness. Taking a deep breath might make you especially aware of the currents of energy flowing through your body.

That energy sensation, or feeling-sense, is the subtle effect of the technique and its real essence. It is the feeling-sense that a technique creates, rather than the technique itself, that opens the door into the Self. For this reason, we want to keep moving into the space created by the practice: into the energetic sensation of a mantra as it drops into our consciousness, into the felt sense of the breath as it pauses between the inhalation and the exhalation, or into the vividness of the object we are visualizing. As you do this, you'll automatically release yourself into a subtler level of your being.

Another way to discover the inner essence of a technique is to work with *bhava*. *Bhava* is a Sanskrit word that means "feeling" or "attitude" or "conviction" about oneself. According to Indian tradition, bhava is so powerful that it can transform our experience of reality.

> *When a man meditates on the thought that he is rooted in the divine, and he prays to God, then he performs an act of true unification.*
>
> —BAAL SHEM TOV [6]

We are always holding onto one bhava or another. It is just that we don't think of our identification with being a woman or an accountant, our feeling of discomfort, or our sense of being responsible for the universe as attitudes or convictions. Instead we think that they are the truth, that they are who we are. We look at the world through the glasses of our particular set of bhavas and imagine that what we see is the way things really are, when actually we are seeing only the reflection of our bhavas. That is why a shift in your attitude makes such a change in your daily experience of the world. Any time you decide to focus on forgiveness instead of anger, or look at a situation from someone else's perspective, or dwell on your own good qualities instead of brooding about your failings, you discover the power of bhava to transform your experience.

The practice of consciously creating an internal bhava, or articulating a specific spiritual feeling, is called *bhavana,* sometimes translated as "creative contemplation." Each bhavana has its own effect on us. For example, if you practice the bhavana of offering your practice to God or for the benefit of others, it creates a feeling of selflessness in your practice and helps take you beyond grasping for a particular experience or inner state. Remembering love or grace—as in the practice of breathing in with the feeling that you are breathing in love—expands the heart and gives a sense of contentment and protection. Feeling that everything is a part of your own Consciousness loosens the grip of limitation.

If you practice a particular bhava long enough, it will become natural—meaning that it will become your actual experience. That's because your consciousness is so creative that it can shape itself completely around any feeling you hold, and recreate itself in that image. Once the feeling that you have been practicing begins to arise spontaneously as experience, you will discover the truth of what Tukaram Maharaj meant when he wrote, "God is in your bhava."[7]

Tukaram was an impoverished grocer from a tiny village called Dehu in western India. He had nine children and a fiercely disappointed wife—such dedicated yogis often don't make satisfying spouses. Despite everything, he spent his days chanting and singing to God, until he eventually attained a state of God-realization. A master of bhava, he used to talk to God in a different mood every day. Sometimes he called out to God with love, sometimes he railed in angry frustration, and sometimes he declared that he belonged to God and God belonged to him.

It was Tukaram who articulated the secret of bhava. He understood that our spontaneous feelings are what connect us to the higher power. In short, when you love God, you actually experience divine reality in your love. If you are afraid of God or angry at God, you experience God as fear or anger. When you feel one with God, God's presence reveals itself as your inmost being. When you long for God, you discover that God is in your very desire. By practicing these bhavas, you bring them alive inside you.

As we look now at some basic meditation techniques, we will also look at how we can merge them with different bhavas.

MANTRA REPETITION

The word "mantra" means "a tool for the mind." Specifically, mantras are articulated sounds that approximate the "unsounded sound," the vibration of the Infinite that throbs in the silence of pure Consciousness. These inner vibrations are far too subtle to be heard by the physical ears or articulated by the tongue. However, the lineage mantras of the different spiritual traditions—heard by sages in deep meditation and then transmitted to their disciples—carry that high, subtle vibration embedded in their syllables. Such mantras are called "awakened," enlivened by the power of Consciousness, because the full power of pure, universal Consciousness is within them. Repeating such an enlivened mantra gradually draws the mind inward, back to the source of the mantra—which is the spaciousness of the original great mind, the deep Self. That is the basic principle of mantra practice. However, the way the mantra works and the secrets of how it works are quite subtle. To understand the inner practice of mantra, we must turn to the texts of the Indian tantric tradition, where the science of mantra is explained in all its complexity.

Tantric teaching texts like the *Shiva Sutras* tell us that the words of a mantra are only its shell, a kind of jacket. The real essence of a mantra is the subtle energy embedded in its syllables, rather like the code in a computerized keycard. As in the keycard, that energy needs to be activated in order to work for us.

There are two ways that a mantra gets activated. One is through your practice: you repeat the mantra with focus and feeling until it gradually sinks into your body and mind at deeper and deeper levels. The

The Word without a word, the Word within The world and for the world; And the light shone in darkness and Against the Word the unstilled world still whirled About the centre of the silent Word.

—T. S. ELIOT [8]

second method, which the tantras agree is not only easier but more powerful, is to receive a mantra that has been empowered by a teacher or a lineage of teachers. This is like having the mantra activated at the source, because then it is imbued with the effort and the inner experience of the teachers who have practiced with it over the centuries.

The more direct the transmission, the more power is embedded in the mantra. But the transmission doesn't have to come in the form of a whisper in the ear, as in the old guru–disciple stories. The transmission can be verbal, it can come through writing, or it can be received in a dream or meditation. When you receive a mantra through transmission, the key code has been unlocked for you.

Practicing with a Mantra

The simplest, most basic way of working with a mantra is to combine it with the breath. You breathe in softly, thinking the mantra with the inhalation. You exhale gently, thinking the mantra with the exhalation. If you're practicing with a long mantra, like *Om Namah Shivaya* or *Om Mani Padme Hum,* you might find it difficult to coordinate the mantra with your breathing. One solution is to adjust the speed of your mantra repetition to the speed of your breathing. If you begin by mentally repeating the mantra rather quickly, you will probably find that your repetition slows automatically as you get deeper into meditation and your breath slows. Another solution is not to try to coordinate it with the breathing, but simply to think the mantra to yourself over and over again.

The one truth, formless ... eternal ... infinite, imperishable, inaccessible to mind and speech, shines forth in the conjunction of the great mantra and its profound meaning.

—KULARNAVA TANTRA [9]

Many people find there is a lot of power in enunciating the syllables of a mantra precisely and distinctly. But I've always found that the mantra opens up more easily if I don't try so hard to enunciate. Instead, I allow a slight slurring, a blurring together, of the syllables. I've noticed that when I repeat a mantra with "hard" focus, trying to keep each syllable separate, I tend to create a sense of difference between myself and the mantra, and this can become a barrier that keeps me from releasing into meditation. In mantra practice, as in any technique, the effort you make needs to be soft and subtle—the effortless effort about which we spoke in chapter 3. You focus, yes, but your focus is not a grasping concentration, not a mental fist gripped around the technique. Instead, you hold the mantra in your awareness as delicately as you would hold a bird that had alighted on your arm.

The Levels of Mantra

As you become more intimate with a mantra, you begin to experience it on progressively deeper levels. A mantra has three basic aspects. On the simplest level, of course, a mantra is an object of focus. It is a thought you can cling to in order to keep other thoughts at bay. On a deeper level, the mantra is an energy that comes from, and connects you to, a specific grace-stream, to a teacher or teaching lineage, or to the energy of a deity. At this level, it channels subtle energy into your system, and functions within you as a subtle force of transformation. On the very deepest level, the mantra is pure radiance, pure silence, and pure love. According to the *Shiva Sutras*, this is the *rahasya*, or secret, within the mantra. At its core, a mantra is the light of supreme Awareness itself.[10] The *Parasurama Kalpa Sutra*, one of the esoteric texts of the North Indian yogic tradition, says *"mantra maheshvara,"* or "Mantra is [a form of] the supreme Reality." In the tantric traditions, mantras are regarded as sound-forms of specific deities. A practitioner will repeat a mantra as a way of connecting with the subtle power personified in a deity-form like Durga or Tara. In fact, the tradition says that mantra is actually the most powerful form of deity energy, because it connects to the essential vibratory energy at the heart of the deity-form. Certain mantras, however, are said to hold within them the light of the formless reality beyond all forms. *Om* is one of those, as is *Om Namah Shivaya.* That's why practice of these mantras can offer such a direct and immediate experience of the sacred. The tetragrammaton YHWH, sometimes used as a mantra in Kabbalistic meditation, is said to be encoded in the DNA, and to connect a human being to their inborn spiritual essence. Similarly, the breath mantra *Hamsa* or *So'ham,* which corresponds to similar mantric sounds found in Hebrew and Arabic, is traditionally believed to be embedded in the subtle cellular structure of the energy system.

How the Mantra Works

Of course, all this is not necessarily apparent at first. When you initially begin to practice with a mantra, you are usually working purely with the syllables, and you seem to spend much of your time in meditation losing track of them. You try to stay with the mantra, but without even knowing how it happens, you keep finding yourself somewhere else—thinking about the laundry, worrying about what your brother-in-law said yesterday, wondering whether to drive to the city or take the bus. This moment when you catch yourself thinking, however, is a powerful point of practice. At such a moment, there are a couple of possibilities.

You could follow the original thought or let yourself get caught up in an inner commentary on the process—such as berating yourself for thinking—or you could choose to bring yourself back to the mantra. The practice, clearly, is to bring yourself back. Without surrendering to the reverie or getting upset with yourself for thinking, you just come back to the mantra. After a while, the mantra begins to act as a sort of magnet that aligns the particles of your scattered attention. This practice of gathering up the rays of your mental energy and bringing them into alignment is referred to in Patanjali's *Yoga Sutras* as *dharana,* which literally means "concentration."

At any point in this process, the shakti embedded in the mantra can plunge you into meditation—sometimes right in the middle of a particularly nagging thought! Here is where the right bhavana can often help, quickening the mantra energy by adding feeling to your practice.

During worship,
all the actions performed
merge into the mantra.
The mantra, which
is the name,
merges into the mind.
When the mind merges,
everything dissolves.
Then the world of the
seen, along with the seer,
assumes the form
of Consciousness.

—LALLA DED [11]

Someone once told me that the mantra given by her teacher seemed impenetrable—"just Sanskrit words with no meaning"—until she was asked to repeat the mantra with the feeling that she was gently dropping the syllables into her heart. That bhavana made the mantra more personal for her. She began to notice that when she dropped the mantra into her heart region, she experienced a soft expansion of tenderness there, as if she were receiving an inner caress. Love began to arise in her. The mantra syllables seemed to merge into her heart.

For this woman, a devotional bhavana helped open the mantra. For someone else, repeating the mantra with the feeling that the syllables pulsate with enlightening energy, or offering the mantra to the inner Beloved, might provide the opening. You could think of the mantra as light or even visualize the syllables in letters of light inside your awareness. If you are a visual person, in fact, you may need to do a visualization as you repeat the mantra before you succeed in opening the mantra for yourself. If you respond more to sound, try having the feeling that the mantra is being sung to you; try to hear it being chanted inside. If you tend to be kinesthetic, feel for the pulsation in the mantra, the energy experience of it. I'm a kinesthetic meditator, and mantra practice only began to work strongly for me after I learned to think of the syllables as energies and to feel each syllable pulsating inside me as I repeated it. Then the energy of the mantra began to open up for me into a pulsing sweetness, a feeling of gathering love.

Eventually, as we become sensitized to the feel of a mantra, we learn to hold the syllables within our awareness in such a way that we can actually sense the vibration, the throb of shakti, in the syllables. At this point, we begin to be able to merge our attention into the mantra energy, and as we do, we feel the mantra beginning to sink through the layers of our subtle being and to affect us at deeper and deeper levels. The mantra moves from the conscious level, where we have to repeat it distinctly with every breath, to a more subconscious space, where we can at times feel the mantra throbbing beneath our conscious awareness. Eventually the syllables seem to pulsate with love, with Awareness, with an expansive feeling, or even with light. In other words, we begin to experience a palpable sense of Presence in the mantra as we repeat it. One of the important Shaivite texts, the *Spanda Karikas,* refers to that Presence as the *spanda* (throb)—the original pulsation of divine energy that creates the universe and remains embedded within every particle of it. The mantra is actually one of the main vehicles we can use to become aware of that ground energy.

Once you start to feel that energy, you begin to love repeating the mantra. Like the poet-saints Tukaram and Namdev, whose essential practice was to repeat the names of God, you experience deep joy in simply turning the syllables over and over in your mind.

That experience of an energetic presence in the syllables is a sign that the mantra has cracked open for you and that you are experiencing the "real" mantra, the inner mantra. Ramana Maharshi once said, "Mantra is our real nature. When we realize the Self, then mantra repetition goes on without effort. What is the means at one stage becomes the goal at another." [13]

If you want the truth,
I'll tell you the truth:
Listen to the secret
sound, the real sound,
which is inside you.
The one no one talks
of speaks the secret
sound to himself,
and he is the one who
has made it all.

—KABIR [12]

89

This experience can happen quite early in your practice. When you are deep in meditation, you will sometimes feel the mantra dissolving into light, into pure energy, or into bliss. People have "seen" the form of a deity arising out of the mantra. In meditation, one man saw himself riding astride the mantra syllables, which had formed an arc of light that ended in an ocean of radiance. A young woman repeating the mantra *So'ham* began to hear the mantra repeating itself spontaneously, then felt her awareness open until she experienced herself as pure vastness.

When I repeat my own mantra with great feeling, I sometimes find that its energy will fill my body, and then seem to turn into a human-sized white lingam—the pillarlike form worshiped in India as a representation of the formless Absolute. Then that form will disappear, and I will be left with a feeling of silent, pulsing presence.

Try to gain one moment in which you see only God in heaven and earth.

—ABU YAZID AL'BASTAMI [14]

When the mantra begins to reveal itself at the deepest level, both the syllables and the feeling of pulsation disappear completely, and we experience only pure Awareness, the mantra as pure silence. This is a *samadhi* state—a conscious state of absorption in love, power, and crystalline Awareness.

Unpacking a Mantra: So'ham

For the basic practice given below, we'll work with one of the great Sanskrit mantras, *So'ham*. However, if you've already practiced with a mantra, please feel free to use the one with which you're already familiar.

So'ham is sometimes called the natural mantra, or the mantra of the breath, because its sound is like the natural *susurra* that the breath makes as it flows in and out of the nostrils. *So'ham* (the "a" in *ham* is pronounced like the "u" in "cup") means "That am I." "That" refers to the pure Awareness at the heart of reality. So the mantra *So'ham* reminds you that your true self is identical with pure Consciousness. It expresses the realization of enlightened beings. When you coordinate it with your breathing, you can begin to feel that your own breath is reminding you of the deepest truth of who you are. However, if breath practices are uncomfortable for you, feel free to simply think the mantra in a relaxed rhythm, letting it become part of the stream of your consciousness, and gradually allowing *So'ham* to become your dominant thought.

Exercise: Basic Mantra Practice with So'ham

Sit in a comfortable, upright posture and close your eyes. Focus on the flow of the breath. Gently and with relaxed attention, begin to think the mantra *So'ham*. Coordinate the syllables with the breathing—*so* on the exhalation, *ham* on the inhalation. Or simply think the mantra to yourself in a gentle, relaxed rhythm.

Listen to the syllables as you repeat them. Allow your attention to focus more and more fully on the mantra's syllables.

Feel that each syllable is softly dropping into your awareness. Gently tune in to the energetic sensation that

> the mantra creates inside. When thoughts arise, as soon as you notice yourself thinking, bring your attention back to the mantra. If your attention wanders, bring it gently back to the mantra. Little by little, let the mantra become the predominant thought in your mind.

The Essential Bhava: Feeling the Presence in the Syllables

Any mantra will work much more quickly if you can remember that the radiance of supreme Awareness is present inside the syllables. This is a core instruction that applies not only to mantra repetition, but also to every practice that we do. It is the ultimate bhava, and yet it can seem quite abstract and difficult to practice at first.

The best way to work with this instruction is not to try to eat it whole, so to speak, but to use it as an invitation to investigate your experience of the mantra. Working with an instruction like "Feel the presence of God, of universal Consciousness, in the mantra syllables" confronts you with the gap between the teaching and your experience. It challenges you to understand how pure Consciousness could possibly be present inside a word. The answer you come up with needs to be a real answer, not just an intellectual formulation. For that to happen, you need to question yourself, to inquire, "What am I really experiencing? How do I need to hold myself so that the mantra will reveal its inner essence? How can I get deeper into the mantra?"

Holding this kind of awake, contemplative awareness as you repeat a mantra makes your practice very alive. It keeps it from becoming mechanical. It leads to insight. I recently talked to a man who told me that when he first heard the instruction "Feel divine presence in the mantra syllables," it drove him so crazy that he finally began asking the mantra itself to help him out. "What do they mean when they say you are divine?" he asked over and over again. One day the mantra "answered" him. It began to vibrate waves of ecstasy all through his chest. The feeling of ecstasy expanded, and along with the mantra, the man's awareness and his sense of being began to expand outward, until he felt as though his body contained a vast spaciousness.

The Kashmiri sage Somananda gave a key instruction on mantra repetition. He said that you should do it with the feeling that you, the mantra, and the goal of the mantra are not different. In other words, it's all about identification. The idea is that you should think *the mantra describes who you are, just the way you might normally assume that your body or your personal history is you.* When someone calls your name, you respond. In just the same way, if you identify with the mantra, with the light and transformative energy in the mantra, it shifts you into a meditative state immediately. Again, this instruction is an invitation to contemplation. It is a way to enter into a more vibrant relationship with the mantra.

As you think about how to go about identifying yourself with the mantra, you might find yourself discovering a lot about what you are and what the mantra really is. How do you practice identifying yourself with a word? I've asked many people over the years how they practice identifying themselves with a mantra, and I've heard many imaginative responses. One way is to imagine that the mantra is a cloud that surrounds you on all sides. Another is to imagine it as water, or as light, and to see yourself immersed in it. Still another is to bring yourself as energy closer and closer to the mantra until you feel that you are inside it. All of these practices help open the experience of repeating a mantra.

Exercise: Sensing the Mantra as Light

Sit quietly, and begin to breathe with the mantra *So'ham*. Let your focus be soft, and don't try to control the breath in any way. Breathe in with the subtle thought *ham* and out with the thought *so*. (Or simply think *So'ham, So'ham* to yourself at a relaxed pace.)

Consider that as you focus on the mantra, its syllables are reminding you that you are Consciousness, that in your essence you are the light of Awareness itself. Let yourself take this in. The mantra is calling your name, the name of your true Self. Take a moment or two to feel and contemplate what this means.

Then let go of that contemplation, and simply focus softly on the energy within the mantra syllables as they drop into your inner space.

Sense the energy that pulses within the sounds, and imagine that the mantra syllables are pulsating light. Let the light appear in its own way. It might be golden or white, or you might sense it simply as an energetic lightness. Even if you aren't visual, you can often sense light as an energy within the mantra syllables.

Feel that this light, this energy, carries infinite blessing. Feel the light-energy in the mantra syllables pour into and through your body with each breath.

As *ham* flows in with the inhalation, it pours into your your body as light and blessing. As *so* flows out with the exhalation, it expands through your body as light and blessing. With each breath, let the light energy within the syllables expand. Begin to feel that you are inside the mantra's energy and that the mantra's light is pouring through your body until it fills you and surrounds you on every side, like a river of liquid luminosity, or like a pulsating cloud of energy. Relax into the sensations, taking rest in the mantra as it fills your being.

If thoughts arise—even great insights!—let them go as soon as you notice them, and bring your attention back to the mantra and to the expanding sense of its energy and light.

The Space Between the Breaths

The Kashmiri sage Kshemaraja, in his book *Pratyabhijna Hridayam (The Heart of Recognition),* offered in just a few words one of the great mystical secrets, saying that the way to experience the fullness of the ultimate reality is to expand the *madhya,* or the center.[15] Madhya is a technical term for the still point between two phases of movement. When a pendulum swings, there is a fraction of a moment at the end of each swing when the movement stops, before the pendulum begins to swing back.

That moment of pause is the madhya, the central still point out of which the pendulum's movement arises. All movement—whether the swing of an axe, the movement of the breath, or the flow of thought—arises out of such a point of stillness. That still point is an open door into the heart of the universe, a place where we can step into the big Consciousness beyond our small consciousness. As the medieval English saint Julian of Norwich wrote, "God is at the midpoint between all things."[16]

One of my favorite descriptions of this reality is from the poem "Burnt Norton," in T. S. Eliot's *Four Quartets:*

> At the still point of the turning world. Neither flesh
> nor fleshless;
> Neither from nor towards; at the still point, there the
> dance is,
> But neither arrest nor movement. And do not call it fixity,
> Where past and future are gathered. Neither movement
>   from nor towards.
> Neither ascent nor decline. Except for the point, the
> still point,
> There would be no dance, and there is only the dance.
> I can only say, there we have been: but I cannot say where.
> And I cannot say, how long, for that is to place it in time.[17]

Tripura Rahasya, a wonderful text of Vedanta, calls these pregnant still points "fleeting samadhis."[18] Such points exist at many different moments. One of these is the pause between sleeping and waking, the moment when we first wake up before we become fully conscious. Another is the moment before a sneeze or at the high point of a yawn. Another is the space between thoughts. If we focus our attention in one of these gaps, it may open up for us, and we will find ourselves in the madhya, "the still point of the turning world," the placeless place where we leave the activity of the manifest universe and enter the emptiness at the heart of manifestation.

This is, in fact, the inner realm that Ramana Maharshi, Abhinavagupta, and other sages have called the Heart—meaning not the physical heart or even the heart chakra, but the mystical Great Heart that contains All-that-Is. This is the place of ultimate stillness, where the microcosm of human consciousness expands into the macrocosmic vastness of the ultimate. It is the Consciousness that underlies all forms. The divine mind. The Self.

One of the most accessible points of entry into the madhya is the space between the inhalation and the exhalation, and between the exhalation and the inhalation.

In the next exercise, you will be given the opportunity to access the space between the breaths by focusing on the sound of the breath itself. The secret of entering this space is awareness and subtle, relaxed attention. The space between the breaths is tiny and subtle—so subtle that at first it seems barely there at all. So to enter it, we need to pay close attention.

Exercise: The Space Between Breaths

Sitting in a firm, upright, yet relaxed posture, softly focus your attention on the movement of the breath. Let your inhalation come into the heart region in the center of the chest, and let the exhalation arise from there.

As you breathe, let the breath make a little sound as it passes through the nostrils. You might notice a slightly audible *ham* sound on the in-breath and something like *so* or *sah* on the out-breath. As we saw earlier, in Sanskrit *ham* means "I" and *so/sah* means "that." The sound of the breath is a natural mantra, as if we are being reminded with every inhalation and exhalation to remember our identity with the Infinite. But it's not necessary to hear the sound as a mantra. Just hearing the sound as it is, is enough.

Listen to the sound that the breath makes and notice that when it comes to an end in the region of the heart, there is an infinitesimal pause, a tiny "space" of stillness. Focus on that pause. Don't try to lengthen it; just note it.

Then when the exhalation starts, follow the sound of the breath until it comes to an end in the space outside. Again note the pause. Focus softly there, but don't try to lengthen it.

Keep following the breath in this way, gently focusing on the space inside and the space outside. Let the practice itself absorb your attention.

There is no need to worry about whether or not you feel something happening, and no need to feel frustrated if the space doesn't immediately open further. The doorway to the madhya opens by grace, by its own will. If you simply stay with it, the expansion will happen.

For me, it opened with a tap on the head! A few weeks after my teacher first instructed me in this practice, I was sitting in the meditation room in his ashram, trying to feel the space between the breaths. Try as I might, the space wouldn't lengthen. It was so small that it seemed nonexistent.

Suddenly the door swung open, and my guru walked in. He walked up to me and tapped me sharply on the head. In the next moment, a vast chasm opened between my in-breath and my out-breath. The breath stopped, and I was inside a huge space, a kind of ocean of Awareness.

Admittedly this is a rather dramatic example of how a guru might help a student open the inner space. You don't need to get whacked on the side of the head by a guru or a Zen master in order for the inner space to open. It is enough to sit, to practice the technique, and to wait. In time, you will become sensitive to the feel of the space there. Then one day, perhaps at a moment when your thoughts have thinned out and slowed down enough for you to perceive in a more subtle way, you will notice the space lengthening. You will be able to feel the gap between the breaths and enter into it for a little while—even while the breath continues going in and out.

One way you know you're entering deeply into the practice is when you begin to feel that your breath is moving "horizontally." Instead of feeling the whole arc of the breath coming in through the nostrils, going to the heart, and moving back out, you seem to be breathing in and out of the chest. Sometimes, instead of a horizontal breath, the breath comes in and out in a circling motion that seems to operate completely independently of the body. At that point, you might begin to experience how the space inside the body is connected to the space outside. You might realize that one field of Consciousness connects both the spaces, and that the separation we normally make between inside and outside is nothing more than an illusion.

In general, it is better to let the breath come in and out naturally—not to hold your breath or try to force the breath to extend itself. Yet, I've found that at certain times—perhaps at the beginning of a daily practice—the following exercise can help jump-start the process by giving you a feel for the space between the breaths. It re-creates the state that we would like to have arise spontaneously, in this case the moment when the *madhya* begins to reveal itself in meditation.

Exercise: Finding God at the End of the Exhalation

When you come to the end of an exhalation, let the breath stay out for thirty seconds or as long as it feels comfortable to you. Rest in that space where there is no more breath. Then name the space "God" or "the Self" or "pure Consciousness." Letting yourself stay in that moment of emptiness at the end of the exhalation is a way of entering into the space of the Self. Notice how in that space you are fully in the present. There is no past, no future—just the experience of now.

MEDITATION ON CONSCIOUSNESS

Meditation on pure Consciousness is usually considered an advanced practice, mainly because Awareness is so elusive and insubstantial that a beginning meditator can have a hard time finding a foothold in it. But once the mind has shed some of its surface agitation and acquired a bit of subtlety, this practice tends to suggest itself naturally. In fact, it often happens on its own.

Any technique you meditate with will eventually disappear for you, even if you try to hold on to it. In India, there's a saying that a technique is like the car you drive to the temple: when you get to the temple, you leave the car behind. In fact, the "car" of your meditation technique usually gives out long before you get to the temple. At some point, the mantra syllables will dissolve into pulsations of energy, the visual form will melt into the space that surrounds it, and the breath will slow down or stop. Then you will be left with your own bare consciousness, your own inner sensations, the basic pulsation of your own energy.

Some people worry when they get to this point. They think that they have lost the technique and that something has gone wrong. In fact, it means that the technique is bearing fruit. Once the mind has become centered and relatively quiet, our deeper Awareness naturally emerges and presents itself as the primary object of meditation. To use Emily Dickinson's metaphor:

The Props assist the House
Until the House is built
And then the Props withdraw

101

And adequate, erect,
The House supports itself.[19]

Consciousness, of course, is not a house, nor is it any kind of object. It is the eternal subject; it is what Meister Eckhart called the "ground of being." Because this technique is so direct, it can create a big shift in our understanding, even if we are only able to hold it for a moment or two.

Most days I begin my meditation practice by working with a form, as discussed in the mantra techniques earlier in this chapter. Sometimes I focus on a mantra; at other times, I follow the breath or look for the space at the end of the exhalation. At some point, usually half an hour to forty minutes into the meditation session, the thought-stream slows to a trickle, the object of focus melts back into the Awareness from which it has arisen, and my attention becomes focused on the subtle, pulsating energy that underlies my thoughts. At that point, my meditation becomes centered directly on the energy field of my own consciousness. For me, this is the heart of my meditation practice—simply being present with the pulsation of energy that throbs constantly inside Awareness.

Let's look for a moment at that pulsation. It is one of the most important clues to deeper meditation.

Exercise: Finding the Pulsation in Your Consciousness

Sit in a comfortable, upright posture. With eyes closed, regard your inner consciousness. You are not looking for anything. You are just observing your own inner world with your inner eye, becoming aware of what your inner eye actually sees when you close your eyes. Perhaps you see blue light or a field of gray, or perhaps you see a haze of darkness filled with tiny points of light, like a pointillist painting. You are looking at what in Sanskrit is called the chitta, the mind-stuff, the inner consciousness. This is the energetic ground from which all thoughts, feelings, perceptions, and sensations arise, and into which they subside.

Now notice the dynamic quality of this inner consciousness. Notice how there is a constant shimmer of subtle movement, a kind of vibration or pulsation within it. Your inner consciousness is made of energy. It vibrates, and it is that vibration which gives rise to thoughts and feelings and images.

See if you can become aware of the pulsation of your consciousness. In its physical form, that pulsation manifests as the heartbeat, but if you pay close attention, you can sense a subtler pulsation that underlies the heartbeat.

If you do not immediately feel the subtle pulsation, focus on the throb of your heartbeat.

Stay with the heartbeat until you begin to feel its subtler level, or to feel how its pulsation actually reverberates through the body. Or if you feel a pulsation of energy somewhere else in the body, focus on that until you gradually become aware of the subtler pulsation that underlies it.

In Sanskrit, the subtlest level of this pulsation is called spanda, meaning "throb" or "vibration." According to the *Spanda Karikas (Stanzas on Vibration),* one of the key texts of Kashmir Shaivism, the spanda is the original impulse of energy that creates all life and all worlds, and that keeps them going. When you sense the pulsation inside yourself, you are sensing your own personal spark of that huge, primordial life force. It is the energy behind the breath, the heartbeat, and the movement of our thoughts and feelings. It is also the source of all our experiences in meditation. When you get deep into meditation, you realize that this throb, this subtle pulsation, is actually meditating *you.*

The tantric texts speak of this pulsation as the pure expression of kundalini, the evolutionary power within us. One medieval Shaivite text, *Tantra Sadbhava,* says that the same power that enlivens a mantra is actually inherent in the mind of an experienced meditator. You notice its throb as you get quiet in meditation. That throbbing energy gradually draws the mind into meditation. If you focus on it and follow it, it will lead you to its source, to the ultimate silence of the Self.

Thinking of the magnitude of the sky, Meditate on the Vastness with no center and no edge.

—MILAREPA[20]

Once you sense that subtle pulsation, stay with it. Let it become your point of focus, just as if it were a mantra. When you get out of touch with it, bring yourself back to it. As you stay with the pulsation, it will keep releasing you deeper into the field of your own being.

Of course, there are several other ways to practice directly entering Consciousness. Some of these practices, such as becoming aware of Awareness or being the observer or knower of thoughts, can be found in chapter 2. The one that follows is adapted from the *Vijnana Bhairava*.[21] It is a practice that yogis have been using for several thousand years.

Exercise: You Are in an Ocean of Space

Sit in a comfortable, upright posture, close your eyes, and gently merge your attention with the flow of breath coming in and going out through your nostrils. Keep returning your attention to the breath each time it wanders away. Do this until you feel the breath gently slow and the thoughts become quieter.

Imagine that your body is completely empty. It is as though your skin were a thin membrane, like the skin of a balloon, and inside it is nothing but space. Not only is your body full of space, but space also surrounds you on every side. As you inhale, have the feeling that you are breathing space in through the pores of your body. Exhale with the same feeling. Your skin is a delicate, porous membrane, and you are breathing through it. You are in an ocean of space. With each breath, gently let go into the ocean.

CLOSING YOUR PRACTICE

Just as preliminary practices help you turn within, a formal practice for ending your meditation session helps you transition from inner space to outer focus. The closing is a kind of ceremony that creates a container for the energy you've generated in meditation, and that can also help its benefits spread to others.

Here are three simple steps for closing:

First, fold your hands and silently offer thanks to your body and mind for supporting you in your practice. (Without the grace of your body and mind, your meditation would never get off the ground, so it's important to get in the habit of saying "Thank you," even if your body fidgeted and your mind ran all over the place!)

Second, offer your thanks to the grace and energy that lend power to your practice and allow it to unfold.

Finally, you can end by offering up your practice. Bowing your head, you might inwardly ask, "May this act of meditation bring benefit to all beings." Or "May my meditation contribute to the peace and harmony of the world." Or you could simply offer the blessing, "May all beings everywhere be happy and free."

You may also want to offer the benefits of your practice for the well-being of a particular person, for the benefit of the earth, or to bring peace, harmony, or healing to a situation that needs it.

You'll find more practices for closing your meditation in chapter 10.

FOLLOW YOUR INSTINCTS

Any of the practices in this chapter will open up into the Self. All are empowered, infused with the energy of many lineages of enlightened meditators. I suggest you spend some time experimenting with each one. Notice how each practice affects your meditation. If one practice doesn't seem to fit, try another.

Of course, you don't want to become a technique junkie, flitting from practice to practice without ever entering deeply into any particular one. However, if you clearly understand that a technique is not an end in itself but simply the doorway into the greater Awareness, you can begin to sense which doorway is going to open most easily for you at a particular moment. Some practices will energize you or pull you out of stagnation. Others will kindle love. Others, you'll find, will help quiet an agitated mind.

Playing with different practices helps us get to know ourselves and what works best for us. Everyone's road is unique, and ultimately no one else can tell us what we need. That's why there aren't any rules about the "best" way to meditate, except that a practice should soothe the restlessness of the mind and make it easier for you to enter the interior silence. You find this out only through practice.

There is one more principle to remember in working with a technique. Nearly always, when people have difficulties going deeper into meditation, it is because they are keeping some sort of separation between themselves and their technique, and between themselves and the goal. The antidote for nearly every problem that arises in meditation is to give up the feeling that you and the technique and the goal are separate from each other. The bhavana of oneness is so powerful that just thinking about it, even if you don't believe it, will change the quality of your meditation.

The mind, turned outwards, results in thoughts and objects. Turned inwards, it becomes itself the Self.

—RAMANA MAHARSHI [22]

107

CHAPTER FIVE

*M*oving Inward:
The Practice of Oneness

*Y*ears ago, when I was first beginning to meditate, I found myself swimming in an ocean of light. The light was all around me, dazzling in my inner vision, seemingly without limits or shores. Experiences like this come from time to time in our meditation journey, like gifts or beacons that show us what is possible. Though they usually don't last, they reveal truths about the nature of reality that we can contemplate for years.

In this particular meditation, as I sensed the light around me, an inner voice said, with great conviction and authority, "Become the light!" I felt that if I could manage to do that, my journey would be over, or at the very least, I'd have made a breakthrough. But I couldn't. The problem wasn't that I was afraid; I was simply caged, enclosed in the feeling of being "me." My sense of limited personal identity was too stubborn to let go.

As I came out of meditation, feeling vastly disappointed in myself, two words arose: "Practice oneness." My inner being was telling me that if I couldn't realize the Truth, at least I could practice it, contemplate it, and remember it. Since then I have become convinced that even if we were to forget every other instruction about meditation, we could never go wrong if we would just remember that whatever we experience is part of one great field of light, of energy, of Consciousness.

Oneness is the Truth. All the teachers of the great non-dual traditions say the same thing in their own way. Jalaluddin Rumi, classical texts of Advaita Vedanta like the *Avadhuta Gita,* the Tibetan teachers of Dzogchen, and the German mystic Meister Eckhart all have told us that there is only one reality, one Awareness in the universe, and that we have never been separate from that. They have also pointed out that all our problems, from fear, to craving, to feeling abandoned, from selfishness, to aggression, to loneliness, to carelessness toward each other and the earth, arise from the feeling of being separate. So even an instant spent remembering oneness strikes at the root of our human dilemma. Even better is to follow the advice of the Kashmiri sage Somananda, the author of *Shiva Drishti (The Viewpoint of God),* an important tantric text. Somananda's position was this: "I am God, and all the instruments of my *sadhana* [spiritual practice] are God. Being God, I will attain God."

Of course, just to know this intellectually is not enough. One famous Vedantic parable tells of the sage-king Janaka, who used to repeat "*So'ham*—I am That" (meaning "I am the

Absolute")—over and over to himself. One day, as he stood by the local river saying *"So'ham, So'ham,"* he heard a man on the opposite bank shouting over and over, "I have my water bowl, I have my stick."

First Janaka became annoyed. Then he became curious. "Why do you keep shouting that you have your water bowl and your stick?" he called out. "Who said you didn't have them?"

The man (who, as is often the case in these stories, was actually an enlightened sage in disguise) called back, "That's just what I wanted to ask you! You already are the Absolute, so why do you have to keep shouting about it?"

The point he was making was that it isn't enough just to practice oneness. We need to realize it, to get it, to let ourselves *be* That.

The knowledge of one's identity with the pure Self . . . sets a person free even against his will, when it becomes as firm as the person's belief that he is a human being.

—SHANKARACHARYA [1]

Still, practicing oneness helps increase our chances of experiencing it. That's the basic law of inner transformation: practice creates an inner climate within which grace can reveal the reality you are trying to discover. If you keep feeding the bhava of unity into your mind, intellect, and imagination, your consciousness will eventually respond by generating its own spontaneous intuitions and realizations of oneness. That is one reason why it is so important for meditators to read and study the teachings of realized beings who speak from the state of oneness. Our sense of duality is so tenacious, so deeply ingrained, that holding on to a feeling of unity is not easy. The mind might grasp the concept for a moment, only to skitter off when a really gripping emotion or fear seduces its attention.

THE SHAIVITE PHILOSOPHERS OF KASHMIR

At this point, I would like to say a few words about Kashmir Shaivism, the philosophical system that is the basis for most of the teachings in this book.

Take a pitcher full of water and set it down on the water— now it has water inside and water outside. We mustn't give it a name, lest silly people start talking again about the body and the soul.

—KABIR [2]

Kashmir Shaivism has a rather remarkable history. Between the seventh and thirteenth centuries CE, a lineage of yogi-philosophers flourished in northern India. They belonged to a cloistered brahmin community called *panditas,* centered in the city of Srinagar. No one knew of them outside the Vale of Kashmir, though their tradition was linked to schools of nondual teachings in southern and western India, as well as to other northern Indian schools of Hindu and Buddhist Tantrism.

The teachers of Kashmir Shaivism were not just theoretical philosophers. Many of them were siddhas, enlightened yogis, who used the system as a way to clothe their inner experience in words. Their path was a juicy amalgam of metaphysical doctrines, maps of human consciousness, yogic practices, and devotion. They worshiped the ultimate Reality as one great divine Consciousness, with two inseparable aspects that they called Shiva and Shakti, the former being supreme Awareness and the latter being its intrinsic creative Power. Since their realization showed them that Shakti becomes all the forms, subtle and physical, in this world, they had no trouble loving the absolute Reality as a personal deity, as all-pervading formless Awareness, and as their innermost Self. Shiva, as the ultimate divine intelligence, was also considered the original teacher of the tradition and the ultimate source of its core texts—the *Shiva Sutras,* the *Malini Vijaya Tantra,* and the *Vijnana Bhairava.* These texts were, at the very least, inspired by the deep meditational experiences of awakened sages.

The unique quality of the Shaiva system is its radical nondualism. Rejecting the Vedantic view that the material world is illusory, an empty dream, the sages of Kashmir Shaivism saw all forms of the universe as manifestations of divine creative energy, of Shakti, the dynamic female principle. They worshiped Shakti in themselves, in the earth, and in every substantial and insubstantial thing, and they looked for the pulsing heart of divine bliss within all domains of experience. Astute seekers of the tradition knew innumerable pathways for uncovering the experience of the divine. They knew how to extract it from states like terror or pleasure or in the high point of a sneeze; they knew how to find the pulsation of ecstasy in empty space, in fixed attention, and in the sensations that come from swaying or twirling, or enjoying music or the taste of food.

But the crucial insight of Shaivism is its recognition that when human consciousness lets go of its identification with the body and reflects back on itself, it is revealed as a perfect, if limited, form of the supreme "I," which is God. By expanding their own I-consciousness beyond its limits, past its tendency to cling to narrow definitions of itself, yogis of the Shaivite path experienced God as themselves.

Because they saw the world as divine, the Shaivite yogis of Kashmir had no difficulty enjoying life in all its different flavors. In this they differed from their Vedantic cousins and from the Madhyamika Buddhists who inhabited the same region of India. Shaivism was not a traditional renunciant's path. Abhinavagupta, the pre-eminent genius of the tradition, was not only a philosopher and a widely revered guru but also an aesthetician, an artist and musician, and the center of a circle where sensory experience—including art, music, and drama—was constantly being trans-muted into yoga.

Can you coax your mind from its wandering and keep to the original oneness? . . . Can you cleanse your inner vision until you see nothing but the light? . . . Can you step back from your own mind and thus understand all things?

—LAO TZU [3]

It is this insight—that a serious practitio-ner of yoga does not reject their world, but instead transforms daily experience through their practice—that sets Kashmir Shaivism apart from many Indian yogic traditions, and has made this system particularly reso-nant for our time. Yet Kashmir Shaivism had all but disappeared as a living tradition when a series of synchronous events rescued it from obscurity.

In the early years of the twentieth century, the Maharaja of Kashmir encouraged important local scholars to bring together some of the texts of the tradition. These were printed, in Sanskrit, in a limited edition called the *Kashmir Series of Texts and Studies*. Sent without fanfare to university libraries in India, Europe, and the United States, the books gathered dust, unnoticed until the 1950s. It was then that a few scholars around the world—a Bengali Sanskritist in Benares, a French scholar at the Sorbonne, an Italian professor— picked up some of these texts and began to go through them. Translations began to appear in French and in Italian. Some graduate students traveled to Srinagar to sit at the feet of Swami Laksman Joo, one of the last living masters of the tradition.

You who want knowledge, see the Oneness within. There you will find the clear mirror already waiting.

—HADEWIJCH II [4]

In the early 1970s, an Indian scholar named Jaideva Singh began bringing out annotated English versions of key Kashmir Shaivite texts. Among them was *Pratyabhijna Hridayam (The Heart of Recognition)*, a pithy tenth-century distillation of the essential teachings about the identity of the individual and the divine, written by Kshemaraja, one of Abhinavagupta's disciples. The *Pratyabhijna Hridayam* condenses the heart of the philosophy into a form that is particularly easy for the ordinary practitioner to grasp. The twenty sutras and commentaries in this small book describe the stages by which the divine creative energy (called in Shaivism *chiti*, or creative Consciousness) becomes the world, creating the illusion of separation within its essential unity, descending into the state of a limited human soul, and finally recognizing itself again. (Hence the book's title, which means "The Heart of Recognition.") Its most radical point is that the entire spiritual process—the process of recognizing one's intrinsic divinity—is brought about by the very same creative energy that caused us to forget who we are. In short, it is a teaching of absolute nonduality.

One of the teachers who recognized the radical importance of this text was Swami Muktananda, who saw his own experience of the post-enlightenment state described in it. When he began teaching in the West, he brought the *Pratyabhijna Hridayam* with him and introduced it to his students, some of whom helped to bring these texts into the Western spiritual world. He also became instrumental in getting it published by the Indian press Motilal Banarsidass.

DISCOVERING THE TEACHINGS

For me, as for many others who discovered Shaivism in those years, this teaching created a shift in awareness that was almost as radical as the experience of kundalini awakening. From the beginning, just reading some of the aphorisms of the *Pratyabhijna Hridayam* would instantaneously transform my state of mind. One moment I would be out of sorts, worried, and off-center. Then I would remember one of the teachings of Shaivism— perhaps "Universal Consciousness manifests this universe out of its own freedom, upon the screen of its own being"—and my perspective would immediately expand. It was like being in a small room and suddenly having the roof blow off to expose the sky. Even to consider the possibility that this could be true, that everything could be made of one Awareness, demanded a complete reframing of my ideas about myself.

One afternoon in the mid-1970s, I overheard a discussion between two friends. We had just been working with a practice for recognizing our identity with divine Consciousness. This involved looking at our own mental process—in which thoughts are constantly coming into being, staying for a while, then dissolving—as a mirror of the cosmic process of the creation, maintenance, and dissolution of natural forms.

One of my friends had been practicing this understanding with a lot of diligence and inspiration. On this particular afternoon, with persuasive excitement, he began to describe his experiences. He'd realized, he told us, that everything inside him is a manifestation of divine Consciousness—that in every moment and in every mood he could recognize the presence of divine energy, of Shiva, the supreme Lord.

A woman who was listening became more and more uncomfortable as he continued talking about how we are all Shiva, how we are all God. Finally, she burst forth with her objection. "But what if you're depressed?" she asked. "How can you be Shiva if you're depressed?"

"If I'm depressed, then I'm depressed Shiva!" he said.

"No way," retorted the woman.

I could sympathize with her problem. I, too, had a hard time feeling that my unhappy, uncomfortable states were divine, that they were inseparable from the wholeness of Consciousness.

Like this woman, I held the deep assumption that I could only be close to the Truth (let alone one with it) when I was "good," happy, pure, and feeling positive about myself. It was difficult for me to understand that divinity could also exist inside feelings like depression and anger. As another friend once put it, "How can I be God when I don't get along with my mother?"

The magic of looking at yourself as intrinsically divine— divine even in your flawed humanness—is this: it gives rise to a kind of unconditional self-love that has a way of changing your attitude toward your mother, and also toward your depression. It isn't that negative feelings disappear overnight. Depending on our mental habits and tendencies, they might continue to arise for some time. Nor can we let our understanding about intrinsic divinity become an excuse for indulging in anger, greed, and the rest of our darker emotions. (Ramakrishna Paramahamsa used to say that milk and muddy water are both God, but we don't drink the muddy water!)

Whether through immense joy or through anguish, Whether from on a wall or in an earthen jug, Whether from external objects or from within, Reveal yourself to me, O Lord!

—UTPALADEVA [5]

Still, if you can remember that divine energy, pure Awareness, God-ness, is present even in the midst of your fear, anger, and depression, it becomes easier to let these feelings come and go without clinging to them, letting them derail you, or rejecting yourself for having them. There will be times, in fact, when your remembrance of oneness dissolves these feelings entirely. Remembering oneness helps make love arise.

It takes a lot of contemplation and self-inquiry to hold on to the understanding of oneness. As you practice it, you'll see—over and over again—the gap between your intellectual convictions and your underlying conditioning. Over the years, I've repeatedly been humbled by seeing how tenaciously I've clung to identification with my body and my personal agendas, and by my own resistance to the force that wants to expand me.

Yet these obstructions begin to disappear when you confront them. Rather than backing down before the force of your conditioned habits of mind or giving in to your fear of seeing your own largeness, you can simply ask yourself, "What lies behind this resistance? What deeper feelings might be there?" Once you discover what the resistance is made of, you can do the practice for working with intense emotions on page 157, and let go of each successive layer. You can keep on investigating what the sages meant when they told us that we are not different from Consciousness, that we are not different from God. In fact, you can do this every time you sit for meditation with whatever technique you happen to be practicing.

PRACTICING ONENESS

A good place to begin with practicing oneness is through one of Shaivism's basic teachings: the idea that when you repeat a mantra, you should understand that there is no difference between yourself, the mantra, and the goal of the mantra, which is the experience of the Self. Like most high teachings, this instruction sounds simple. The challenge comes when you try to do it. How do you go about identifying yourself—your solid, physical, personal self—with a mantra, with a Sanskrit word? How do you make that instruction real for yourself?

You have to begin by disengaging yourself from your feeling of being a particular personality and physical being. It is hard to identify with a mantra if you are thinking of yourself—even very subtly—as Martha, the 122-pound brunette who grew up outside Louisville, Kentucky, the person who secretly worries about her weight and whether or not she is lovable. On the other hand, if you think of yourself as energy or Awareness, and if you also think of the mantra as energy or vibration, it is a different matter entirely. Then you can begin to bring your own energy into alignment with the energy in the mantra.

How do you do this? You might try working with the pulsation in the syllables and in your mind. Feel how the syllables vibrate in your inner space when you say them. Let yourself tune in to the sensation of that energy. Then tune in to your internal space, your own Consciousness, and feel the shimmer of vibrating energy there. Become aware of the natural energy that is you. Once you mentally bring these two things together, you can feel that the energy in the mantra is no different from the energy of your Awareness. You can mentally merge your own energy into the energy of the mantra.

So to practice oneness, it helps to let go, at least provisionally, of the idea that you are simply a body. You will need to sense your own energy and begin to contemplate what it means to identify yourself with energy or Awareness, rather than with your body or your thoughts or your personality. Initially, this is the best way to make sense of the concept of oneness: realize that it is your Awareness, your energy, and your love that exist as one with others. (Eventually, we do come to realize that the body, too, is energy, but in the beginning it is easier to work with the energy whose subtlety we can easily sense.) When you and I are identified with our bodies, we are miles apart. When we are thinking of ourselves as individual personalities, we are wildly different. Only as energy, as Awareness, can we experience our unity.

Once we see and begin to remember that "I" am not a body but a center of Awareness and energy, all sorts of ways to practice oneness suggest themselves.

Exercise: Your Awareness Pervades the World

Sit in a comfortable, upright posture, close your eyes, and become attentive to the rhythm of your breathing. Observe the flow of the breath as it moves in and out of your nostrils. When thoughts arise, let them flow out with the breath. Keep your attention on the breath for a few minutes.

Now shift your attention from the breath to the Awareness that knows you are breathing. As you become aware of your Awareness, notice how everything you are experiencing in this moment is actually contained in this Awareness. It is not that Awareness is inside your head or inside your body. Your body, your breath, and your thoughts are all inside Awareness.

Now allow Awareness to expand outward. With each exhalation, feel that your Awareness expands more and more. Let it fill the room, then the building, then the surrounding area, expanding out into the sky and the universe. Let Awareness expand as far as it can go. Rest in the spaciousness of your expanded Awareness.

ENTERING THE EXPERIENCE

One potent and kinesthetic way to involve the experience of oneness in meditation is to practice entering into whatever presents itself to you, whether it is a mantra, a visual image, your heart-space, or an image of the Buddha; whether it is a pain in the knee or pressure in the forehead; whether it is the space between the in-breath and the out-breath; or a vision. You can change your relationship to whatever appears in your meditation if you enter it.

I like to use an imaginative process to do this. I think of a doorway or an opening, and I take myself through it. I keep on doing this until I have the feeling that I have entered the inner cave of the Self, the cave of the heart, the cave of Consciousness. This often takes several entrances through several successive inner doorways. But if I keep imagining doorways or openings or corridors, and keep taking myself through them, I eventually find myself in the deeper layers of my being. Consciousness seems to recognize this image of the doorway as a signal to release into the subtler and deeper layers of itself. It is an amazingly simple and powerful process. What waits on the other side of the doorway, finally, is the Self.

You can work with this principle in nearly every situation. Whatever appears before you in meditation and whatever technique you are practicing, you can enter it. You can create a "doorway" inside the pulsation of breath as it moves in and out of the heart by imagining an opening in the space between the breaths. Or you can enter the breath or the mantra by imagining that it surrounds you, like a cloud, or that you are immersed in it, like water. Or you can simply remind yourself, "This is a part of my own consciousness."

When, with a one-pointed and thought-free mind, a seeker contemplates his whole body or the entire universe all at once as being of the nature of Consciousness, he experiences the supreme awakening.

—VIJNANA BHAIRAVA [6]

I often use the awareness of oneness as an antidote to feelings of blockage or discomfort. Sometimes in meditation, I'll come to a point where I can't go further. It is as if an inner wall, an energy block, bars the way. There might be a strong feeling of pressure or even pain. Trying to move past it doesn't work. If I can let go of my resistance to the feeling of discomfort, stop trying to push it away, and instead go into the pain, I often find within it an entryway to a deeper level of energy. Often at that point, the block simply dissolves.

When we practice oneness, we are practicing the Truth. That is why it has such power to change us. Thousands of enlightened teachers from countless lineages have realized this Truth and passed on the experience to their students. Their wish for us to experience it is very strong, and the force of their well-wishing moves through us every time we remember to let go of our feelings of separation. A single moment of remembering oneness connects us to the stream of knowledge that flows from the enlightened ones and opens us to revelation.

Of course, if the understanding of oneness is to be more than an intellectual exercise or a dutiful remembrance of a beautiful teaching, we need to come to terms with our own tendency to create separation. That means coming to terms with the discursive mind—*manas* in Sanskrit—whose innate tendency to rove among thickets of thought and perception effectively blocks us from seeing the unity behind our experience. Like Cerberus, who guarded the threshold of the underworld in Greek mythology, the mind stands vigilantly at the doorway to deep meditation. If we don't befriend the mind, it will never let us enter. That is why the texts of meditation devote so much space, so much attention, and so much effort to the eternal question: how do I deal with the mind?

CHAPTER SIX

Working with the Mind, Part I: Navigating the Thought-Stream

*E*ver since the artists of the Indus Valley carved their famous statue of the horned god sitting in meditation—back around 5000 BCE—meditators have been grappling with the same basic scenario. We sit for meditation. We focus on the breath or practice mindfulness or begin repeating a mantra. We try to hold on to the feeling of oneness. Then the thoughts come. The thoughts come.

Thethoughtscomethethoughtscomethethoughtscome. Quickly or slowly. Flooding or trickling. Steady or intermittent. Apparently endless. Thoughts about the phone calls you have to make, thoughts about what your son's teacher said to you yesterday, thoughts about your aunt. Thoughts about the thoughts. Thoughts on the order of "Am I really meditating? This can't be meditation. My mind isn't still. And why is nothing happening?"

This is a universal human experience—like birth and leaving the body at the time of death. Even great meditators go through it. We tend to assume that a good meditator, a really successful meditator, never gets disturbed by thoughts. Somehow a real meditator just sits down for meditation and—*wham!*—they are in a deep state of stillness, merged in the witness, or watching golden lotuses of light waft gently through the inner spaces.

The Mind is ever a tourist Wanting to touch and buy new things Then toss them into an already Filled closet.

—HAFIZ [1]

But this is not true. Even great meditators have to wrestle with thoughts. Without a doubt, the Buddha himself spent hours sitting with closed eyes, thinking of one thing or another and wondering why he didn't seem to be making progress. But in that process, he learned how to move through these thoughts, and into meditation.

One of the game-changing recognitions for a meditator happens when you realize that meditation can go on even when there are thoughts in the mind. This is a big idea, so let me repeat it: the mind *need not be completely still for you to experience the state of meditation.* Often when you are deeply settled inside, thoughts continue to drift across the screen of your awareness. Even when the actual thoughts slow down, a subtle buzz of mental static might remain. This is only a problem when you don't understand what thoughts are and how to deal with them. Much of the meditator's art lies in knowing how to work with thoughts and ultimately how to let them dissolve into the subtle fabric of the mind.

This much should be obvious: you can't deal with thoughts by taking them out and shooting them. The delicate, intelligent energy we call the "mind" does not respond well to harshness. There is good reason for this, as we will see further in the next chapter, since the mind is essentially nothing more than a thought-clogged form of the pure Awareness that is the goal of our practice. ("Consciousness plus thoughts is the mind," says the *Yoga Vasishtha,* a text of high Vedanta. "Consciousness minus thoughts is God.") Consciousness filled with thoughts is Consciousness nonetheless, and Consciousness by its very nature is free, powerful, and elusive. That is why when we try to suppress thoughts or stamp them out, or even when we try to bring our attention forcibly to one point, the mind reacts rebelliously.

Indian tradition compares the mind to a king who has not been given a proper seat. Until the king is seated on his rightful throne, he will be restless, dissatisfied, and even quarrelsome. Once he is seated, however, he becomes calm and begins to manifest his royal qualities. The mind's proper seat—in fact, the only place the mind will be satisfied—is in the Self, in the deep abode of pure Consciousness. The mind's restlessness actually comes from the fact that it is searching for the throne room, looking for the place where it can experience its true grandeur, as Consciousness. Our job in meditation is simply to keep it pointed in the proper direction. As you direct the mind toward its seat again and again, it will begin to settle down into being Consciousness and eventually take a seat there on its own.

Seating the mind, like much else that we do in our meditation practice, involves equal parts of rigor and subtlety, practice and understanding. Usually when we begin a meditation practice, and often for several years thereafter, we spend most of our time bringing the mind back to an object of focus. A thousand times, our thoughts run us from here to Paris. A thousand times, we bring our attention back—gently, softly, without straining. It is boring and frustrating sometimes, but there is a reward. In time the mind begins to listen to us. At first, it might have toured all around Paris or replayed your entire relationship with your mother before you catch it. But if you keep stopping it, bringing it back, eventually it will only go halfway to Paris. Then it might go as far as the airport. Eventually, it will wander just a mile away. And if you stay with it, a time will come when the mind stays quite comfortably in meditation.

Focus is a kind of mental muscle. When you strengthen it by learning to hold your attention in one place for a while, instead of remaining trapped on the surface, you automatically strengthen your ability to hold subtle states in meditation and to find the inner pathways that lead you deeper. Eventually, this basic practice of catching yourself in distraction and bringing your mind back begins to affect your whole life. Not only does the mind become more stable in meditation—so that you can actually sit for a long time in the space of the heart, or remain in stillness for longer than a minute or two—but the mind also acquires a new ability to focus on things like driving your car, writing a report, or perfecting your golf swing. Learning to resist distraction makes you more resistant to boredom, worry, and depression; more grounded; and less prone to being driven by untamable fantasies. That is why there is no way you can dispense with this basic practice of dealing with the mind, any more than an athlete can dispense with his or her warm-ups.

CONFRONTING THE INNER DIALOGUE

Ironically enough, when we begin practicing seriously, the mind often seems to become more troublesome. Some people get scared by this. I know people who actually stopped meditating because they found it so uncomfortable to confront that inner dialogue. "I don't care what anyone says," one man told me. "My mind never used to be this bad. Meditation just makes me more restless. In fact, I feel better when I don't meditate."

His mind wasn't getting more restless, of course. It's just that when he sat down to meditate, he noticed how restless it really was. Normally, we aren't aware of the intensity of our inner dialogue. Our attention is focused on what is going on around us, so unless we are unusually introverted or introspective, the wild and crazy scenarios running through the mind generally escape our notice. But when we sit for meditation—ah, then we see them.

Besides becoming more conscious of our normal state of distraction, we may also experience something that we could call "samskaric burn off." *Samskaras* are mental and emotional tendencies, residues of our habitual thoughts and feelings, the ones we replay so often that they have made tracks in the field of our consciousness. As meditation releases energy into that inner field, those buried samskaras rise up and are burned away by the energy of our Awareness, the kundalini.

At one point early in my career as a meditator, I noticed that my morning meditations had become fogged with irritation. I was living in an ashram then, with several hundred other people, and in that atmosphere had no way to hide from my mood. Finally, I put a question to my guru: I asked, "What should you do if meditation makes you irritable?"

"It's not that meditation makes you irritable," he told me. "You have irritability inside you, and meditation is helping you see it so you can let it go."

PURIFICATION: THE INNER STEW

One reason we meditate is precisely so that this letting-go can happen. Our personal unconscious is a murky stew, filled with a huge array of tasty and untasty items. All these things have to come out of the stew. Otherwise their presence bubbling around inside us blocks our experience of the pure, clear water, the pure light, that is our real substance. Meditation allows these buried feelings, obstructive ideas, and painful emotions to float to the top of our consciousness, where they can be recognized and removed.

Once kundalini is awakened, this work of purification goes on more or less continuously under the surface. However, it is during the time of sitting practice that our inner energy gets a chance to work full throttle. The act of sitting quietly and focusing inward invites the shakti to leap into action, churning up the ocean of our consciousness and dislodging whatever is buried there. So as we sit in meditation, we may experience not just random, stray thought-lets, but huge, charged ice floes of heavy emotions and old buried complexes. When these things come up in meditation, it is a sign that certain tangled webs of memory, belief, and emotion, the known and unknown blocks to our freedom, are ready to move out of our system. Our part in the process is to let them go. There is no need to get involved in these feelings or analyze them—at least not while we are meditating. Instead, notice them and breathe them out, releasing them with the exhalation. Or repeat the mantra, letting the shakti embedded in the mantra move through the emotions and negativities and melt them away.

As our meditation practice deepens and becomes more stable, we get the strength to stand aside from all these feelings and to witness our process of purification. In fact, as we will see in the next chapter, the inner witness can become a platform from which we can look at and begin to heal these buried feelings. But many of us, especially in the early years of meditation, find our thoughts are too thick, fast, and uncontrollable to allow us to stand back from them for long. This is another reason why an empowered or enlivened mantra is so helpful for most meditators.

SWEEPING YOUR HEART WITH MANTRA

An empowered mantra acts as a sort of cleansing force, a subtle but extremely strong broom that sweeps the basement of your subconscious. The yogic texts speak of kundalini as an inner fire, a transforming heat that burns up mental detritus and melts away psychic debris. An empowered mantra is filled with this transforming fire. When you rub the mantra against your thoughts, it generates an inner friction. The Sanskrit word for this friction is *tapas,* meaning "heat." *Tapas* is also the word for the yogic austerities that refine and purify the mind. The subtle fire in the mantra generates the heat of tapas in the mind. That is what cleanses your inner ground.

During the first year after my kundalini was awakened, the effect of the inner purification process was sometimes so intense and uncomfortable that I could hardly bear being in my own skin. Some days, the uprush of buried negative feelings—guilt, unworthiness, anger, and the like—would begin the moment I opened my eyes and would roil around all day long. More or less in desperation, I used to repeat "my" mantra as a way of distracting myself from these feelings. I would begin the moment I woke up and repeat it all day long, whenever there was space from ongoing activities and sometimes even during conversations.

As I kept this up, I began to notice that the emotional charge behind the feelings had lessened dramatically. The feelings still came up, but they didn't knock me over. The mantra seemed to create a counterforce. It released an energy of light, repose, and happiness in my mind that swallowed up the painful feelings. After some time, this layer of deep-seated, painful feelings—feelings that had troubled me all my life—was gone.

Every time we sit with an empowered mantra in meditation, we go through a small-scale version of this clearing process. Little by little, as we sit with the mantra, the combination of our own focused intention and the mantra's intrinsic power dissolves the day's residue of thoughts and images so that the mind can settle into stillness. Once this settling has occurred, then the natural process of meditation takes over. The inner shakti begins to draw us inward and to dissolve our ordinary waking mind into pure conscious energy.

LETTING GO: THE PRACTICE OF VAIRAGYA

Patanjali, in his *Yoga Sutras,* has told us that there are two aspects to the process of steadying the mind. We have just discussed the first one: *abhyasa,* or practice—the effort to stay with our object of focus. The second part of the process is *vairagya,* or detachment.[2] Vairagya is a way of putting the gears of the mind into neutral, disengaging ourselves from the thoughts, feelings, and desires that normally hook our attention.

A few years ago, I heard this story from a young woman at a meditation retreat in upstate New York. She had been planning a trip to Japan, and her mind was already running through her checklist for departure, wondering how many sweaters to take and whether she needed to pack a winter coat. Suddenly, a voice inside her mind spoke up loudly. "Drop it!" the voice said. Startled, she let go of her plans and began to focus on her breath. No sooner had she done so than she was overwhelmed by a feeling of sadness. She thought of how much she had received from the retreat and how sorry she would be to leave.

Then she heard the inner voice again: "Drop it." She let go of her sad thoughts. Still, the voice came again: "Drop it." She asked herself, "What shall I drop? What's my biggest block right now? My sense of unworthiness. Okay, I'll drop that." The voice said again: "Drop it." She didn't know what else she could drop. She gave a big sigh—and fell into a deep state of meditation. It was as if a field of bliss had opened in the ground of her mind. She felt as if she were swimming in the oceanic tide of this bliss, lulled on its waves. "Oh, please," she said inwardly, "don't let this stop." Immediately, the voice came again: "Drop it." "Drop the bliss?" she wondered. "No, drop wanting to keep it," the voice responded. She let go of her feeling of clinging to the bliss. With that she fell into the deepest, quietest state she had ever experienced. She felt utterly present, completely loved, and as clear as limpid water.

As you can probably see, this woman's experience points out a pathway we can follow. If we move through the stages she went through, we also can discover how much peace arises when we just drop everything—our plans, our thoughts, our doubts about ourselves, and even our desire to hold on to our beautiful experiences. Ultimately, of course, we want to let go of the tendrils of deep-seated identification, attachment, and aversion that reinforce our sense of separation and that clothe our false personality in an appearance of permanence. We want to drop—at least for a while—the feeling of being a particular "me," separate from all others. That is the key, the sages have told us, to entering our own essence. The experience of our innate wholeness and freedom naturally arises when the ego of separateness has dissolved. Of course, few of us can dissolve the separative ego just like that, especially if we aren't entirely sure we want to. But practice helps, and there are three levels of vairagya that we can practice in meditation.

Letting Go of Tension

The first level of vairagya involves releasing the tension in the body. As we saw in chapter 3, we can do this at the beginning

134

of any session of meditation by scanning the body, noticing where we feel tight or uncomfortable, and then breathing out the tightness.

Breathing out the tension in the body does more than relax us physically. It also relaxes the mind, because every physical tension has its inner counterpart. Sometimes when I work with seasoned meditators, they will tell me afterward that the most helpful part of the process was not the actual meditation instructions, but the time we took in the beginning to breathe out tension. For some people, this is all they need to do to enter deep meditation.

Letting Go of Desire

In the second level of vairagya, we let go of the layers of desire and its many offspring— hope, expectation, fear, and worry.

I like to begin meditation sessions by making a conscious decision to leave everything else aside for a while. I mentally set aside my work and all my personal agendas, and I make a resolution not to let myself get distracted. That is the first step. The second step is to keep renewing the intention every time the mind begins to throw out tempting morsels of desire.

Our desires and dislikes are two apes living in the tree of our hearts; while they continue to shake and agitate it, with their jogging and jolting, there can be no rest for it.

—YOGA VASISHTHA [3]

Practicing this level of vairagya shows the seams of desire that are layered throughout our mind. It's only when we try to let go of desires that we begin to realize how pervasive and distracting

135

they are. In fact, this is one of the great teachings we can receive in meditation. Each time we sit, we give ourselves the opportunity to come face to face with all the disguises desire takes, and with the power that even a simple desire has to throw us off-track.

Here is an example: How many times have you been pulled out of meditation by the smell of coffee brewing in the kitchen? Or by the thought of the coffee? Your mind is just beginning to get quiet, and then you remember that besides the coffee, you have a croissant waiting in its waxed-paper bakery bag, and that if you get up from meditation now, you can put it in the oven and heat it up so you can have a hot croissant before work. Before you know it, you are off the mat and halfway to the kitchen.

Desires have a way of filling the mind with wonderful reasons why you should follow their siren song. Of course you need to have breakfast now—otherwise you might have to rush to get to school. Of course you should get up and watch that video now instead of waiting until later—because, after all, it is better not to clutter the mind with images too close to bedtime. Of course you need to write down that terrific idea that just came up—in fact, you need to turn on your computer and start exploring it, since you are feeling so inspired. (Actually, it's not a bad idea to keep a notepad by your meditation cushion, so you can jot a note to yourself when an idea comes up. Then you can go back to meditation.) Or even more compelling, isn't this the right moment to go look up the phone number of your high school boyfriend, Timmy, whose face just surfaced so meltingly in your vision? He was surrounded with blue light, and you heard he just got divorced . . .

Even if you resist the temptation to get up off your mat and swing into action behind one of these impulses, letting yourself dwell on them can seriously throw off your practice. (This is just as true when the desire you follow is a subtle one—like those tempting philosophical speculations that some of us enjoy indulging in, or the various plans and life scenarios that play like movies through the mind if you don't catch them.) As we meditate, we see this again and again. And we do have to face the consequences, the immediate costs, of getting caught up in desire. On the other hand, each time you drop one of these desires, you lessen its grip on you. Just as focusing in meditation helps to develop your power of focus in daily life, your practice of dropping desires in meditation trains you in the practice of detachment, which helps keep you from being tossed around by distracting impulses in your waking life.

This kind of letting-go is an essential act of meditation.

Exercise: Breathing Out Thoughts, Desires, and Emotions

Sit in your meditation posture, paying attention to the grounding of your sitting bones and allowing your spine to elongate. Close your eyes and focus your awareness on your breath until you feel yourself becoming settled and centered.

Now begin to notice the thoughts as they arise. Whenever a thought, desire, or emotion comes up, breathe it out. Breathe in, and breathe out the thought.

Another thought arises. Breathe it out. A desire, an impulse arises. Breathe it out.

There are variations on this practice. If you like dynamic visualizations, you could imagine a sword made of your subtle will with which you lop off each thought. You might create an inner fire and throw the thoughts into it. (Neither of these are gentle practices, of course, but as meditators working with our thoughts we must sometimes enter warrior mode.) I also like to imagine that I have a Trash icon in the corner of my mind, and I mentally drag the thoughts into it.

Afterwards, contemplate the effect of this exercise. What do you notice about your inner state? What was the effect of this intense focus on dropping your thoughts?

Letting Go of Identifying with the Thinker

In this nakedness the spirit finds rest, for when it covets nothing, nothing raises it up, and nothing weighs it down.

—JOHN OF THE CROSS [4]

The third kind of vairagya is more subtle. It involves letting go of your attachment to being the thinker, the one who identifies with the thoughts and desires, the one, in fact, who constantly, if unconsciously, chooses to think. Instead, you identify yourself with the witness, the watcher of the thoughts. You don't try to cast out thoughts. You let them be there, but you pull back from them. You identify with the one who watches the thoughts.

A classic way to do this is to look at thoughts as if they were clouds passing in the sky. Clouds don't touch the space of the sky. The sky isn't affected by clouds racing across it. It isn't changed if the clouds are big and black and full of thunder, or if they pour rain. In the same way, your Awareness—the real you—isn't touched by thoughts. Your Consciousness is completely unaffected by anything that arises.

Pure Consciousness cannot say "I."

—RAMANA MAHARSHI [5]

Becoming the watcher of thoughts instead of the thinker is simply a matter of shifting your perspective. Here's a very simple way to practice taking this perspective shift: Say to yourself, "My name is _____." Then notice that another part of your mind notices that thought. That's the witness. When you're "noticing" the thought, you are in the witness. Being the witness is simply identifying with the noticer rather than with the thought.

Or you might like to work with the image of the sky and the clouds.

Exercise: Watch Your Thoughts Move Like Clouds through the Sky of the Mind

Sit quietly and close your eyes. You can focus your attention on the flow of the breath as it moves in and out of the body. As you do, become aware of the space inside your mind. Imagine that your mind is a sky, an open space. Thoughts move through it like clouds. Let the thoughts arise and let them depart. You are the watcher, not the thinker, observing the thought-clouds as they move through the sky of your Awareness.

Once you begin to identify with the sky of Awareness rather than with clouds of thought, a great sense of spaciousness arises. You can let the thoughts be there without being caught by them.

From there, it is just a small step toward understanding the great truth about the mind: even your thoughts are part of that underlying field of Consciousness.

CHAPTER SEVEN

Working with the Mind, Part II: Liberating Your *T*houghts

*L*etting go of distractions, bringing your attention to a point of focus, and witnessing the rising of thoughts and images are all basic techniques in mind-training. The only problem is that they can entangle you in a subtle feeling of duality. When you keep trying to discipline your thoughts, you'll often begin seeing them as adversaries. Then meditation can turn into a battle between your striving for quiet and the very mind that you are hoping to coax into stillness, and you find yourself out of relationship with your inner realm.

The ultimate practice for dealing with the mind is to let it be. Not to let it lead you around by the nose, but *to let it be,* a tactic that truly becomes possible only when we get what the mind actually is.

What is the mind? According to the tantras, the phenomenon we experience as "mind" is actually a particularly vibrant and subtle kind of energy. An ocean of energy, in fact, in which waves of thoughts and emotions arise and subside. Your thoughts and feelings—the difficult, negative, obsessive ones, as well as the peaceful and clever ones—are all made of the same subtle, invisible, highly dynamic "stuff." Mind-energy is so evanescent that it can dissolve in a moment, yet so powerful that it can create "stories" that run you for a lifetime. The secret revealed by the tantric sages is that if you can recognize thoughts for what they are—if you can see that a thought is nothing but mind-energy—your thoughts will stop troubling you. That doesn't mean they'll stop. But you'll no longer be at their mercy.

You lose sight of the original mind and, seeing the thinking, discriminating mind, take that as your own. But that is not your real mind.

—SUTRA OF PERFECT WISDOM [1]

One of the more exciting findings of contemporary brain research has been the recognition of the brain's inherent plasticity. Neuroscientists have long seen that neurons and their dendrites—the physical structures behind thought and perception—act together to create brain patterns that we experience as thoughts and feelings. What they have now discovered is that this brain patterning is utterly fluid, plastic, and malleable. Even deeply embedded patterns can be changed through practices like cognitive shifting, and especially through meditation.

The tantric sages, of course, had no access to fMRI scans and knew nothing about neurons and dendrites. But they did have a vision of why the fluidity and creativity of the human mind is essentially limitless. They recognized the human mind-energy, human consciousness, as a contracted, miniaturized form of the great Consciousness of the universe, the cosmic mind itself. In the quantum world, energy can appear as both a particle and as a wave. We might say that the individual mind is a wave in the ocean of consciousness, while each thought is a particle.

Just as waves, eddies, and bubbles arise in the ocean without ever leaving the ocean, your mind assumes the unique colors of your individual thoughts, your perceptions and memories and tendencies, but never stops being one with the oceanic love-intelligence that is the source of all this. The power in an individual wave is the power of the ocean. The power of the mind is the power of Consciousness itself.

As mentioned earlier, the Sanskrit word for our individual human consciousness—the mind—is *chitta.* The word for universal Consciousness is *chiti.* (*Chiti* is also another word for shakti or kundalini.) Both words, *chiti* and *chitta,* come from the root *chit,* meaning Awareness or Consciousness—but not in the limited sense in which we usually use the word "consciousness" in the West. Chit is Consciousness as an absolute intelligence, an intelligence that is unlimited in its knowledge and creativity, omnipresent, and blissful, with a boundless capacity to do and to become whatever it wills. It is, in short, Consciousness as the creative force of the universe.

In Sanskrit, the root of a word describes its essence. The essence of chitta—the individual consciousness—is the same as chiti, the great intelligence that creates the universe. The only difference is one of scale. Chiti is boundless, free, and omnipotent; it's capable of creating and dissolving solid planets, stars, galaxies, sea anemones, and porcupines. Chitta, on the other hand, is limited, contracted, and relatively powerless. Nonetheless, chitta does exactly the same thing that chiti does. Even though it only operates on a small scale, the consciousness-stuff in your mind keeps endlessly creating. Just as chiti creates landscapes, people, planets, and solar systems and keeps them going, chitta creates ideas, thoughts, fantasies, and moods, not to mention novels, poetry, philosophical systems, designs for buildings, piano concertos, software programs, and mischief.

If you could fully recognize this truth about the mind, you would instantly free the mind to expand back into its original vastness. In short, your chitta would start to emerge from its disguise and reveal itself as chiti. The ramifications of this are literally mind-blowing, but you will feel them only if you start to practice this awareness.

YOUR THOUGHTS ARE NOTHING BUT CONSCIOUSNESS

When I was first meditating, and feeling like a complete victim of my vagrant and uncontrollable thoughts, this teaching offered me the first hint that there might be a path through the thicket of my mentalogue. I had been looking at thoughts as the enemy—especially the negative thoughts, the angry thoughts, and the irreverent, ungodly thoughts. But something radical happened when I remembered to look at thoughts and feelings—the difficult, negative, greedy ones, as well as the peaceful, loving, and smart ones—simply as constructions of the same subtle, invisible, highly dynamic "stuff." For the first time in my life, I could let go of my fascination with the content of a thought.

My neighbor's five-year-old eats Froot Loops for breakfast, but he will only eat the red Froot Loops and won't touch the green. He doesn't yet see that the red ones and the green ones are both made of the same sugary stuff. In just the same way, we get so bamboozled by the stories our thoughts are telling us—by the content of them—that we neglect to look at what is actually *inside* a thought. I often do an exercise with students. I ask them to imagine a chair, and then "look" at the image of the chair that has formed in their mind. Then I ask them what the chair is made of. Many people will answer "wood" or "metal." It takes a moment for them to recognize that the chair in their mind has no substantiality at all, but that it is made of energy, energy that their mind has shaped into a particular pattern.

Once you can see that the chair you have formed in the mind is made of the stuff of your own mind-energy, then you can also dissolve that image back into the mind, just as you can dissolve the distracting fantasy or even the emotionally painful

The Essence of Mind is like the sky; Sometimes it is shadowed by the clouds of Thought-flow. Then the wind of the Guru's inner teaching Blows away the drifting clouds; Yet the Thought-flow itself is the illumination. The Experience is as natural as sun- and moon-light; Yet it is beyond both space and time.

—MILAREPA [2]

memory. It's also possible to let the thought-forming energy in the mind relax back into its underlying substance, to deconstruct itself, to become naturally loose and free. To be able to recognize this is literally to be liberated from the tyranny of thoughts.

You might want to try this now.

Close your eyes and observe the thoughts going through your mind. Now create a thought—a beach, perhaps, or the name of someone you like.

Hold the thought for a few seconds. Now focus on the thought's substance. Notice the energetic space the thought creates in your mind. If you like, you can formally label the thought "energy" or "thought-stuff," just the way, if you were practicing mindfulness meditation, you might label it "thinking." Now notice what happens to the thought once you recognize it as energy.

For many people this practice has an almost magical effect on meditation. First of all, it tends to dissolve the worried, conflicted attitude that we often have toward thoughts. Even more amazingly, the thoughts themselves tend to dissolve. After you've sat for a while with the understanding that your thoughts are Consciousness, you might have to look hard to find a thought. They will have melted back into the energy that was their substance, just as clouds melt back into the sky.

THE MIND IS THE GODDESS

The practice of recognizing thoughts as energy becomes particularly juicy if you take the step of looking at thoughts as the sages of Kashmir did: by revering them as manifestations of the divine dancer, of shakti, or Goddess Consciousness. One of the most significant facets of Indian metaphysics is its understanding that spirit is both utterly formless and impersonal—and at the same time totally capable of taking a personal form. Because the old sages understood this, even the most anti-dualistic of them could relate devotionally to the divine. When we think of the world-creating energy, the shakti, as an abstract force, it might seem awesome but never approachable. Think of that same energy as a goddess, however, and suddenly the whole situation becomes more personal, more playful. You can pray to a goddess, talk to her, honor her, and love her. When you think of the energy of the mind as a divine "person," you can have a relationship with her. In fact, a relationship becomes imperative.

O wavering mind,
awaken your upward-
flowing awareness.
Become the sublime
warrior Goddess Kali,
who moves with graceful
power through the vast
landscape of the body . . .
She is none other than
primordial bliss,
this great swan ever
swimming through the
lotus jungle of the
subtle body.

—RAMPRASAD [3]

Try this for a moment: Think of your mind, your extraordinarily powerful mind, as a glorious feminine entity, a goddess who has forgotten she is a goddess and is going around collecting rags and bottles from the scrap heap of thoughts, piling them up and obsessing over them, chewing them like bones and spitting them out at you.

She acts a bit wild, but who can blame her? After all, even

though she has forgotten who she is, she still knows she is someone pretty important, and she doesn't understand why she is not being treated with the respect she deserves. Can you imagine how such a great divinity feels when you get impatient with her, when you angrily shove your thoughts away, when you treat her as your enemy? Or when you behave like a limp victim of every vagrant thought-let or fantasy? Naturally she gets outraged at your harshness, and naturally she runs wild when you meekly give in to her. Both these attitudes toward the mind simply encourage the goddess to demonstrate her creative power in all sorts of unproductive ways.

When you entertain the idea that shakti is dancing in the form of the mind, it is as if you free the goddess. She can then reveal herself as she truly is and expand back into her original form. It is like the legends of enchanted princes and princesses in old fairy tales who are freed by a moment of recognition. One of my favorite versions of this archetypal situation is the story of the crone Dame Ragnell from the Arthurian legends.

The story of Dame Ragnell begins with an ambush. King Arthur is traveling alone through a forest when he is surprised by a dark knight. The knight unhorses Arthur, which technically makes the king his prisoner. Instead of holding him for ransom, however, the knight makes a bargain. He will give Arthur a riddle, and Arthur has one week to come up with an answer. If the king fails, the whole kingdom will be forfeited to the knight.

The knight's question is this: "What does a woman really want?" Like other men throughout the ages, Arthur hasn't a clue. As he rides away, however, he is accosted by an aged hag who hangs on to his bridle and insists that he stop to listen to her. The crone is shudderingly ugly—hunchbacked, covered in warts, and bald except for a few gray strands sticking straight up out of the crown of her head. She walks like a duck, and her voice is somewhere between a cackle and a screech. "I am Dame Ragnell," she croaks. "I can give you the answer to the knight's riddle—if you agree to my price."

"There would be a price," says Arthur with a sigh. "Still, anything is better than handing over my kingdom to that wretched knight."

"Then promise me the hand of Sir Gawain in marriage," cackles the hag.

Arthur hesitates for a moment, weighing the fate of the kingdom against the prospect of blighting his friend Gawain's life, and then chooses the kingdom.

"If you can solve the riddle," he says, "Gawain is yours."

"Such a simple riddle," Dame Ragnell tells him. "Really, it should be obvious. What a woman wants is to have her own way!"

Sure enough, this turns out to be the right answer. The kingdom is saved. And Gawain, being a loyal subject of his liege, agrees to go through with the marriage.

On the appointed day, he meets Dame Ragnell in the palace chapel. In her bridal gown, she looks like a dressed-up skeleton. The ladies of the court break into tears when they see the woman this noble knight is to wed. Gawain, being the model of courtesy, gives no sign of distress. But after the ceremony, he escorts his bride to her chamber, bids her good night, and turns to leave.

"Not so fast," cackles the crone. "You've married me this day and, by God, you shall bed me this night."

Gawain is appalled. Still, his good manners do not fail him. Taking a deep breath, he clasps the old woman in his arms and kisses her. As his lips touch hers, a miracle happens. Dame Ragnell's warty, hunchbacked shape falls away, and she is revealed as a stunning beauty, the very incarnation of a medieval knight's feminine ideal.

"You have saved me," she tells Gawain, looking up at him through long, curling lashes. "I was under a curse that could only be lifted when a gentle knight kissed my lips. Now I am free to be my beautiful self—but only for half the day. Husband, which would you prefer? Would you rather have me beautiful by day or beautiful by night?"

Gawain is in a quandary. If she remains beautiful at night, he will have to look at Dame Ragnell all day. But if she is beautiful only during the day, he will have Dame Ragnell's crone form in his marriage bed. "I don't know what to do," he says. "You choose."

"Ah," says his wife, "now you've lifted my curse completely. Because you gave me the choice, you've freed me to be my beautiful self all the twenty-four hours!"

This is what we do for the mind when we recognize the beautiful Goddess Chiti beneath her skin of thoughts. We free her to reveal the beauty and power that lie behind those thoughts. It was Gawain's willingness to treat his ugly wife with kindness that made the difference. In the same way, our respect for the goddess-within-the-mind allows her to reveal her sweetness and glory.

> ## *Exercise: Seeing the Mind as Shakti, the Energy of Creation*
>
> Sit in a comfortable posture and close your eyes. Allow your attention to center itself on the breath. As you do, say to yourself, "My breath is a manifestation of shakti, the divine energy of creation." Each time a thought arises, say to yourself, "I honor this thought as an aspect of the Goddess Consciousness. I honor this thought as shakti: divine, conscious energy."
>
> Continue this for at least ten minutes and notice how it affects the flow of thoughts in the mind.

DISARMING NEGATIVE THOUGHTS

It is fairly easy to do this practice with ordinary, random thoughts. It becomes more problematic when the thoughts are of something you strongly desire or when they are negative or unwelcome. Negative thoughts exercise a particular power over us, partly because we tend to judge them more harshly than other thoughts. Most of us have a secret yardstick that we apply to our mental content. Some thoughts we deem acceptable, usually because they fit our image of ourselves as intelligent, mature, kindhearted, good people. Other thoughts, however, contain too much negative charge for us or reveal us to be less evolved or loving than we would like to be. These we judge and do our best to push away.

The habit of judging our mental content is a congenital disease for meditators. It is one of the more insidious manifestations of the inner judge, the fearsome parent figure so many of us hold inside, whose fulminating criticisms we sometimes confuse with the voice of God. That inner judge rises up in self-righteous condemnation of anything that seems weak, immature, or "bad," constantly on the lookout for more evidence of our general unfitness. The inner judge is the one who has us convinced that having negative thoughts makes us bad people.

One deluded thought and we are all dull and ordinary. But with the next awakened thought, we are as wise as the Buddha.

—HUI-NENG [4]

But from a nondual point of view, your negative thoughts are also manifestations of shakti. Even your ugliest feelings—your jealousy, your anger, and your hatred—are created by the Goddess. Your anxiety, your fear, and your painful memories—all these are waves arising in Consciousness, all these are forms and figures in the Goddess's great dance. If you can realize that a thought or an image—whatever it is—is just a bubble or wave rising out of the sea of Consciousness, then even the most embarrassing, fearful, hostile, frightening thought need not disturb you. Consciousness is so creative that she can transform herself in a moment from a state of contraction and rigid negativity to a state of expansion and love. Just as the Goddess Chiti can manifest any thought, she can drop any thought. The moment we genuinely recognize a thought or an emotion as part of our Consciousness, it automatically resolves back into its original state.

Let me give you an example. I am writing this early in the morning after a long session of meditation. Because I'm engaged in this writing process, my mind is busy these days; it is filled with ideas about what I'm writing and also with a driving compulsion that I recognize as the creative urge. That urge, however, often gets derailed into irritation, anxiety, and fear. This morning as I sat in meditation, I began by focusing on the breath, merging my awareness with the space between the in-breath and the out-breath. Usually after I have done this for a while, the space between the breaths begins to lengthen, and I find myself slipping into a state of spaciousness, a state that I identify as the Self or my own free Consciousness. Today, however, the space felt choppy, like an ocean in a storm. The energy was sharp and uncomfortable, almost unpleasant. Then in the midst of the ocean, a wave of overpowering anxiety arose and took the form of words. They went something like "Omigod, the structure, the structure—I haven't figured out the structure."

At that moment, I experienced a flash of recognition. I saw that the anxiety was just energy and that the words were simply the form that the anxiety-energy was taking. In short, I realized that I didn't have to pay attention to the content of the thought. Instead, I focused my attention on the energy bundle that was the feeling of anxiety and its verbal expression. I regarded it with the feeling that it was simply energy. In that instant, the energy dissolved, imploding back into itself, and the

Wherever the mind goes, whether turned inward or toward the outside world, everywhere there is the divine. Since the divine is everywhere, where can the mind go to avoid it?

—VIJNANA BHAIRAVA [5]

surface of my Consciousness resolved itself into a thick, palpably blissful, and undulating sea of energy.

Sometimes, of course, the overpowering thoughts that come up in meditation are messages that need attention. If you have a feeling that something needs to be attended to, it probably does. Still, you don't have to let it derail you. Make an inner note of the thought. Promise yourself that you will attend to it later. Then go back to meditation. If it really seems important, write it down; I keep a pen and notepaper handy for insights that I don't want to forget. When they come up, I pick up the pen, scrawl a reminder, then go back to meditation.

WORKING WITH INTENSE EMOTIONS

Once you discover how to let thoughts and feelings dissolve into their own energy, not only have you learned the secret of dealing with thoughts, you also have a way to work with the real heavies: your charged emotional states. Sometimes people say that they are afraid to meditate because heavy emotions come up and ambush them as soon as they close their eyes. Usually it turns out that they have been sitting on a backlog of unprocessed feelings that they find unacceptable and therefore overwhelming.

You can make it safe for yourself to let these feelings come up in meditation if you keep part of your attention on your wider Consciousness, on your "real" Self. On pure Awareness. Then when strong emotions arise in meditation, you can acknowledge them, hold them in the spaciousness of Awareness, and let your own Consciousness dissolve them. When you are very afraid or grief-stricken, or when you are flooded with anger, jealousy, or anxiety, Awareness can become both a cradle in which you hold these feelings and a cauldron in which they dissolve. It is one of the most important things you can teach yourself through meditation: how to hold strong feelings in Awareness and how to allow Awareness to dissolve them. Once you know how to do it, you'll no longer fear your own feelings. There is nothing you can't process, even the most extreme and shocking life events.

The Crucible of Awareness

A few years ago, a friend of mine was blindsided by her husband's announcement that he had fallen in love with someone else and wanted a divorce. She had not suspected there was anything wrong with her marriage. She loved her husband. Feelings of grief, anger, insecurity, distrust, betrayal, and confusion erupted inside her. Understandably, they seemed nearly uncontainable.

Meditation was especially difficult because then she had nothing to distract her from the emotions churning through her mind. At last she decided to sit with her feelings without trying to push them away. She would let herself feel the burning sensation of anger and notice how it made her chest hot and her breathing rapid. She would feel how grief caused pressure to build up behind her eyes, as if from tears wanting to be shed. She observed her inner recitals of betrayal and revenge until she knew every word of them.

One day as she was sitting in meditation, reeling under the onslaught of feelings, she suddenly became aware of her own Awareness. She could feel how her Awareness surrounded and held her feelings. Then an image arose. She saw a container like an old-fashioned warming pan. She realized that this was her Awareness. It could hold her hot feelings the way a warming pan can hold burning coals.

When you are fiercely angry or feeling joy beyond description, when you are at an impasse, not knowing what to do, when you are in terror or running for your life, know that such intense states of mind are fully permeated with the spanda, the creative vibration of divine shakti. Find her there.

—SPANDA KARIKAS [6]

She let the feelings be there. She let herself feel them and all the physical sensations associated with them. She let her Awareness hold them. After a while, the feelings began to slowly dissolve, as if they were melting into her Awareness. When she got up from meditation, she was free of them for several hours.

Every day after that, she sat in meditation and let her feelings come up, held them in her Awareness, and let them dissolve. As she did, different layers of grief revealed themselves. She saw that this new pain was fueled and supported by ancient griefs, old feelings of loss and hurt and anger. Sometimes her breathing would change as she saw a flash of childhood memory. Sometimes she even saw scenes that seemed to be glimpses of past lives. As she held the feelings in her Consciousness, each layer eventually dissolved. After several weeks of these daily meditations, she found that not only had she processed her anger and hurt at being left by her husband, but she had also become free of a subtle sadness that had been controlling her moods from beneath the surface. Layers upon layers of old hurt, old anger, and old suffering had dissolved.

Admittedly, this process is not easy. To stay with it takes courage. The key is to let go of the content of the feelings, the plot of your internal drama, and to focus first on the feeling itself and then on the energy of the feeling. As you learn to do this in meditation, you get to the point where you can do it in action. Anger, jealousy, or grief will come up, and you will be able to hold the feeling in Awareness and let the edges of the heavy emotional energy dissolve into the wide and calm energy of your Awareness.

Exercise: Allowing Your Consciousness to Dissolve Intense Emotions

Sit in a comfortable, upright posture and close your eyes. Focus on the flow of the breathing, allowing the breath to bring your attention into the heart center, the place where the inhalation comes to rest. This is not the physical heart, but a subtle center located in the center of the body, beneath the breastbone, at a point four to five inches (approximately eight finger-widths) below the collarbone. Let yourself enter the space inside the heart center. Let that inner space of the heart expand with the breathing, softening and widening.

As you hold your awareness in the heart-space, remember a situation that brings up intense feelings such as anger, grief, pride, fear, or desire. If there is no current situation, see if you can remember an experience that triggers a particularly strong emotion. (Even though it may not be as powerful for you as something current, you can still practice the exercise with a remembered emotion.)

As the emotion begins to fill your mind, let go of the thoughts you have about it. Let go of the story line, the drama of it, and your tendency to obsess on the situation that triggered it. Focus purely on the energy of the emotion, on the feeling of it within your body. Where is the feeling located? Is it in your head, your heart, your belly, or somewhere else? What sensations do you notice? Is there heat? Sharpness? Heaviness? What other sensations do you feel?

As you focus on the feeling-experience of your emotion, become simultaneously aware of the heart-space, the field of Awareness that contains the feelings. Hold the emotional feeling within the heart-space as though you were cradling it in your Awareness.

Sit with the emotion, feeling its energy while simultaneously keeping your focus opened out into the widening spaciousness of the heart.

Sit until the energy of the emotion dissolves into Awareness.

ALL THINGS ARISE OUT OF YOUR OWN CONSCIOUSNESS

As we practice looking past the content of our negative thoughts and intense feelings, and seeing into the energy that is their essence, we eventually begin to see ourselves in a profoundly liberating way. We realize that everything that appears in our meditation—every single thing—is pure shakti, pure Consciousness. Every image, every thought, every feeling—everything is made of energy. The ugliest, scariest thought is Consciousness. So is the most beautiful vision. Ultimately all of it, even our most exquisite inner experience, has to dissolve back into Consciousness.

In the Tibetan tantric tradition, advanced practitioners are assigned to meditate on a particular deity. They have to visualize the deity, giving it a form inside their own consciousness. The idea is to get so good at the visualization that you eventually see the deity step outside your mind, as it were, appearing before you in a moving, speaking form.

Your own mind is originally as pure and empty as the sky. To know whether or not this is true, look inside your own mind.

—PADMASAMBHAVA[7]

Accomplished practitioners of this difficult and complex visualization report that it is possible to get the deity to actually appear. That is because Consciousness is infinitely creative. When you focus on something with enough intention, it does become a real entity within your mind. The stuff of your mind takes that shape and gives reality to that object of focus. Then depending on what kind of object you are focusing on, you have an experience of it.

An entire complex of thoughts, feelings, images, and bodily sensations makes up an experience. When the form you are focusing on is a negative one—the thought of the insensitive remark someone made to you yesterday or the latest news about global warming—you experience feelings of anger, sadness, or fear. Your heart feels hard or your cheeks get tight. You feel pressure behind the eyes from held-back tears, or your breath gets choppy with held-in resentment. Your inner consciousness contracts around the feeling much the way your hand contracts into a fist, and before you know it your whole world is sadness or anger. The negative thought is creating emotions and tension in the body; it is even affecting the immune system.

In the same way, when you focus on a mantra, on a loving or positive thought, or on a visual meditation object like a flame or the form of a deity, this form creates its own complex of thoughts and feelings—usually feelings like love, reverence, happiness, relaxation, and fullness. Most of us, of course, prefer the complex that goes with the positive thoughts and images over the one we associate with negative thoughts.

Yet even the most beautiful image or form eventually has to dissolve back into Consciousness. That is the point of the Tibetan exercise with the deity. Once a meditator has made the deity real enough to actually appear, she is supposed to deliberately let the form of the deity dissolve back into her own Awareness. The ultimate purpose of the exercise is to reveal that everything, including the divine forms that religious people love, is actually a manifestation of and within our own Consciousness. As the sages of Vedanta say, "Everything exists because you exist. Everything is within your Self."

The tantras remind us that whatever object of focus we choose to meditate on, however we decide to meditate, we should do it with this understanding: all thoughts, feelings, and images, all emotions, and all the forms we focus on in meditation, are made of Consciousness, of shakti. They are manifestations of the underlying energy, the shakti that is bubbling up from within us.

Once we begin to acknowledge this truth, we are close to the heart of meditation. In fact, we are ready to begin following Sir Gawain's example.

We are ready to let the Shakti show us how she wants to meditate.

CHAPTER EIGHT

Letting the Shakti Lead

A few years ago, a friend asked me to spend an afternoon meditating with her. She had been having a hard time with her practice and hoped that I could help her find a way to give it a jump-start.

"What's the problem?" I asked her.

"I don't know. I think it's that my heart feels dry," she said. "There's no energy there."

"Where do you feel energy?" I asked her.

She closed her eyes for a minute, and then reported, "There's a sort of pressure between my eyebrows. It gets stronger when I close my eyes."

"Why don't you try focusing there?" I said. "Let yourself be in that energy, and try to breathe in and out of it."

Half an hour later, she opened her eyes.

"How was it?" I asked.

"Fabulous," she told me. "I kept breathing through the energy, and after a while it opened up. I was in a pasture made of emerald-colored light. The sun was so bright that I could hardly look at it. Then it became huge, and I was just in the light. It was terrific."

Although kundalini shines brilliant as lightning in every individual, yet it is only in the hearts of yogis that she reveals herself and dances in her own joy.

—SHARADA TILAKA [1]

At that moment, I felt as if I had been handed the ultimate secret of meditation. "Of course," I thought. "Find out where your inner energy is playing and let it guide you." Let the subtle energy in your body determine how you meditate. That way, the kundalini, the spiritual energy, the awakened Presence within you, will get behind whatever you do and impel it forward.

Like so much of what I've discovered during my journeys through the inner country, this was not a new idea. It was basic, and it was one of the core instructions I'd received at the beginning of my journey. In the tantric traditions, it is known that one of the ways you know that you have awakened kundalini is that meditation begins to unfold naturally. This happens differently for everyone, and the unfolding is often very subtle, so subtle that we have to be very attentive to tune in to it. After the conversation with my friend, I realized that it had been some time since I thought to investigate exactly how the kundalini shakti was working inside me.

Of course, I always felt her presence, especially when she took over in meditation and dissolved my thoughts into an emerging witness state, or pushed me into a hatha yoga posture and held me there, or simply turned my inner consciousness into such an ocean of happiness that I couldn't help letting go into it. I had noticed how she gave impetus to certain practices and how she enlivened teachings so that they became experience. Yet at the same time I tended to take her for granted, the way as a child I took for granted that my mother would be there to cook supper and make my dentist appointments. The one thing that had never occurred to me was to ask the energy within me where she wanted to take me, and to follow her lead.

When kundalini is awakened within us, this is what we are constantly being invited to do: to move beyond technique into the sweet and mysterious expanse of spontaneous meditation. Our meditation will deepen and open to the exact degree that we pay attention to the shakti's signals and allow it to lead our practice.

What does it really mean to let kundalini lead? Does it mean becoming passive, sitting back, and waiting for something to happen? Or is there a way to actively work with kundalini, to follow her like a dance partner? Beyond following the basic disciplines of meditation—sitting, directing our attention within, and invoking grace—what do we need to do to be in the correct relationship to our own shakti?

As usual, it is a matter of attention. To dance or flow with kundalini, we need to keep ourselves attuned to the felt sense of the shakti as she moves within us. Kundalini pulsates. Through her pulsations, she is always communicating with us, drawing us inside, and showing us the pathway that will lead us deeper into ourselves.

THE LANGUAGE OF KUNDALINI

The inner shakti communicates with us through subtle impulses, feelings, and sensations, through insights, images, and realizations. Some of these communications are immediately recognizable once we tune in to them. For example, you might feel the urge to meditate. At different times during the day, you might notice a strong inward pull, a longing to focus inside. This is the natural meditation urge, and for an awakening meditator, it can be as strong a natural impulse as hunger or thirst. The stirring of the inward-flowing current can happen at your desk or on the bus, and it often manifests as a sensation of heaviness or even sleepiness. If you aren't attentive, you may think that you need a nap or a cup of coffee. But what you really need is to give in to the impulse that wants to draw you into meditation—even if only for a minute or two. (Lock yourself in the office bathroom stall if you need to, or pull the car over to the side of the road.)

Here are some of the more dramatic signs of kundalini's workings: Perhaps a light appears in your inner field. Or you find yourself in a natural witness state, observing your experience. A feeling of love arises and grows stronger as you focus on it. Your awareness begins expanding, pushing aside the energy walls that make us feel confined within the boundaries of the body. The breath speeds up or stops. The head shakes or moves backward or forward. You might feel yourself dropping or rising to a different inner state, shifting "levels" within yourself. The Awareness that has hovered behind your surface mind seems to move to the foreground. A vision appears.

Other signals of the shakti are much subtler. Perhaps you feel a pulsation in the heart, a slight tingling in the forehead, a sensation of energy on one side of the body, or a realization that the mantra "wants" to stop being repeated.

These subtle signals are easier to ignore than the more dramatic ones, so we often fail to pay attention to them. Nonetheless, they are as significant as dramatic manifestations. They are our own personal trail markers, footprints that reveal the direction that our inner shakti is opening for us. We need to learn to recognize them for ourselves, because there is no rule book that can possibly describe each of them.

I have realized at last the true nature of prayer and meditation. They are simply your own play as longing and as aspiration.

—RAMPRASAD [2]

You might like to close your eyes at this moment and tune in to the energy within your body.

Exercise: Sensing the Shakti

Close your eyes and allow your body to move into a relaxed, upright posture. Turn your attention inward and scan your body. Where do you feel the currents of energy in your body now? How do you experience your inner energy? Do you notice it throbbing in particular areas of the body? Are there feelings associated with the sensation of energy—feelings like tenderness or heartache or longing? Inner sensations like pressure or heat or hardness or softness? Sounds or lights? Notice them and see whether they are familiar to you.

FOLLOWING THE SHAKTI'S PATHWAYS.

Just as we each have our own style of feeling emotions, processing information, and solving problems, each of us experiences the inner world of meditation in our own way. Until you recognize the validity of your own personal mode, you often doubt your meditation experience, especially when it doesn't conform to the experiences described by your teacher or in the classical texts of your tradition. If you have been taught to identify true meditation with a dead-quiet mind or to imagine that good meditation means seeing visions or entering into dramatically altered states of consciousness, you might discount the other insights, the subtle movements of energy, and the various shifts in mood and feeling that are equally important signposts in the inner world.

Theravada and Zen Buddhist meditation teachers will often tell you to ignore these experiences as mere phenomena, and move beyond them. Certainly, it's important not to get stuck in them, or to take them as the goal of your practice. But in the tantric traditions, contemplative traditions, inner phenomena are taken more seriously. Inner sensations like tingling or pressure or the expansion of energy past the walls of your skin, changes of temperature, sensations of inner pleasure and blissfulness, visions, hearing inner sounds or even poetry, and spontaneous physical movements are all signs of the inner transformative process that is taking place. They are gifts and signposts that can signal a shift in awareness, or even point out a path to follow.

RECOGNIZING THE SHAKTI'S PATHWAYS

All these sensations, whether visual, auditory, or kinesthetic, are manifestations of one particular aspect of the kundalini: its power of action, which is called *kriya shakti*. For this reason, they are often called *kriyas*, or yogic movements.

But kriya shakti is not the only power of the kundalini. Four other aspects of this powerful inner energy awaken in us when the kundalini becomes active, and their manifestations are as significant as those of the kriya shakti. The teachers of Kashmir Shaivism described these energies as the power of Awareness *(chit shakti)*, the power of bliss *(ananda shakti)*, the power of will *(iccha shakti)*, and the power of knowledge *(jnana shakti)*. These powers are inherent in the universal energy, the shakti that creates and supports life. Shaivism tells us that every action that takes place in this universe is performed by one of these powers of the shakti.

The most exalted experience of bliss in any realm of being is directly knowing the universal Mother, the supremely blissful one.

—RAMPRASAD [3]

Now here is the point: When the kundalini becomes active in us, all these powers naturally come into full play in our inner world. As they play inside us, they give us experiences. Every experience we have in meditation is brought about by one or another of these five powers.

For example, our experiences of expanded consciousness come from the chit shakti, the power of Awareness. Chit shakti might manifest as a spontaneous experience of the witness, or as a realization that one Awareness pervades everywhere, or as the experience of pure being, beyond the ordinary sense of body or personality.

Ananda shakti, the power of bliss, unfolds within us as an upsurge of spontaneous love, contentment, and joy, the feeling of an ever-expanding heart. The joy of awakened ananda shakti is different from ordinary pleasure not just because it is much deeper, but also because it is independent of our moods and external experiences. Once the ananda shakti begins surging, we are capable of feeling a pulsation of joy not only when things are going well, but even in times of sorrow or frustration.

When the force of iccha shakti, the power of divine will, is moving inside us, it enhances our own power of will and makes it easier for us to practice yogic discipline, stay focused on a subtle state in meditation, or do our daily tasks one-pointedly. We might feel it as a force that pulls the mind inward, drawing us into meditation. Some people say that when their kundalini becomes active, an inner force will sometimes bring them fully awake at an hour much earlier than they are used to arising. It is as if the force is suggesting that it is time to get up and meditate. Iccha shakti can also manifest as guiding impulses, as feelings about the rightness or wrongness of a particular action, as stirrings of conscience, or as powerful intuitions that come both in and out of meditation. One of the ways we learn to tune into the guidance of the inner power is to follow these guiding signals and observe the results until we learn to distinguish them from the ordinary (and often unreliable) impulses that come from the mind.

Jnana shakti, or the power of knowledge, brings insight, understanding, and a subtle ability to know what is true. Jnana shakti reveals the difference between our limited self and what is sometimes called the True Self, the pure awareness of being. It shows the meaning of our experiences and gives us instructions, hints, and realizations about subtle truths. Jnana shakti is the power that answers our questions from inside and, ultimately, lets us recognize the Truth.

Again, we need to recognize and honor the form in which kundalini is manifesting in us. A friend once told me that he had always devalued his own experience because it didn't pulse with light, bliss, and drama. Then one day an insight arose, almost as though his kundalini were speaking to him. It said, "Your way is not the way of the kriya shakti. It is the way of the jnana shakti, the way of understanding." After that, he began to recognize the significance of the subtle realizations that often arose in his meditation. He would focus on and contemplate them. As he did, his meditation became more centered on his underlying Awareness, and he began to experience powerful, lasting contact with his essential Self. Once he recognized and began following the pathways that the shakti was opening up for him, his meditation went deeper than it had in ten years of practice.

Why do so many people struggle to recognize the pathways and guidance that unfold in meditation? One reason is that we tend to objectify our experience. We watch our meditation passively, as if we were at a movie. When our experiences are subtle, especially if they are purely energetic, we often ignore them or take them for granted. If they are big and dramatic, we may treat them as spiritual coinage, as signs that something special is happening and that we are succeeding at meditation. In both cases, we separate ourselves from the experience. We might try to hold on to it as if it were some kind of trophy, or we might push it away, or we might get caught up in analyzing it, trying to figure out what it means.

On the other hand, if we take our experiences as directional signals from the shakti, as doorways into deeper meditation, and then follow them, any one of them can take us deeper.

Practicing with Your Spontaneous Meditation Experiences

Suppose a soft glow appears behind your eyes. Very gently you bring your attention to the light. You don't try to hold it or cling to it to make it stay. You just softly move your attention close to it. (Often, the best way to do this is not to observe it frontally, but as if you were watching it from the side.) Perhaps you gently breathe into it and let the breath merge your awareness into it. Or you explore it. How does it look? What is its texture? What do you see or hear? You might also try shifting your perspective. Instead of feeling that you are outside this vision, observing it, imagine that you are inside it. With a sound, imagine that you are hearing it all around you.

Letting yourself be with an experience allows you to move much deeper into your inner field. Perhaps there is a sensation of expanding awareness, but the expansion stops at a certain point. You can let yourself linger on the edge of that expanded awareness, sensing the subtle texture of the consciousness that is expanding, or you can enter the field of consciousness that stretches within you, unfurling itself to the inner senses. The way to enter it is to become it.

It's not your physical self that becomes the expanded awareness, of course. It's your mind-sense, your subtle self. You become
it by identifying yourself with it. First, you identify yourself as
awareness, as attention. (For some people,
this may mean quickly going through a
process in which you disengage from identifying with your body, perhaps thinking,
"I am not my skin, my bones, my blood,
or my organs. I am not my senses, my
breath, my mind, or my thoughts. I am
not my emotions or my sensations. I
am Awareness. I am energy.") Then you
move as awareness into this subtle field
within yourself, as if you were a snowball
picking up more snow as you roll.

*Often when I step away
from otherness into
myself, I behold a most
wondrous beauty. It is
then that I believe most
strongly in my belonging
to a higher destiny.*

—PLOTINUS [4]

As you focus on and move into the pathway that the shakti reveals, the inner pathway often changes or disappears. The energy
sensation widens or diffuses. The light dissolves. The inner sound
shifts its tone, becomes a subtle throb, merges into silence, or becomes light. If you stay with the feeling of it—the felt sensation of
the experience—you can still follow it.

Exercise: Following a Pulsation of Energy

Suppose, for example, you begin by noticing an energy
pulsation in the middle of the head, or the space between the eyebrows. This, you feel, is the opening that
the shakti is revealing to you now. So you focus gently

173

on it, breathing in and out of it. Or you remind yourself that it is your own energy and let yourself feel an identity with it. At some point, you might feel that the energy opens and takes you inside. Perhaps you find yourself in a large ball or field of energy, or in a cavelike space. You might sense or see colors or sensations inside the space. As you let yourself be with it, the energy might draw you deeper into itself. It might manifest as forms, faces, or colors, as feelings of love, or as an expanding sensation. There might be a sudden rush of insight.

Then at a certain point, you will probably find that whatever arises—whether it is a light, an inner understanding, or a feeling of love—has dissolved, evanesced, become attenuated into pure energy. Into space.

As the shakti moves us inward, its natural tendency is to dissolve forms—to lead us from the gross to the subtle, and then to the subtler, deeper, and finer realms of consciousness, where the threads of form disappear into the formless, and the surface mind merges into its source. As the landmarks on the shakti's pathway melt, you can let yourself melt with them. You can keep breathing out the inner sense of holding in your consciousness, relaxing the tightness of your mental "muscles," and moving toward and into each new space as it opens up. The principle is to keep entering more deeply into the place where the shakti is playing. As you do that, it will keep moving you deeper into the inner world.

Some people lose their awareness at this point or fall into a sleepy, unconscious state. It's good to try to stay aware, but don't worry if at this point you lose awareness. As your attention becomes more stable, you will be able to hold the state—ultimately, to rest in spaciousness.

INVOKING SHAKTI

Learning how to follow the shakti's lead is such a core practice for entering the heart of meditation that in some schools of traditional kundalini meditation practice, students are told not to try to practice any technique at all. Instead they simply sit and wait for the shakti to take them where it wants to take them. To do this successfully, though, you need to keep yourself vigilant; otherwise you might wind up suspended on some seductive thought train. It's said that the Goddess has two faces—her *mayic* face, which creates separation and identification with the small self; and her liberating face, which dissolves duality. We want to stay in touch with her liberating face.

Ramakrishna Paramahamsa, who was a great lover of the divine Mother, used to pray to the shakti the way a child speaks to its mother. He would beg, "Please, show me your liberating face rather than the face of your *maya,* your delusion!"[6] This

You are no longer able to conceal yourself or appear distant from me. My very breath and being bond with your potent mystery, and I experience your power alone as my own inviolate strength.

—RAMPRASAD [5]

175

is a powerful little prayer. I often try it when meditation feels particularly thick and agitated. As I utter the words, I begin to experience a radical shift of perspective. I see how thoughts are taking form out of my underlying consciousness, how they stay awhile and then dissolve. Instead of being lost in thought, I find myself watching the play of the energy of the mind. This instantly frees me from identifying with the thoughts, so I am able to move into a deeper state.

In fact, whenever we want to invoke the shakti, the best way to begin is with a prayer and an invitation. Like the invocations to the guru that we looked at in chapter 3, our petition can be very simple: "O Kundalini Shakti, please show me how you want to meditate today." It can also be elaborate and imaginative, like the praise-hymns of the devotional poets: "Mother Kundalini," you could intone if that were your mood, "you are the very foundation of inner experience. You shine like the sun within my body and purify the mind. Please be gracious to me. Guide my meditation."

There is also a kind of prayer that is actually meditation. Here we seek out the shakti's presence in the depths of the mind, feel it intimately present inside us, and move with it. The most natural and immediate way to do this, I have found, is to meditate on the spanda, the inner pulsation that we looked at in chapter 4. You may notice that we keep returning again and again to pointing out this pulsation. That's because it is such a direct way of becoming familiar and intimate with our own shakti.

The following exercise takes a little time. Before you can discern the subtle inner pulse, you need to give the mind time to let go of its surface busyness.

Exercise: Invoking the Shakti's Guidance

Step 1: Settling the Mind

Close your eyes and sit in an upright, relaxed posture, following the steps on pages 75–77.

Focus your attention on the breath. Observe the breath without trying to change its rhythm. Instead of feeling that you are breathing, have the understanding that you are being breathed. The breath is being drawn in and out by the energy within your body. Kundalini is breathing you.

As thoughts come up, name each thought as Consciousness, as shakti.

Continue this for fifteen minutes, or until you begin to feel the mind relaxing and becoming quieter. Now let yourself rest in your own inner consciousness, the field of your inner experience.

Step 2: Experiencing the Pulsation

Feel the slight shimmer of movement, the subtle vibration, the pulse of energy that is always throbbing inside your consciousness. Notice where in your inner field of awareness you feel that vibration, and focus your attention there.

The pulsation of the shakti may manifest as a subtle vibration, a pulsing throb, but it may also manifest as a sound or as a glow of light. You may notice that the pulsation is especially strong in one area of your body—in the heart, between the eyebrows, in the throat, or at the top of the head. If that is the case, gently allow your attention to go to that center. Or focus on the sensation of the heartbeat as it diffuses itself throughout your body.

As you sense that pulsation within your awareness, begin to honor it. Say to it, "I recognize you as the inner shakti, divine kundalini in this form. I honor you. I know you as the Goddess, the mother of the universe, who pulses within me. I know that out of you comes all my thoughts and all feelings. Out of you comes the mantra, the divine sound. Out of you comes visions, lights, and experiences of bliss."

Now speak inwardly to the divine pulsation, this form of the Goddess within you. Ask for her guidance and help. Ask her, "Where do you wish to play today? Where do you wish to take me? In what direction should I follow you? How do you want me to meditate now?"

Once you have asked these questions, wait, with great alertness, for the answers that arise from inside. Wait without expecting anything, without having a program.

An answer may come as an insight, as a verbal direction, as a very subtle feeling, or as an impulse to do a particular practice or focus in a particular way. Don't worry about whether you have the right answer. Trust that whatever comes up is your answer from the shakti.

When an impulse, a direction, a practice, or an experience arises, follow it. Focus on it. If nothing else arises, continue to focus on the vibration, on the shakti as you are experiencing it. Allow yourself to feel at one with the pulsation of the shakti. Let it draw you deeper and deeper into its shimmering field of vibration.

Permission to Unfold

Even though I have worked with the process of invoking the shakti for years, I'm always slightly awed at how much it enlivens practice. The simple act of asking your inner meditation energy for guidance seems to create space for new openings and deeper meditation. Often these openings come when someone focuses on a phenomenon that they have never even noticed before.

During one meditation, a student of mine asked the shakti to lead him, then felt a movement of energy on one side of his head. Ordinarily he would have ignored it, but because he was looking for a signal from the shakti, he focused on it and tried to enter it. The energy softened, widened, and expanded. He found himself in a plane of soft, vibrating energy, surrounded by waves of love. It was like resting in subtle water. His sense of being a physical body dissolved, and he realized that he was this expanded body of Consciousness.

Holy Spirit, giving life to all life, moving all creatures, root of all things, washing them clean, wiping out their mistakes, healing their wounds, you are our true life, luminous, wonderful, awakening the heart from its ancient sleep.

—HILDEGARD OF BINGEN [7]

A young woman told me that the first time she invoked the shakti's help, a field of light opened up before her. Now whenever she sits for meditation, she experiences this field.

> *Trust the divine power, and she will free the godlike elements in you and shape all into an expression of divine nature.*
>
> —SRI AUROBINDO [8]

Another woman felt a strong pressure in her third-eye center, between the eyebrows, which resolved itself into a blue ball of light. She focused on the light and found herself in a huge ocean of radiance, where she floated for the rest of the meditation period. After that, the pulsation in her forehead continued to grow stronger. Not only did she experience it in meditation, but she also kept feeling the pressure throughout the day. She described how, along with the sensation of pressure, there was a new clarity in her mind: "Sometimes when I close my eyes during the day, I feel as if I'm looking through crystal. Even when my mind is very busy, there's lightness underneath it."

Other people have reported spontaneous physical movements, yogic kriyas, or the feeling of witness-consciousness descending over them. For some there was simply a feeling of sweetness and depth in meditation. As one meditator put it, "I began to be drawn to meditation in a way I hadn't been before. My experiences became precious to me."

The Power of Surrender

This process of invoking and following the shakti is powerful because when you do it, you participate in three of the most important practices in the meditation of grace: recognition, worship, and surrender. As you begin to recognize the intrinsic divinity of the energy that pulses within your mind in meditation, you free your inner shakti to reveal her love and her liberating intention. When you take a devotional, worshipful attitude to the energy inside by communicating with her, praying to her, and invoking her grace, you enter into a loving relationship with kundalini. As you give her your attention and ask for her help, you get access to wisdom and guidance that you may not have known you had available. When you surrender—that is, when you genuinely commit yourself to following her guidance—you give her permission to show you the depths of her love for you. Kundalini cannot do this unless you allow her to act. Before she can fully reveal herself to you, you need to have given her permission to guide the program.

This is not always easy. Most of us have a deep inner need to control things—in meditation as much as in daily life. When the shakti presents us with an opening into deeper meditation, there is usually a moment when we want to resist or back away from the opening. At such moments, we have to consciously remind ourselves to let go or to surrender.

Emerging into her thousand-petal reality, O meditator, become the Goddess consciously. She is your essence, you her expression.

—RAMPRASAD [9]

Ultimately, surrender isn't something we can "do." It's a natural movement of Consciousness, a deep release that happens over time and often only in deep meditation. Yet there are practices that allow us to release our hold. One works with the breath—which, as we have seen before, is the great engine of release in meditation. You breathe in, and then exhale with the feeling that you are breathing out the distracting thoughts, the feelings of resistance, and the sense of separation and limitation. That inner gesture of exhaling resistance not only helps release the mental muscles that create constriction in our breathing, but also releases constriction in the mind and loosens our feeling of separation from the shakti.

It is important to remember when you practice surrender that you are not surrendering to something outside. The shakti who guides you into meditation is your own higher energy—the power of your evolving consciousness. She is the energy of your soul who, out of love, is drawing you to complete your journey into the essence of what you are. By her very existence, she asks you to stretch, to expand, to grow, and to become your best and highest self. She does this out of love. She does it because she is, truly, your Self.

So as we invoke shakti and become aware of her signals, as we learn to surrender our meditation agendas and follow shakti's footprints into the inner world, we can periodically stop to breathe out our feelings of resistance and tension. We can stop to remember the reality of oneness, the seamless congruity between the consciousness of our mind and the great Consciousness. We can remind ourselves that the energy of the universe is our energy, that the great Awareness is our awareness, and that God's mind holds, contains, and encompasses our own mind and ultimately dissolves all of it into the vastness of pure chiti, pure Consciousness.

CHAPTER NINE

Where Do You Find Yourself?
A Road Map of
the Meditation Journey

*W*e have been examining a series of practices for coming into relationship with the inner world. We have also looked at several principles that make it easier to swim in its waters—principles like devotion, playfulness, opening to and entering into techniques rather than trying to "do" them, feeling one with your practice and its goal, learning how to sense and follow clues that your inner energy reveals.

In this chapter, I'll attempt to describe some of the states, signposts, and "geographical" landmarks that you might encounter in meditation. In other words, this chapter offers a partial road map of the issues and inner experiences that show up when you journey through the inner territory. I've tried to include the obvious—the basic stages that nearly everyone experiences. But I also, with considerable humility, offer a brief survey of some of the advanced stages in the journey. Because meditation is a journey as well as a practice, it moves through stages and takes us into many different states.

Of course since inner experience is more holographic than linear, the journey of meditation isn't like climbing stairs or traveling on a highway. In other words, as you follow along, it's important to remember that the map is not the territory.

THE MOVEMENT INWARD

As we have seen, when we turn our attention to the inner world and sit with the intention to sink back into ourselves, we open ourselves to the natural inward movement of Consciousness. By now, it should be apparent that this inward tendency is a kind of dissolve. It is a process of allowing the relatively dense state of our ordinary mind to resolve itself back into its own ground, into the natural state of clarity and awareness that the Indian tradition calls the Knower, pure Consciousness, or the Self. This process happens differently for everyone and brings with it a great variety of inner experiences.

Here is where most of our questions arise. First of all, we want to know the meaning of our experiences. We want to understand whether it is important that we see visions of faces, or what that light means, or why our head keeps dropping forward onto the chest, or whether the feeling of joy that surfaces fleetingly is the ultimate joy of the Self or some lesser pleasure. If we seem to lose consciousness in meditation, we want to know whether or not we are just asleep. If we remain in our normal waking state, we are afraid we aren't meditating.

Behind all questions is the great question, the one we all eventually want an answer to: am I actually making any

progress in meditation at all? During the years of experimenting with my practice, this particular doubt would periodically
seize me. I would wonder whether I was really moving deeper
in meditation or simply indulging myself,
drifting through realms of dreams and
moving energy. To deal with these doubts,
I began looking carefully at what the sages had to say about the inner realm, and
comparing my own intuitive sense of the
journey with the maps found in different
meditation texts.

*Be strong then, and enter
into your own body;
there you have a solid
place for your feet.
Think about it carefully!
Don't go off
somewhere else!
Kabir says this: just
throw away all thoughts
of imaginary things,
and stand firm in
that which you are.*

—KABIR [1]

Fortunately, great meditators from every
tradition have left us accounts of their own
experiences and pointed to certain experiences as signposts, signals that we are actually
moving forward. Of course, the indicators
of what the *Shvetashvatara Upanishad* calls
"success in yoga" differ in certain particulars
from tradition to tradition. And ultimately,
most of the great teachers of meditation
would agree that the most important signs of
spiritual progress are revealed in our charac-
ter, our ability to maintain equanimity, our power to keep the mind
clear and still, our compassion and kindness, our clarity, and our
capacity to hold our center.

Nonetheless, there is value in looking at the maps that different traditions offer us when we are trying to understand where
our inner experiences fit and what, if anything, they mean. If

we don't understand them, we are liable to discount significant experiences or to short-circuit yogic processes that are not only normal, but profound and helpful. Or we can fall into the opposite trap and become inflated about experiences that are only signposts, thinking we have reached the final goal.

One friend of mine often describes an early meditation in which she saw a blazing golden light rising out of her heart. "This is it!" she thought. "I'm enlightened. Now what?" She was musing about her possible future as a spiritual teacher when she realized that the light had disappeared. Later her teacher explained that her vision, though profound and meaningful, was not by any means a sign that her journey was finished. It was instead a gift, one of many she might discover along the way.

Another woman wrote a book about the painful confusion she suffered after being catapulted into a state in which she was suddenly and, apparently, permanently freed of any sense of identification with her personal self. Lacking reference points or guidance, she assumed that her condition was pathological and suffered for nearly ten years until she met someone who could put it into perspective. And in recent years, many of us have known or heard of people who experienced a long period of clarity or expansion or blissfulness and assumed, like my friend, that they were now Self-realized beings—until the "awake" state disappeared.

So the maps are essential. Even more essential is our own contemplation, our willingness to examine our experiences in the light of the various yogic paradigms.

In the Indian tradition, the most famous map of the spiritual journey traces our progress up the *chakras,* the energetic centers that lie along the spinal column. Most spiritual practitioners are familiar with the names and locations of the main chakras and are also aware that each chakra is related to certain systems in the physical body, as well as particular emotional or spiritual states.

In *Shat Chakra Nirupana,* one of the authoritative tantric texts on kundalini and the chakras, the basic paradigm places our more purely human experiences in the heart chakra and the chakras immediately below it:* the *svadhisthana* (sacral) *chakra,* near the gonads, which is said to be the seat of lust and fear; and the *manipura* (navel) *chakra,* where our power urges are said to be seated.

At the fourth chakra, at the level of the heart, the *anahata,* we begin to move into the energetic centers that govern higher stages of awareness. Our experience becomes subtler as our awareness ascends higher in the inner body. After the anahata, we move to the fifth chakra, the *vishuddha* (pure) *chakra,* which is at the throat; and then comes the *ajna* (command) *chakra,* which is in the center of the forehead between the eyebrows. When awareness becomes stable in the crown chakra, called the *sahasrara* ("thousand-petaled"), we experience the full expansion of awareness into identity with the divine; we become, according to the tradition, fully awake, or Self-realized.

Recent Western literature on the chakras tends to focus more on the psychological and psychophysical aspects of the chakras

---

*In this text, the *muladhara,* or base chakra, since it is the seat of the sleeping kundalini, is described simply as a center of bliss.

than the original tradition does, but the basic idea is that we "ascend" through the chakras to different developmental domains and stages.

Another yogic map comes from the tradition of Kashmir Shaivism (see appendix 2) and traces our movement in meditation through thirty-six *tattvas,* or stages of mani-festation. According to this paradigm, the spiritual process is one in which you move from identification with the physical body, mind, and separate ego, through progressive-ly subtler recognitions of your identity with the wholeness of Consciousness. In the low-er stages, we experience reality as dense and fixed, and ourselves as limited and separate from the whole. In the highest stage, we re-alize that all of reality exists within our own Awareness. We know ourselves to be not different from the creative Consciousness itself, in all its freedom and natural joy. As we move through the stages in between, we experience progressively subtler and more inclusive states of being.

> *In this body . . . are seers and sages; all the stars and planets as well. There are sacred pilgrimages, shrines, and presiding deities of the shrines . . . The sun and moon also move in it. Ether, air, fire, water, and earth are also there. All the beings that exist are also to be found in the body. He who knows all this is a Yogi.*
>
> —SHIVA SAMHITA [2]

These two maps are related and actually can be fitted together, as the experience of each group of tattvas corresponds to a par-ticular chakra. Both are related to the map I will look at in detail in this chapter: the paradigm of the four states and four bodies offered by Shankara, the great teacher of Vedanta.

I decided to look at meditation experience along this particular grid for three reasons: because it is simple and easy to follow, because it was the one I learned in my early days of practice, and because it helps us understand progression in meditation as a process of moving inward, or of "unpeeling" different layers of our being.

THE FOUR STATES AND THE FOUR BODIES

The texts of Vedanta speak of the physical body, the mind, and the other aspects of our being as "sheaths," or "bodies," superimposed like layers of an onion over the subtle energy of Consciousness that is our core Self. Linked with these sheaths are four states that the texts identify as basic human experience: waking, dreaming, deep sleep, and the state of transcendental Awareness we experience in meditation. Normally we live in one or another of these states, or to put it another way, we live in the "body" that corresponds to that state. So when we move inward in meditation, we actually move through these four bodies, or if you prefer, layers—each one subtler that the last and each interpenetrating the others.

When we are awake, we are normally grounded in the physical body *(sthula sharira)*. In dreams and reverie, when we are lost in thought or fantasy, or during certain stages of meditation, we lose awareness of the physical body and move into the subtle body *(sukshma sharira)*. We experience the causal body *(karana sharira)* in deep sleep and in certain types of deep, formless meditation. The supracausal body is the place we inhabit when we are fully absorbed in the Self. This state normally reveals itself in meditation, though, as we saw in chapter 2, it can also open out when we are wide awake.

Everything that happens to us in meditation happens in one of these four bodies. Of course, this is just a map, a convenient lens for looking at our experience. In yoga, all categories, all paradigms, are simply ways of putting names to levels of experience that are so subtle and personal that any description of them can only be partial. We are, after all, in the domain of the wordless, trying to fix in words experiences that are often beyond the reach of language. Because concepts can trap us here, we always need to remind ourselves to take them lightly, so as not to allow the limitless world of meditation to be limited by our definitions. The world we enter in meditation has so many corners, so many realms, and so many flavors of experience that we can never describe them all or fit them into any one paradigm.

Another trap to be careful of is the assumption that spiritual progress is linear. Sometimes we imagine that consciousness rises or descends step by step, as if we were climbing a ladder or riding an elevator with the operator calling out each floor. In reality, we move in a much less linear manner. You may experience extremely subtle states during the early days of your practice, and then, ten years later, find yourself being drawn to sink your awareness into your physical body. When kundalini guides the inner process, it moves in the direction and at the pace that is appropriate for you at a given time. It works in different "layers of the onion" and not necessarily in sequence. However, for the sake of convenience here, we will look at our meditation experiences in the four bodies from the outside in.

The First Body: The Physical Body

One of the most universal meditation experiences in the physical body is pain. When we are first learning to sit in a yogic posture, our knees and hips and back show their resistance to this unaccustomed discipline by manifesting all kinds of mysterious aches and tremors. The body tends to complain every time we try to sit longer than usual or otherwise push it past its limits. So most of us have a rather ambivalent attitude toward our experiences in the physical body, and when we become aware of the body in meditation, we often assume that we aren't meditating deeply or that we are stuck.

This isn't true. The pain or discomfort we experience in the body during meditation can be a genuine and, believe it or not, significant meditation experience: it can be a sign that the body is being purified. Because the body is the support for our meditation practice, it needs to be stable, clear, and strong in order to contain and conduct the energy that pours through us when kundalini leads us into the subtler stages of meditation. So when we sit for meditation, the awakened shakti will move through the muscles and joints, and open them up.

The unpracticed one will be pulled out of meditation by the senses, even if he forcefully tries to control them. His meditation may be disturbed by such distractions as cold, heat, pleasure, pain, mental upsets, and mosquitoes, which create bodily pain and cause the mind to wander.

—YOGASHIKHA
UPANISHAD [3]

191

This process can be accelerated or helped along—and may even be initiated by—hatha yoga and skillful body work, massage, somatic therapy, and traditional movement practices like qi gong or contemporary movement practices like Feldenkrais. The physical body is layered with memories of old wounds, sicknesses, environmental toxins, unhealthy food, and emotional upheaval. The awakened shakti removes all of this, along with the tensions, both recent and ancient, that we have accumulated.

One friend of mine swears that when her neck gets stiff, not even the chiropractor can do anything with it, but when she sits for meditation, the inner shakti moves her head in circles and releases the kinks. Other people simply experience a gradual release of tension as they sit. Sometimes the experience of release can feel mildly uncomfortable or even intensely unpleasant. But somehow the discomfort seems to be part of the process, because the experience of opening is an experience of learning how to feel.

When our bodies are deeply blocked and tense, we often feel numb. We may not even be conscious of our physical discomfort. As the surface layers are moved away, as we break through some of this surface physical pain, we literally open up to the stored pain that is deeper within the body. We may feel aches that we have never been aware of before—and along with aches in the body, a corresponding emotional pain. This pain is not the pain of sickness but the pain of healing. Though much of kundalini's work takes place below our awareness, much of it must necessarily go on within our awareness. By allowing ourselves to feel the spontaneous release that kundalini inspires, we learn how to release and open up on our own. We can't do this when we are unconscious. So the pains that we experience in the body during meditation are actually teaching us, helping us to become more conscious of what is going on in our bodies.

Many of the physical signals of the shakti that we mentioned in chapter 8 are signs of this purification. The intense pressure that some people feel in the forehead or in the crown of the head is a sign that the energy is working to open the spiritual centers in the head. When the energy is moving in the heart chakra, you might feel a heaviness around the heart; one person described it to me as a sensation of having an elephant sitting on her chest. We sometimes experience heat or a piercing sensation at the base of the spine or at other points along the spinal column as kundalini activates the chakras.

When a particular chakra is being activated, you might feel its effects in the organs associated with that center. The spiritual center at the navel is associated with the digestive system, and when it is being purified, some people go through digestive upheavals. (Of course, before deciding that your digestive problems are associated with kundalini purification, it is highly advisable to have yourself checked out medically!) When the center at the throat is being opened, you may feel a kind of exaggerated tension in the muscles there or even a sore throat. As the energy moves to open the center between the eyebrows, people will often experience it as intense pressure. Understanding the nature of this discomfort helps us to bear with it. Instead of defining it as "pain," we can see it as the pressure of the awakening force within. We can realize its benign intention. We can relax into the pressure and move toward it and into it, instead of away from it. Often just relaxing will shift our experience out of the discomfort zone.

For more than twenty-five years, whenever the shakti became particularly strong in meditation, my head would bend backward and then lock in that position. Sometimes it would jam up against the spine. In my early years of practice, I had a lot of tension in my neck, so this posture was excruciatingly uncomfortable. In fact, it sometimes hurt so much that I would try to come out of it—only to find that the moment I straightened my head, it would move right back again. Once, as if to underscore the value of this pose, my teacher came up to me during a meditation retreat, put his hand on my head, and bent it back into that position! Another time, an orange-robed sage appeared in one of my dreams, pushed my head into the head-against-the-back lock, and said, "This is the golden posture."

One evening I found myself thrust so tightly into this posture that I couldn't move. I had no choice but to give into it. It soon became obvious that my resistance to staying in the posture made it more painful than it had to be, but I didn't know how to stop resisting. Then a thought arose: "This posture is a gift of kundalini. The divine energy in my body is doing this out of love, in order to free me. Even though I don't understand it, still it is an act of love." As I held that thought, a great feeling of love washed over me and, simultaneously, something released in my neck. The posture, which had been sharply painful, became easy and sweet. A few minutes later, my head spontaneously straightened. It was as if that letting-go, my moment of understanding and acceptance, had opened the way for kundalini to free my neck of its tension.

Later I read in a hatha yoga text that this posture is a classical position for opening the heart center. As it spontaneously manifested year after year, the center in my heart did open.

Physical Kriyas: The Movements of the Awakened Shakti

Spontaneous physical movements like my neck-lock—called yogic kriyas—can range from a gentle swaying of the torso, to wildly flailing circles of the head and neck, to spontaneous hatha yoga asanas easily performed even when your body is not used to such positions. Each one of these kriyas has both a physical and a subtle effect. As they release tension in the physical body, they also remove subtle energy blocks.

For example, many meditators experience a kriya in which the energy causes them to bend forward from the hips and place the forehead on the floor. This posture is called *mahamudra*. It is one of the most important hatha yoga postures for activating kundalini and opening the central channel, the sushumna nadi, in the center of the body. The sushumna nadi is the pathway that kundalini takes as it moves through the chakras. Once it opens, the breath, which normally flows in and out of the nostrils, can begin to flow in the *sushumna*. This is when both the breath and the mind become still, and we are able to go into deep meditative states.

On a physical level, the mahamudra posture opens the hips. When the forehead presses against the floor, it not only clears the sinuses, it also opens the ajna chakra, the third-eye center between the eyebrows. That center is the junction point for many different *nadis,* or subtle channels of the life force, the *prana.* It is also the seat of one of the inner *granthis,* the subtle energetic knots that block access to higher states of consciousness. The knot at the third-eye center, called the *rudra granthi,* is a kind of inner gatekeeper that prevents our awareness from entering the spiritual centers in the crown of the head. This knot holds us in the illusion of separateness. Once this knot is opened, there is a profound change in our awareness of ourselves. We begin to realize directly, through experience, that our consciousness is not confined to the limits of the physical body. We can know ourselves as much larger and subtler than we ordinarily believe ourselves to be. We stop clinging to ego limitations, fears, and constrictions. We begin to experience our unity with others and our unity with God.

There are hundreds of different kinds of kriyas. For example, you may experience the following:

- Your jaw may make rapid lateral movements, as though it were trying to loosen itself up. These movements are helpful in opening the throat chakra.

- Your body may rotate from the hips, or your pelvis may wriggle in circles or back and forth or up and down. These movements are related to the first three chakras: muladhara, svadhisthana, and manipura.

- Your hands may move in dancelike gestures. Your fingers may spontaneously press themselves into your forehead or your heart—again, gestures that help to open these centers.

- Your body may move into a hatha yoga posture like the ones mentioned above. You might fall backward into the yogic posture called *suptapadmasana,* a posture that vitalizes the kidneys and digestive organs.

When kriyas occur (and not everyone experiences them), it is one sign that kundalini is working strongly and that spontaneous meditation is taking place. Usually you have physical kriyas during the early part of a meditation session; at a certain point, the energy will release the body, and you are able to move into a quieter meditation. If possible, it is best to allow kriyas to happen—to witness but not short-circuit them. However, if a particular movement is extremely uncomfortable or if it is disturbing to people around you, you might try dropping your awareness deeper inside, into the heart or another spiritual center, consciously moving past the physical to a more subtle level. Or you can invoke the shakti and ask it to give you a quieter experience.

The discomfort that we sometimes experience when these processes are taking place (and, again, not all of them are accompanied by physical movements) is a sort of growing pain. Being able to sit with the discomfort of growth takes a lot of courage and a willingness to be open to the unknown. There is a great nobility in the attitude that a meditator takes: sitting with the intention to experience whatever the inner energy wants to give. It is the attitude of the spiritual warrior, the warrior of yoga, who dedicates himself or herself (at least for the hour of meditation) to going for it—going for the growth, going for the breakthrough, going for the transformation.

At the same time, you shouldn't feel that you need to go faster, or sit longer, than you want to. It's not that anyone is going to give you prizes for endurance or stoicism. You are not in this to get hurt or to prove how strong you are. Ultimately, you are in it for love. So if something feels like too much for now, trust yourself and give yourself permission to back off. Move when your posture becomes stiff, ask the inner energy to give you a gentler experience, or simply come out of your posture for a few minutes and relax. There are times in meditation when it is right to push through a feeling of discomfort and times when the best tactic is to relax, to back off. As you experiment with your practice, you'll learn to sense all this and also to honor your intuitions.

The Second Body: The Subtle Body

Usually after we've been sitting for a while, our awareness of the physical body lessens. If we are having physical kriyas, they die down. We become more aware not just of our thoughts, but of the images and the shifting energy currents that move beneath the surface of our being.

The subtle body is made of energy—the energy of our vital force, the energy of thoughts and feelings and perceptions. According to the *Brihadaranyaka Upanishad*, it is the subtle body that transmigrates, leaving the physical body after death and going on to experience the so-called afterlife, as well as life in other physical bodies.[4]

The subtle body consists of:

- The prana, or vital energy

- The so-called psychic instruments—the sense-mind, the intellect, the ego, and the subconscious mind-stuff—along with the thoughts, images, and perceptions generated by the mind and intellect

- The powers of sensing—sight, hearing, and so on—that act through the physical organs to let us take in information from the outer world and that operate inwardly in dreams, imagination, and reverie

- The subtle elements of experienceable reality, called in Sanskrit the *tanmatras*. These create the inner world of images, sounds, tastes, and sensations that we experience when our attention is withdrawn from the exterior world; these may correspond to the pattern-making capacities of the physical nervous system

- The system of channels called nadis, which carry the vital energy to the organs and limbs of the physical body and to the chakras, or subtle energy centers

- Kundalini energy

The Vital Energy

The energy aspect of the subtle body is sometimes called the *pranamaya kosha,* or "vital sheath." It is truly a kind of sheath, a layer of pure vitality, the energy that powers your life. Prana is the name that the yogic sages gave to the life force that becomes the sap in the trees, the radiant currents of sunlight, the negative ions in the atmosphere, and the nourishment in water. Yogic texts say that before becoming this world of matter, the creative energy of this universe evolves into prana, a form of energy that is slightly grosser than pure Consciousness and that links the relatively thick and solid physical universe with its subtle essence.

> *Student, tell me,*
> *what is God?*
> *He is the breath*
> *within the breath.*
>
> —KABIR [5]

In the human body, prana forms the energetic bridge between body, mind, and spirit. Prana connects all the systems in the body, and powers the nervous system, the internal organs, and the muscles. It is the force that fires your neurotransmitters as they carry impulses through the brain and into the organs and muscles. Prana keeps the mind moving out through the senses, bringing in impressions and forming thoughts. When we breathe, we take in prana from the atmosphere along with oxygen; and in meditation, we can work with prana directly by working with the breath. When the prana slows down (a state that yogis try to induce through practicing *pranayama,* or breath control), the mind quiets down in response. That is why following the breath in meditation is so helpful in quieting the mind.

The pranamaya kosha interpenetrates the physical body, running through a lacework of subtle channels (nadis) and carrying energy to all the limbs and organs, giving them power and life. Until kundalini is awakened, we are only subliminally aware of the pranamaya kosha. We know when we feel energetic or low in vitality, but unless we practice hatha yoga or tai chi or some type of vibrational healing practice, we often walk around unconscious of the way energy flows in the body. Once kundalini awakens, its greater force begins to move with the prana in the body, and the sensations of that prana become unmistakable.

The subtle "touch" of the shakti, the kinesthetic sensation of inner movement that we looked at in chapter 8, is actually a manifestation of kundalini-activated prana. Sometimes you experience subtle tingling sensations. At other times, there is a light sensation of expansion: your field of awareness seems to expand outward to twice or three times its normal size. On the other hand, the prana may feel heavy and thick. People say, "I feel as if I'm being knocked out" or "It feels as if I'm sinking underwater" or "It's like I'm being pulled into deep sleep." The heavy-headed feeling, the sense of dancing energy under your skin, tingling feelings in your arms and legs, a sense of super-abundant energy, feelings of pressure in the heart or in the forehead—all these are pranic manifestations.

More dramatically, the prana can shift your breathing processes in meditation. Sometimes in meditation, the breath becomes very slow or seems to stop alto-gether. It only seems to stop, of course, because as long as we are alive, the breath never really stops. It is just that in yogic states the breath doesn't come in and out of the nostrils, but actually moves within the sushumna nadi, the subtle channel at the very center of the body. Ordinarily, the breath moves in and out of the body through two subtle

Light
devoured darkness.
I was alone
inside.
Shedding
the visible dark
I was your target
O lord of caves.

—ALLAMA PRABHU [6]

channels, the *ida* and the *pingala,* which run alongside the sush-umna. When the prana moves through these two channels, the mind tends to be outgoing and active. When the prana moves into the sushumna, it means that the vital force is turning inward.

This is an important yogic event because when the breath becomes still, the mind quiets down as well, and you can go into samadhi. The first few times this happens, it can feel un-familiar and frightening. You might be afraid that you won't be able to get another breath. Sometimes you panic, try to take a breath, and succeed in bringing yourself out of meditation.

> *During the period of yoga sadhana, one sees mist, smoke, fire, air, fireflies, lightning, crystal, and forms like the moon and the sun in the inner spaces. All these visions precede the light of God.*
>
> —SHVETASHVATARA UPANISHAD[7]

There really is nothing to be afraid of. When the breath slows or seems to stop in meditation, you are actually being sus-tained from a deeper level of your being by the prana shakti itself. You can trust that when the spontaneous process of medita-tion comes to an end, the breath will begin to move in and out of your nostrils again. The best thing is to let the process happen and to observe how it affects your inner state. Notice how the thoughts become still when the breath is still. Notice how your energy begins automatically to turn inside.

Another classical effect of kundalini is spontaneous *bhastrika pranayama,* or bellows breathing—a quick, rhythmic in-and-out movement of the breath, almost like panting, that is accompanied by contraction and release of the abdominal muscles. Again, if this happens, notice the effect on your mind. In traditional hatha yoga practice, bellows breathing is a process that is often performed deliberately to activate kundalini. When it happens spontaneously, it helps kundalini rise in the body, quiets thoughts, and can be the precursor to deeper meditation.

Often as meditation deepens, the prana seems to become finer and more expanded. Though the breath may still be moving slowly in and out of the nostrils, you can also begin to feel the "inner breath," the gentle rise and fall of energy inside the sushumna nadi. As you follow the currents of the prana, you'll find yourself settling more deeply inside. This is one way the prana creates a bridge between our ordinary waking awareness and the subtler realms. The sensations of prana are threads that connect us to the shakti. Prana is the vehicle we ride as the awakened shakti leads us gently through the layers of our subtle being.

Visions

Meditating in the subtle body often feels like a kind of dream state. Vagrant images pass before our inner eye—a scene, a color, a face, a scrap of landscape, a scene from a movie. The images can be familiar, or something we have never seen before. Sometimes these images play out as little scenarios, just as they do in dreams. In fact, this is exactly what they are: as we pass through different stages of meditation in the subtle body, often we actually enter the dream state and experience our own inner image-bank.

Most of the experiences that arise in this dreamlike state of meditating in the subtle body should be looked on as passing phenomena, like our thoughts. Our subtle bodies are as laden with stored images as they are filled with thoughts and feelings, and as we move deeper, we literally pass through inner fields of imagery, just as we pass through fields of thoughts.

However, just as dreams sometimes have significance, so at times do the images that arise in meditation. Their importance may be psychological rather than spiritual—that is, they may pertain to issues of your personal history and psychological growth processes, or to the work you are doing, or to your current professional or relationship challenges. All kinds of learning come to us in meditation, and the messages from our personal unconscious, even though they should not be confused with the transpersonal images that arise from the higher levels of our being, can sometimes be as valuable—in their own sphere.

Here is an example: Several years ago, a young lawyer was meditating before going to court to argue a patent case. In his meditation, the words "Article 509" surfaced. Being a long-time meditator, he took his inner message seriously enough to check it out. Before going to court, he stopped in the court-house library and looked up article 509 in a book on patent law. That day in court, his opponent raised a point that had been addressed by the article, and the lawyer was able to cite article 509 in refuting it. The judge was understandably impressed by his careful preparation, and the lawyer has always felt that his knowledge of article 509 was the thing that turned the judge's decision in his favor.

Another example: In a meditation group, we were doing an exercise that involved dissolving thoughts into Awareness. One man was surprised when, as his thoughts melted, they were replaced by an image of demons coming up out of a well. He sensed the presence of a higher being near him and asked that being to defend him from the demons. When he contemplated the image, he realized that the demons were deeply buried feelings that were beginning to emerge as his meditation went deeper. Because he was afraid of these feelings, he demonized them. He also saw that because he had a strong feeling of connection with a protective divine Presence, he tended to expect that higher power to protect him by "killing" his negative feelings. Contemplating the image later, he realized that he could take a different attitude toward his "demons"—he could see them as aspects of Consciousness rather than trying to kill them. This led to a far more loving and permission-giving attitude toward his inner world.

One reason it's so useful to write down your experiences each time you sit for meditation is precisely because even the apparently silly stream of non-spiritual images that come up can have significance for you. On the other hand, you also need to realize that even when these images are worth contemplating, you should not act on them without a great deal of thought. Until the mind has been fully purified, messages from the inner world are often unreliable or misleading. As a friend of mine says, they are "100 percent accurate, 50 percent of the time."

Our Lord opened my spiritual eye and showed me my soul in the middle of my heart, and I saw the soul as wide as if it were an infinite world, and as if it were a blessed kingdom.

—JULIAN OF NORWICH [8]

The Tandra State, or Yoga Nidra

Sometimes, however, the images that appear in meditation are of a very different quality. The colors are brighter, and the light is different. The content of the images has a "true" flavor that distinguishes them from the random series of images that ordinarily run across the inner screen when we are journeying through the subtle body.

This experience of having richer, brighter, and generally more objective images and visions in meditation is called *tandra*. The images of the dream state usually come out of our personal unconscious, while the images of tandra are true visions of inner or outer landmarks, symbolic figures, or events that are playing out in the world. In fact, many meditators enter the tandra state not only when sitting for meditation, but also from the state of dreaming sleep. Like Joseph in the Bible, or the ancient Greeks seeking advice from the Delphic Oracle and getting it in dreams, many of us have had such "true" or even sacred dreams. The Jewish tradition calls these dreams "prophetic," not necessarily in the sense of being predictive, but because they come from an inner center of wisdom, from the transpersonal realm.

One lovely contemporary description of this can been seen in this poem by Antonio Machado:

> Last night, as I was sleeping,
> I dreamt—marvelous error!—
> that I had a beehive
> here inside my heart.
> And the golden bees

were making white combs
and sweet honey
from my old failures.
　　Last night, as I was sleeping,
I dreamt—marvelous error!—
that a fiery sun was giving
light inside my heart.
It was fiery because I felt
warmth as from a hearth,
and sun because it gave light
and brought tears to my eyes.
　　Last night, as I was sleeping,
I dreamt—marvelous error!—
that it was God I had
here inside my heart.[9]

Awakened meditators of many traditions have left us accounts of such visions and dreams, and of the inner lights and sounds that can appear in meditation. Experiences like these can bring insight that changes people's lives forever. Often they are harbingers of a great inner shift in perception, waystations on the path that transform an ordinary person into an individual capable of holding the light of the truth inside her. From the prophet Mohammed's famous account of his night journey to the heavens, to Saint Teresa of Avila's inner visitation from the angel carrying a golden, fire-tipped lance that pierced her heart and sent her into ecstasy, to the visions painted by Hildegard of Bingen of blue-tinged divine beings and egg-shaped lights, we see how much power these experiences have to inspire not just the person who went through them, but also those who hear or read about them.

When meditation is empowered by awakened kundalini, experiences like these are available on a scale that convinces us that mystical experience is a natural realm of human life. Not only saints and mystics have these experiences—so do people like you and me.

In that moment, by divine favor and the spiritual assistance of the sheikh, my heart was opened. I saw that within me was something resembling an overturned cup; when this object was stood upright, a feeling of limitless happiness filled my being.

—TEVEKKUL-BEG [10]

Here is how a man described an experience during a guided meditation with a teacher:

"As I sat listening to the instructions, kundalini was released. I could feel a sensation at the base of my spine. It began to spiral up my back, and as it did, that area of my body was filled with shakti. As it rose, I became more and more aware of the shakti. At first I laughed, the sensation was so wonderful. As kundalini rose further, I began to weep. Who can contain such an experience? Soon I was filled with shakti. I was shakti. I stayed in meditation in this state, and the experience was indescribable. I soon found myself on the shore looking out over a vast white ocean. It was the whitest white you can imagine. I began to wade into the ocean until I was completely submerged. I began to experience a freedom beyond anything I've known. I was free. Free from all limitations. I was swimming and rolling in the ecstasy of the ocean."

This vision, the man said later, created a shift in his sense of self, his priorities, and his understanding about his life.

Not all meditation visions have such a powerful effect. Some are merely curious and odd. Yet all of them reveal the incredible variety of the inner world:

A woman in meditation feels herself rising out of her body into the center of the universe, where she sees the form of Jesus, whom she has loved all her life.

> *The soul is not in the universe; on the contrary, the universe is in the Soul.*
>
> —PLOTINUS [11]

A New York man sees in his meditation an undulating pattern of energy circling around a core. That morning he sees the same pattern on The Weather Channel—it is the energy pattern of a hurricane that is making its way along the Atlantic Coast.

A woman in Hawaii sees a wall of blue light rising before her eyes. In it she sees her housemates cooking breakfast in the next room. She can see everything they are doing and later is able to confirm it.

A woman in a meditation retreat was instructed to meditate on the witness. She later wrote:

"I heard the instructor say, 'You are the eternal witness.' Each time I focused on the word 'witness,' I would slip behind my thoughts to the place that was listening. I kept dropping back further, further, and further into a deep, deep silence. It was all-encompassing and infinite, so full and peaceful that the thought arose, 'If I can be here, why act?' As if in answer, I had a vision. First, there was the infinite space of the night sky—full yet empty, full of energy yet formless. Then, from this endless space many hands were reaching

209

down to the earth. The hands were performing an infinite variety of actions. Sometimes the hands were alone, sometimes together. Sometimes they would become entangled and fight with each other. As the image unfolded before me, these words arose: 'No matter what actions you do, they all arise from the same place; they arise from the Infinite.'"

Divine Moods: The Emotional Flavors of the Inner World

Most of our meditation experience is in the realm of subtle feeling-states. Harder to categorize and describe than visions, yet often more fulfilling and transformative, they are the spontaneous moods (bhavas) and flavors *(rasas)* of the inner world. Some people's entire meditation experience is in the realm of mood and feeling. "After I've been meditating for about twenty minutes, this tremendous feeling of peace comes over me," a man told me. "It's my baseline experience. Occasionally I'll see a vision or something. But I treasure that feeling of peace because I can take it with me when I leave meditation." A woman related to me that she will often experience a transformation of one feeling-state into another while she is sitting. An initial feeling of depression or anxiety will begin to break up into shimmering particles of light that seem to float away from her, leaving her in a state of serenity.

Other people have described how at certain moments they will feel a spontaneous sense of surrender or trust in the benevolence of the universe, knowing, "Everything is all right. I'm taken care of. I'm loved." Or they might fall into a sense of unity-awareness—a realization that the world around them is a part of them or that they are fully connected to every being in the world. Insights might arise: "All that matters is love" or "I can forgive" or "This is how to deal with the situation." Often the content of the insight is neither new nor startling, but it comes with a certainty and an energy that give it transformative power.

Looking back over our meditation experiences, we often realize that insights like these have had a powerful long-range impact on our lives. That is because the deeper insights that arise in meditation actually come from the realm of pure Consciousness, the realm of the Self. The way of the Self is to teach us from within. Once we see in meditation that the source of love is within us, we are no longer quite so liable to get caught in emotional dependency. Once we realize that by inwardly blessing an enemy we can melt our own anger and resentment, we no longer feel like such victims of our feelings. Meditation insights can change our lives.

The realm of the subtle body is huge and contains an almost endless storehouse of experiences. It is a vast universe in itself; in fact, the texts of yoga assert that everything that can be seen in the outer universe can be found within the subtle body of a human being. Many of us linger for years in the different corners of the subtle realm. And yet, there are other meditators who seem to bypass it altogether and move straight to the next level of experience, the state called the causal body, or the state of the void.

The Third Body: The Causal Body

Sometimes in meditation, we seem to lose consciousness altogether. Describing the experience afterward, we can only say, "I closed my eyes, and the next thing I knew, the alarm was ringing" or "I don't know where I went" or "I just went so deep inside that I didn't know anything; I wasn't even conscious." If we try to remember how it felt to be in that state, we recall nothing but a feeling of rest, of peace, of ease. We sense that we could have stayed there for hours, perhaps with the head dropping forward onto the chest or backward against the wall, and the breath calm and even. It is like being asleep, but we aren't exactly asleep. Perhaps we see a velvety blackness. Or perhaps we don't see anything at all. But it feels good.

> *Darkness within darkness. The gateway to all understanding.*
>
> —LAO-TZU [12]

At the same time, it can be disconcerting to spend so much time in meditation in a kind of void. It might make you wonder whether this is really meditation—especially if you find yourself immersed in this void state day after day for months or years.

It *is* meditation. It is meditation in the causal body, the karana sharira. This is a layer of our being composed entirely of darkness—but a deeply contented darkness. We ordinarily inhabit the causal body only when we are deeply asleep, in the state of dreamless rest. One fascinating hallmark of the causal body experience is that it is a place of great bliss.

The causal body is close to the Self. That is why meditating there can bring us such contentment. Often when we have been meditating in that state of profound blackness, we come out feeling refreshed, happy, and rejuvenated. That is the gift of the causal body. But it is not the final state. The causal body is unconscious, while the state of the Self is a state of super-consciousness, super-awareness.

The causal body got its name for two reasons. First, it is the part of our subtle system that houses the collection of impressions, tendencies, desires, beliefs, and concepts about reality that actually cause our lives to unfold as they do. Second, the causal body is home to the primordial darkness of maya, the veiling power that keeps us from seeing our essential unity and light. Maya is also a powerful energy, the force that gives rise to our experience of limited existence. Maya causes us to experience ourselves as individuals, and it causes us to experience the world as an object outside ourselves. So maya is the "cause" of our existence as individuals. This makes the causal body a very powerful place.

Only when the veil of maya lifts can we experience the world and ourselves as they really are: pure light, Awareness, and bliss. To reach the state beyond maya—the numinous realm of super-consciousness—we must journey through maya's darkness. This is not just a symbolic journey. The causal body literally is a "body" of darkness—the darkness of the deep sea of the collective unconscious described in Jungian psychology, the darkness of the void from which all form manifests, the darkness of deep sleep.

At a certain point, we might experience this body of darkness as a velvety black light, the flame of the void, and if we meditate on this light, it will take us very deep. Even when we find ourselves in the causal body in a relatively unconscious state, something very significant and necessary is happening.

Here is why meditation in the causal body is of the utmost importance. As we know, one of the main functions of awakened kundalini is to clear the accumulated karmas, past impressions, deeply lodged memories, and embedded fears that lurk in every part of our subtle system, especially in the causal body. Most of us have been around for a long time, and we've been through a lot. In some ways, we are a bit like that pair of boots you bought ten years ago and have been wearing every winter since. You get them patched and retreaded because you like them and they're comfortable. But they are pretty beat up. They have nicks, scratches, rips, and holes on the toes, and worn patches in the lining. We are the same way. We have been retreaded and re-cycled many times, and although we are holding up, there's been a lot of wear and tear.

The time of meditation is the time we give kundalini to melt, sweep, dust, chisel, and scrub away not only the tensions in the physical body, but also all the subtle causes for these tensions: the accumulated layers of old forgotten thoughts, opinions, and feelings that we have acquired over years and even lifetimes. Just to give you an idea of how much cleaning there is to do, think about all the opinions you have had in your life. Remember how you used to think that making the soccer team was the most important thing in the world, or that people who practiced religions other than your own were deluded, or that a particular political position was the only truth? Remember the person you were in love with at fifteen, and how that person looked when you saw them ten years later? All this is lodged in your subtle system, along with every song you have ever listened to and all the insensitive things you have ever said to the people who loved you, not to mention the things they said to you. All your good and bad ideas are there. Your dreams. Your hopes. The shame you felt when you were caught stealing candy from the luncheonette at age four. The pain in your throat after you had your tonsils out. Your sympathy for the kid everybody picked on, and the exhilaration of riding your bike downhill, and the grinding feeling in your heart when your marriage was breaking up.

Kundalini will root out every last one of those old memories and usher them from your system if you encourage it to do so by meditating every day. That doesn't mean you will lose your memories. You will still be able to remember the names of your children and what you ate for breakfast Saturday morning. In fact, your memory will be even sharper. What will be gone is the charge in those memories—including the longing that we often feel to get back to times we remember as joyful, and which may remove us from being fully present where we are. What dissolves is the emotional baggage attached to those experiences—their power to hurl you off the emotional cliff. Actually, you probably wouldn't mind so much if some of the memories themselves got cleaned out, too. Who wants to remember the mean things you and your best friend said to Louise Frankovitch when you were in junior high? Some things are best eliminated entirely.

Everything depends on this: a fathomless sinking into a fathomless nothingness.

—JOHANNES TAULER [13]

All these memories and impressions, or *samskaras,* are lodged in different parts of your subtle and physical system. But the bulk of them is in the causal body. That is the residing place of the really deep layers, the *vasanas,* or tendencies, that rule you from within. I once dreamed that I was living in a huge mansion. In the cellar lived a man who never came upstairs. He was the one who ran the place. He made all the decisions, took care of the maintenance, and subtly imposed his will on everyone in the house. This is exactly what these buried samskaras do. They rule us from inside, and because they are so familiar to us, we befriend them.

When we meditate and allow kundalini to work inside the causal body, it roots out the influence of our undercover tyrants, which is why at times in our meditation practice it is important to let ourselves go into that state of deep rest, that state where we are "out," lost in a realm that feels much like sleep. At such times, we are entering the sleep state consciously, as meditators.

Years ago, a friend of mine habitually used to fall into a deep, unconscious state. Eventually, he decided to take steps to stay awake, so one morning before meditation, he drank a cup of coffee, and sure enough, he stayed "conscious" throughout his meditation. Just at the end of the hour, he saw the numinous figure of a woman, who seemed to be sweeping out his heart. She looked up and spoke to him. "What are you doing awake?" she asked. "This is my time to do my work. That's why I always knock you out." He went back to his usual pattern. Some time later, his meditations moved out of the causal level, and he began having a more conscious meditation.

However, since the journey of meditation is not necessarily a straight line, a seamless progression that leads us from one realm of the soul to the next, but more of a two-steps-forward, one-step-back zigzag, we may find ourselves revisiting this deep and apparently unconscious state again and again through the years.

The Fourth Body: The Supracausal Body

When all is said and done, however dramatic or quiet our meditation, we must finally come back to the seer, the pure "I," that is the goal of our practice. In any given meditation session, we might pass through all three of the bodies we have just described. When we first sit down, we usually spend some time settling the posture, breathing into tension, perhaps observing the movements of the kriya shakti as it shakes the head or sways the torso. After a while, as we follow the shakti to a deeper, subtler state, we might find ourselves witnessing the dreamlike images of subtle-body meditation or moving through the currents of energy. A profound vision may burst upon us—a sudden glimpse of light or an insight. And we may spend some time in the velvet darkness of the causal body, completely unaware of where we are until we emerge.

Yet in any of these states, and at any moment, there is always the possibility that the pure I-awareness, the ever-present experience of the Self, may emerge. It can happen in many ways. We might find ourselves lifted into a clear field of Awareness, the thoughts left behind or chattering faintly somewhere beneath or below the expansive, peaceful sky where we are sitting. Perhaps the thoughts dissolve into a well of deep contentment. Perhaps our feelings of being a small self disappear into a larger, expansive sense of being. We might be engaged in some act of remembrance—asking ourselves, "Where is my Self in all this?" or "Who is the *real* I?"—and gradually becoming more and more aware of a witnessing presence, perhaps surrounding and containing the body-personality-self or poised above and behind our head,

217

watching without commentary, simply *there*. When the pure "I," the great Awareness, shows its subtle face, all we have to do is be in it. Merge into it. Allow ourselves to become it.

Gaze intently into the blazing heart of joy and you will perceive my blissful Mother, matrix of all phenomena . . . burning down conventional barriers, pervading minds and worlds with light, revealing her exalted beauty . . . where lovers merge with Mother Reality, experiencing the single taste of nonduality.

—RAMPRASAD [14]

The texts of Vedanta call the state of being in or with our supreme conscious Self *turiya*, meaning "the fourth"—that is, the state that is beyond waking, dream, and deep sleep. In *The Nectar of Self-Awareness*, Jnaneshwar Maharaj, the enlightened poet, described it as "the eye of your eye, where the void comes to an end." It is the furthest shore of human experience, the place where the human recognizes itself as spacious, impersonal, and divine. And though the full experience of this state is an experience of limitlessness and formlessness, some tantric Siddhas (self-realized masters of inner yoga) have told us that this boundless state also has a "body," or a form. To experience the form of this fourth body is one of the most sublime and secret realizations a meditator can have.

Jnaneshwar described how this transcendental body can actually be seen as a sesame-seed-sized blue light, darting quickly in and out of a meditator's field of vision, and sometimes even appearing when he is not meditating. It may have been that which Jesus was referring to when he described the kingdom of heaven as "like unto a mustard seed."

The blue point of light, or *bindu,* is described in the tantras as the manifestation point out of which the universe arises. These texts speak of a moment when the entire creative energy of the universe, the power behind manifestation, gathers itself into a vibratory rumbling, the sound of *Om,* and then into a tiny point of light, a bindu. Out of this point of intensely concentrated energy erupts the universe of matter and energy. (You may notice that this view of creation has a certain correspondence to the Big Bang theory of physics.) When we have a vision of the blue point of light, we are seeing this point of primal, intensely concentrated energy.

Since the sages who wrote these texts based their metaphysics on their own mystical visions, we can assume that they themselves must have seen this bindu, this tiny point of energy. In fact, the image of a blue orb of immense power can be found scattered throughout spiritual literature. Hildegard of Bingen painted the blue light. The sages of the Kashmir Shaivism tradition and the householder-saints of Maharashtra mentioned it in their poetry. A. H. Almaas, a contemporary writer in the Sufi tradition, describes it as a vision of essence; he calls it "the pearl beyond price."

These sages, and others from devotional traditions, also wrote about another kind of vision that comes sometimes to meditators in turiya. These are visions of a personal light-form of God, whom Hildegard of Bingen, like many of the Indian and Tibetan writers, saw as being made entirely of blue radiance.

That form may appear as Jesus, or as Krishna, as a buddha, or a form of the Goddess. When such a form appears in the turiya state, it will often seem to merge into the meditator's own body, so that the meditator actually experiences that specific form of divine presence within. In the tantric traditions, this experience is seen as a revelation of the oneness between the individual and the Absolute. It can bring with it a deep conviction that the human Essence is not different from the divine—that, in the language of the Indian tradition, *jiva,* or the individual, is not different from Shiva, the Absolute.

Yet all the traditions agree that these experiences of the divine in form are not the ultimate experience. They are a profound station on the path, a vision of the light-body of the Reality that is ultimately without any form at all. But the truth at the heart of the meditative experience is beyond all this. We find it in the spacious Presence, the unmoving Beingness that arises when seeing merges into itself, when there is no longer an object in awareness.

> *Eye cannot see it, ear cannot hear it nor tongue utter it; only in deep absorption can the mind, grown pure and silent, merge with the formless truth. He who finds it is free; he has found himself; he has solved the great riddle; his heart forever is at peace. Whole, he enters the Whole.*
>
> —MUNDAKA UPANISHAD[15]

That objectless awareness is pure Consciousness, pure knowingness, pure being—the state of immersion in the seer, the Self. To enter that state is also called, again, samadhi, the state of complete absorption; or *samavesha* (literally, "sameness with divine

Presence"), the state of merging into your own Consciousness. Of course, there are several levels of the experience of samadhi. In the first level, called *savikalpa samadhi* (absorption in a form), one has a sense of merging with an object, however subtle—becoming completely absorbed in a mantra, or becoming one with a light, or merging into a subtle feeling of bliss. In this *savikalpa* state, thoughts can remain.

But in the deeper state, called *nirvikalpa samadhi* (absorption in the formless), there are no thoughts, only complete stillness—an experience of emptiness that is at the same time utterly full and blissful. "*Nirvikalpa* is chit—effortless, formless Consciousness," wrote Ramana Maharshi. He continued:

> To some people whose minds have become ripe from
> a long practice in the past, nirvikalpa comes suddenly
> as a flood, but to others it comes in the course of their
> spiritual practice, a practice which slowly wears down
> the obstructing thoughts and reveals the screen of pure
> Awareness, the "I—I." Further practice renders the screen
> permanently exposed. This is Self-realization, *mukti* . . .
> Samadhi alone can reveal the truth. Thoughts cast a veil
> over reality, and so it is not realized as such in states other
> than samadhi. In samadhi there is only the feeling "I am"
> and no thoughts. The experience of "I am" is "being still."[16]

There is a paradox about this state; one of the great paradoxes of human life. The transcendental state, the seat of the soul, the place of the Self, is both *beyond* our normal consciousness and *within* it. On the one hand, it transcends time and space. It is the innermost eye of the eye, the I regarding itself. It is untouched by thoughts, by the feelings and ambitions and confusions and limitations of vision that we experience in the waking state. The evanescent images of the dream state don't touch it, and it is unaffected by the causal darkness of the void. It is a state of total Awareness, an Awareness so subtle and so fine that it reduces all matter to its essence and reveals a universe made of luminosity. It is, in short, an utterly "extra-ordinary" state.

At the same time, the supracausal body, the transcendental state, is totally and constantly accessible because it pervades every experience and every state of human experience. It is nothing other than the background of our experience. It is what turns back into itself and *reflects* on experience. It is the ever-present knowingness that is present to all our thoughts and feelings—and even to our state of deep sleep. In *Tripura Rahasya,* Ramana Maharshi's favorite text, it is pointed out that we touch that thought-free witness many times a day—in the pause between one breath and another, in the moment when our eyes refocus from a nearby object to a distant one, in a moment of silent contentment. For a person who is aware, any of these "fleeting samadhis" can yield a full-blown recognition of the Self.

His point: that you can experience the supracausal state *at any time.* Because it is always present, you don't have to be in meditation to experience it. I know a woman who regularly "wakes up" at night to find herself in a state of total blackness, without thought or sensation. The experience of being "awake" in deep sleep is an entry into the ever-present witness.

Many of us have our first glimpse of our true reality in a flash and in the waking state, as if the fabric of reality turned inside out to reveal itself as a unity. A friend of mine called it "supermarket samadhi" because she first experienced it in Ralph's Market in Cupertino, California, when the breakfast-cereal packages on aisle ten began without warning to glow with light, revealing that a single intelligence, sparkling with love, was somehow awake within the stacks of dry goods, the shopping carts, the fluorescent lights, and her sleepy daughter nodding off in her stroller.

In a commentary on one of the *Shiva Sutras, Udyamo bhairavaha* (or "The divine flashes forth"),[17] Kshemaraja described how the divine Consciousness, the highest state of intuition, the witness, can sudden-

> *Again the light blazes for me. Again I see the light clearly. Again it opens the skies; again it drives away the night. Again it reveals everything.*
>
> —SIMEON, THE NEW THEOLOGIAN [18]

ly emerge as if out of hiding, flashing forth and taking over our awareness. In meditation we experience this in the moments when the underlying Awareness, the self-knowing knower, the clear spaciousness called witness-consciousness, suddenly swallows up our ordinary consciousness. "My mind melted like a hailstone into the ocean of the supreme Absolute,"[19] wrote Shankaracharya in a famous passage in *Viveka Chudamani*. A contemporary meditator described how in meditation he will be lifted up from his mind until he seems to be sitting above himself, poised in a wide, calm awareness, observing the ordinary mind chattering away as if at a great distance, very small and faint.

So the transcendental state, the state of the Self, enters our meditation in many ways, and it can enter our meditation at any time. It can arise as a feeling of deep bliss or love. Or as an opening into radical compassion. Once, after meditating, after a visit to the Chidambaram temple in India, I could feel the mosquito bites on my driver's body and the sore muscles of the people threshing grain on the road. When I watched some boys splashing in a pond, the water sliding over their bodies seemed to be sliding over mine. I began to weep with the intense intimacy of the world, the depths of its joy and sorrow.

We might experience *turiya* as a field of light. A longtime meditator, asked to describe her experiences, said, "When I sit for meditation, I feel myself going into a peaceful, quiet space. After a while, that space becomes infused with blue light, a wide field of light. Then within that field, different manifestations occur. Sometimes I'll see a burst of white radiance so bright that it blinds me. It's like looking at the sun, only brighter."

Teresa of Avila wrote of these inner lights:

> The light that is now revealed is so different from any
> earthly light that, by comparison with it, the brightness
> of our sun seems quite dim and we never even want to
> open our eyes again to look at it. It is as if we were to look
> at a very clear stream in a bed of crystal, reflecting the
> sun's rays, and then to come out and see a very muddy
> stream in a bed of earth overshadowed by clouds. The
> inner light is a natural light, and all other kinds of lights
> seem artificial by comparison. It is a light that is never

followed by darkness. And nothing can ever disturb it. No one, no matter how powerful his intellect might be, could ever . . . imagine what this inner light is like.[20]

Sometimes simply reading an account like this can trigger an experience of the light, the Awareness that underlies material experience. And so can a practice like meditating on light—perhaps by imagining that a field of blue radiance fills your mind—or through the exercise that follows.

Exercise: The Light of Awareness Behind Your Experience

Close your eyes and focus for a few moments on the breath. Silently say to yourself, "Behind my thoughts is the light of pure Awareness. My thoughts come out of that light and merge back into that light. Behind my breath is the light of Awareness. My breath arises and subsides in that light. The sensations in my body come out of that light of Awareness. It is the light of Awareness that allows me to perceive, and that light of Awareness is in whatever I perceive, whatever I feel, whatever I hear."

As thoughts come up and as perceptions arise, be aware that they are all arising and subsiding within the ground-light of pure Awareness, the divine source. When you open your eyes and begin to look around, have the feeling that it is the light of Awareness that allows you to see and that appears in all that you see.

When turiya arises for me, it often comes as a gradual melting of boundaries between inside and outside until I am experiencing everything, within and without, as a part of my own consciousness. This happens most often in meditation, but occasionally I have experienced it with my eyes open. Sitting in a roomful of people, I notice a sudden shift of vision. Instead of seeing the room around me and sensing myself as being within the room, the entire room is within me. The sounds are happening inside me. The air itself is a pulsation inside me. When someone moves, their movements tickle my awareness. The *Shiva Sutras* say that one of the experiences of the transcendental state is the sensation that one's body has become the universe. In the tantric tradition, a perfectly Self-realized being is said to live in this experience all the time, whether in or out of meditation, always aware of the world around them as an emanation of their own blissful Awareness.

God alone reveals Himself to Himself, the knower being that which is known.

—MEISTER ECKHART [21]

Sometimes intense longing or focus can catapult us into the turiya state. One morning in meditation, a man began to wonder what an enlightened being's inner experience felt like. As his inner questioning intensified, he heard a roaring sound, and his awareness was pulled backward until he found himself in a realm of blue light. Waves of light undulated around him. The sensation of energy increased until he felt

My I is God, and I know no other I than this my God.

—CATHERINE OF GENOA [22]

his consciousness vibrating intensely. The roaring sound got louder. Then, abruptly, the movement of the ocean stilled. The roaring sound resolved itself into the pulsating of an awareness: *I am. I am. I am.* Out of that pulsation, waves upon waves of love coursed through him.

Like all experiences of the transcendental state, this one contained elements that we can recognize from the yogic texts and the writings of the sages. The blue ocean appears in many of the *abhangas,* or songs, of the Indian poet-saints, and Ramakrishna Paramahamsa often spoke of how he experienced Goddess Kali, the form of the divine he loved, as a limitless field of blue. The roaring sound was probably an experience of the *megha nada,* or thunder sound, that the texts of *laya yoga* (literally "the yoga of dissolving," a very subtle form of meditative practice) describe as the sound that ushers us into samadhi, the experience of merging in the Absolute.

I do not know where the "I" is, nor do I seek it . . . I am so plunged and submerged in the source of His infinite love, as if I were quite under water in the sea and could not touch, see, feel anything on any side except water.

—CATHERINE OF GENOA [23]

The awareness "I am," the recognition of yourself as pure being, known as the *purno'ham vimarsha,* or perfect I-consciousness, is described in the writings of the sage Abhinavagupta and others as the ultimate experience of divine subjectivity; it is the "I am that I am" that Moses heard on Sinai, and the supreme state spoken of in the *Vijnana Bhairava* and other texts. The ancient writers used metaphorical language to describe the ultimate paradox of this state, where nothingness contains everything, and the absence of external experience allows the fullest experience of the inner vastness. They describe it metaphorically as light merging into light, as the space that remains after camphor has burned out, or like what remains when one is subtracted from one.

There is no direct way to describe this state, because it is so utterly beyond words. "Here, the intellect, embarrassed, retires along with the mind and senses," writes Jnaneshwar. Saint John of the Cross, in his poem "Dark Night of the Soul," said that to reach the place where one experiences everything, one must go by way of becoming nothing. In *The Nectar of Self-Awareness,* Jnaneshwar Maharaj described that same state by saying: "For a while, the Self appears as an object of perception. But when the seer and the seen unite, both of them vanish. Then the seen is the same as the seer, and the seer is merged in the seen. Both vanish, and only the Reality remains."[24]

The supracausal state is not something we climb into or attain. It reveals itself by itself, through grace. Yet as we have seen before, we can "attract" it because it is always present. When kundalini is awake, that state can and does arise periodically. Many of the practices in chapter 2 help us cross the bridge between ordinary consciousness and that samadhi state. Here is another one, a simple exercise that you can practice with eyes open or closed. If you like, please feel free to substitute a different word—perhaps "Pure Presence," "love," "Awareness," or "emptiness"—for God.

Exercise: God Is in Everything

Sit in an upright, comfortable posture and close your eyes. Take a few moments to relax your body by breathing into any feeling of tightness, then breathing the tightness out.

Focus your attention on the breath, feeling the slight coolness of the breath as it comes in and the slight warmth as it leaves the nostrils.

Have the following awareness: "God, the Presence that gives life to all, is in my breath. God is in my thoughts. Wherever my mind goes, God is there. God is in my physical body. God is in the air. God is in the chair I sit on. God is in the clothes I wear. God is seeing through my eyes and thinking through my mind. Wherever my thoughts turn, wherever my attention goes, God is there. That which sees is God; that which hears is God; that which I call 'I' is God." After a while, open your eyes and look around with this awareness.

Though an exercise like this may not give us a full experience of the transcendental state, it can open doors in our awareness and make us ripe for the emergence of the full experience. Even one such experience can forever change our sense of who we are—especially if we can recall it, hold it in our awareness, and return to it in memory.

As we accumulate experiences of this supracausal state, we also begin to realize that there is more, that the journey of meditation doesn't culminate in indrawn samadhi. There are states beyond turiya. In the Siddha traditions of Hinduism and in the tradition of the Kashmir Shaivites, true Self-realization is described as *sahaja samadhi,* or natural samadhi. In the Siddha's description of the *sahaja* state, your awareness of nonduality never changes. The word "nondual" is significant here. It means not that everything is merged in oneness, as in the indrawn samadhi state, but that you recognize even in your waking experience that there is nothing in which the Absolute is not. In the sahaja state, you are aware of the particularity of people and objects, of the uniqueness and manyness. But you also recognize that they are arising within and as one Consciousness, that spirit and matter, absolute and relative, are not two different realities.

*He who
without hesitation
Views all this tangible
world as your form,
Having filled the universe
With the form of
his own self,
Is eternally joyful.*
—UTPALADEVA [25]

Ramakrishna Paramahamsa, the great nineteenth-century realizer, described ecstasies in which the whole animate and inanimate world revealed itself as divine, as full of light, and as alive with Consciousness—even those parts of it that are supposed to be insentient. Ramana Maharshi would say that in this state, your samadhi is unbroken, whether you are meditating, eating, sleeping, or walking.

Kabir wrote:

> Ever immersed in bliss, having no fear
> in [my] mind, [I] keep the spirit of union

in the midst of all enjoyments.
The infinite dwelling of the Infinite Being is everywhere:
    in earth, water, sky, and air . . .
He who is within is without:
    I see Him and none else.[26]

Realizers of different traditions describe the sahaja state in different ways and often from unique perspectives. U. G. Krishnamurti said, "Each person who comes into this state expresses it in a unique way, in terms relevant to his time." He also described his own experience as a "declutched state," in which thought retires and in which the world is experienced without the mediation of conceptual knowledge, yet action takes place spontaneously as needed. "You can never understand the tremendous peace that is always there within you, that is your natural state," he writes in *The Mystique of Enlightenment.* "It is not a thing to be willed into existence. It is there. It is the living state. This state is just the functional activity of life . . . It is the life of the senses, functioning naturally without the interference of thought . . . What is here, this natural state, is a living thing. It cannot be captured by me, let alone by you. It's like a flower. It just blooms."

It is told of one master . . . that when he wanted to contemplate individual things he had to put on spectacles in order to subdue his spiritual sight, for otherwise he saw all the individual things of the world as one.

—MARTIN BUBER[27]

Meditation's ultimate promise is that it will reveal to us our own inner sahaja, the open-eyed experience of the world shimmering with a single flavor, unconditioned by ordinary thought. That is why, as time goes by, we realize that it isn't enough to experience peace or joy or the taste of our own pure Awareness in meditation. We want that state to seep out into our days, to fill our awareness even in the midst of the comings and goings of life. In other words, we want to know, from our own direct experience, what the sages meant when they said that the Self is always present, that the turiya state, the state of samadhi, pervades our waking and dream life, and even our deep sleep. So we begin to pay attention to the first moments after meditation and to the ways we can carry that awareness into the day.

CHAPTER TEN

Coming Out of *Meditation*: Contemplation, Recollection, and Journal Writing

*I*t is early morning. I'm sitting in a pool of stillness that opens out from the region around my heart. The longer I sit, the more it expands and the softer it becomes, until my body disappears into it and I'm resting delicately in its smooth, vibrant waters. Then the alarm rings—too loudly. It jars me so much that I jump, bumping myself out of meditation, back to a consciousness of the chair and my body and the need to hit the alarm button. Clumsily, I get to my feet and walk to the window. I'm fumbling with the shade when I notice that I'm staggering, that I'm not really in my body, and that I need to go back and redo the entry because if I don't, there will be too much disjunction between meditation and the rest of my day.

> *A person looks,*
> *The blossoms look back:*
> *Plain heart seeing*
> *into plain heart.*
>
> —SUN BU-ER [1]

It took me a long time to learn about reentry, to realize that even when we don't feel that we have gone deep, we still need to take time to come out of meditation slowly. When we do, surprising things often happen in the afterglow. One friend of mine says that if she sits for a while when her meditation session is officially done and then opens her eyes, she sees the world around her emerging out of a pinpoint, recreating itself before her eyes as if for the first time. She knows what it really means to say that everything arises from and subsides within one's own consciousness.

These moments after meditation are often the time when we pluck the fruit of an hour of "work," of focusing and letting the thoughts slow down. These moments are the time when we feel the peace and taste the bliss. At the very least, they give our awareness time to fully return to the waking state. If you sometimes feel irritable or hypersensitive after deep meditation, it is usually because you haven't given yourself enough time to return to waking consciousness.

We need this time for another reason: it is in the moments after meditation that we begin the process of integration, the process of learning how to bring the stillness of the inner world into our day.

If the great question for a beginning meditator is "How do I get into it?" then the question for a person who has meditated for a while is "How do I hold on to it?" Often at the end of a meditation course or workshop, someone will say to me, "I feel great when I'm meditating. But then I open my eyes, and life caves in on me, and before I know it I'm buried in activity, and it's all gone, almost as if I hadn't had the experience at all."

Most of us have our own version of this complaint. It is another of those universal frustrations with meditation: to rise out of deep meditation and enter our day, only to watch the peace and stillness of meditation disappear from our daily mind.

Of course, all experiences, whether they are sweet or painful, exalting or depressing, come and go. Part of what we learn through meditation is to allow one state to give way to the next. We have all known people who tried to stay in meditation all day long. They can usually be recognized by their slightly glazed eyes, by their air of being not quite focused on the gritty reality of dirty dishes and parking spaces and stop signs, by their tendency to forget where they are, and by the way they do everything very slowly, sometimes taking a long time to answer even simple questions. I vividly remember my own space-cadet or bliss-bunny phase, during which I once drove a friend's van thirty blocks before realizing that the emergency brake was still on, because I was trying to stay in meditation while on my way to the grocery store.

So there is bound to be a difference between our states of meditation and our states of ordinary waking consciousness. In fact, we can trust that even when we forget what happened in our meditation, the inner process that began during that indrawn hour is still alive in us, still working its alchemy in our consciousness. In kundalini-inspired practice, inner work goes on constantly beneath the surface of awareness. The inner intelligence naturally integrates our meditation experiences, weaving them into the fabric of our waking state without our even realizing that it is happening.

At the same time, one unmistakable sign of spiritual maturity is the ability to live from the fulcrum of that inner state—to hold the clear spaciousness of Awareness like a pool of rejuvenating nectar that we can dip into at will. In fact, if our meditation practice is to be more than an escape, a kind of inner calisthenics or something we do to soothe ourselves, we will eventually need to discover how to maintain our Self-awareness through the day. That is how we practice for living in a state of wakefulness.

> *A great yogin is still full of the samadhi state even when he is in normal consciousness, because even then he beholds the entire mass of things to be dissolving in the sky of Consciousness like a bit of cloud in autumn.*
>
> —KSHEMARAJA [2]

One difference between an enlightened being and a person on the path is that the enlightened being has learned to hold on to his inner experience and make it a part of the fabric of daily life. The skill of merging our inner with our outer worlds is one of the great arts of spiritual life.

How do we do this? The first step is to get into the habit of consciously recollecting and contemplating our meditation experiences with the help of a journal. The second step is to learn how to return to our meditation experiences by bringing them into future meditations, even dwelling on them between meditations.

THE MOMENTS AFTER MEDITATION

In the *Pratyabhijna Hridayam,* a text of Kashmir Shaivism, a sutra describes how in the moments after meditation we can relish and recall the experience in meditation. By relishing the energy we've collected, we help it integrate. Here is how you might do that at the end of meditation.

First, before you even sit for meditation, set your timer (if you use one) so that it goes off ten minutes before you know you have to get up. When it rings, sit quietly for a few minutes or slide gently into shavasana, the corpse pose: flat on your back with your arms near your sides. This is a good time to begin recollecting your experience.

Become conscious of how you feel at this moment. Notice your state. How does your heart feel? What are the sensations in your body? What do you notice about your mind? How is your energy? Is your body relaxed? Energized? Sleepy? Take an inner photograph of all this. Then go back over your meditation. Recall its quality, its moods, and its texture, noting any unusual occurrences or simply the sequence of your inner experience.

*Be—and yet know
the great void
where all things begin,
the infinite source
of your own most
intense vibration,
so that, this once,
you may give it your
perfect assent.*

—RAINER MARIA RILKE [3]

Then embrace your post-meditation state with your awareness. Have the feeling that you are holding it in awareness. As you slowly let yourself ease back into your ordinary state, try to keep a part of your awareness touching the felt sense of meditation.

At first you may not be able to hold this awareness for more than a few minutes. Through practice, though, you will find that even after you have fully entered waking consciousness, you can feel the presence of your meditative awareness for longer and longer periods. The inner photograph of the meditation state stays with you. Each time you take that photograph anew, you strengthen the impression of it. As you recollect the experience again and again, you eventually learn how to reenter it by remembering it.

RECORDING YOUR EXPERIENCES

The best time to write in your meditation journal is in those first moments after coming out of meditation. If you write as soon as you open your eyes or after you have taken a few minutes to recall and hold your experience, you will still be in touch with the state of meditation, and the feeling of that state will come out onto the paper. Meditation experiences are quite often so subtle that if you don't capture them in written form, they will disappear almost before you open your eyes. Yet these subtle realizations can be life-transforming if we can hold on to them. When we reread our journals months or years later, we realize that the experiences we recorded are treasures that we can return to again and again.

The challenge in recording these experiences lies in finding the language to capture their subtlety on the page. When you meditate, you are in the realm of the mystical, and that means you are moving in an arena where language does not reach. This may be one reason why so many of the available descriptions of spiritual experience are descriptions of visions, voices, or other concrete manifestations of the inner world. It is a lot easier to describe the glowing star that appeared to your inner eye than it is to describe the sense of an all-encompassing, loving presence, or the feeling that you are pushing through veils in your awareness, moving from a thick and contracted state into a state that feels light and clear. Sometimes there are no words to describe these energy shifts and subtle sensations. If you want to avoid falling back on the old standbys like "sweetness," "inner nectar," "deep space," or "bliss"— words that have become tired from overuse—you will need to search for new ways to capture your inner experience.

The effort we make to find words for the spiritual world is profoundly worthwhile because it actually fixes our experiences in the mind. It is simply a fact of human life that what we put into words becomes real to us in a way that the unarticulated often does not. It doesn't matter whether your words are beautiful or even whether they have meaning for anyone but you. You aren't writing for anyone else.

> *. . . the beloved Heart alone is the refuge for the rising and subsiding of that 'I.' . . . Heart, the source, is the beginning, the middle, and the end of all. Heart, the supreme space, is never a form. It is the light of truth.*
>
> —RAMANA MAHARSHI [1]

Besides writing down what happened in meditation, I also like to remember and record the process by which I got there. Was I repeating a mantra? Watching the breath? Do I think the technique propelled me toward a shift? Or was it a *coup de foudre,* a pure act of grace? Maybe I think nothing happened. But what did that "nothing" feel like? Was there a moment or two of separation from the thoughts, a little space that opened up between them? Did I feel the energy change? Did an insight come up, or a feeling of comfort? Or did I become hyperaware of some lingering anxiety or problem? Was there a moment when my awareness seemed to become sharper, brighter? All these things are worth recording.

Here is an excerpt from one of my meditation journals:

> A swelling love in the heart, and the breath began to
> arise from out of the feeling of love. The breath arises
> as if love were breathing. Each exhalation pulsing with
> a soft shakti—sweet energy in the heart. A sense: This
> energy is me . . . I offered mental flowers to the shakti
> in my heart. Worship your Self. Is this what it means, to
> worship the energy pulsating in the heart?

When I reread this passage a year later, on a day when meditation hadn't been so sweet, it took me back to the devotional feelings of that other time. The words reminded me of my connection with the divinity inside me—and that it is always there even when I don't happen to be feeling it.

Another meditator wrote his insight in the form of a poem:

> Become embodied now!
> On the in-breath, the All.
> On the out-breath, love.

In this meditation, he realized that only by being "in" the body could he experience the feeling of love. The practice of breathing in the universe and breathing out love had arisen naturally as a result of his insight.

WORKING WITH EXPERIENCES

Once we write down our experiences, we have the material not only for contemplation but for going even deeper into the experience itself. Looking at the experiences in my journal, it is clear that though they were very subtle, there was much to contemplate in them: realizations arose in them that created one more tiny shift in the sense of self.

Each time you realize something more about your true subtlety—say, that your emotions are actually energy, or that the spaciousness behind thoughts is the real you, or that you are being breathed by a greater force (rather than being the one who breathes)—you let go of another atom of attachment to the limited self. Each tiny realization or insight arising in meditation creates a new pattern in your consciousness that you are free to revisit at any time. The memory is there, and it is a memory of freedom. You will deepen the new pattern each time you return to it. In fact, the experience of one meditation can become a focus for practice in your next meditation.

FOLLOWING THE PATHWAYS

This makes sense when you consider that most of the great techniques of meditation and yoga probably began as someone's spontaneous experience. A practitioner—maybe a sage or future sage—would hear or intuit a direction arising from inside: "Ask yourself, 'Who am I?'" or "Follow the movement of the breath."

Or perhaps a vision or inner sound would arise spontaneously and lead him to a deeper state. Later he would retrace his steps along that same meditation pathway, except that this time he'd do it deliberately. Some of these pathways would become the basis for an entire meditation tradition.

Learn to listen to the voice within yourself. Your body and mind will become one, and you will realize the unity of all things.
—DOGEN ZENJI [5]

You don't have to be a sage or teacher to use your own experiences as techniques for practice. Suppose your attention is drawn up into the center of the head during one meditation, and your focus becomes laser-like as you "watch" thoughts and feelings passing before you. In a subsequent meditation, you could station your attention in that center, and practice witnessing your thoughts from that place.

Or suppose you have the experience that "I am being breathed by a greater force." In another meditation, you could recover that insight and practice it. As you train your awareness on your own breath, recall the sensations of being breathed. Feel for the presence of the greater force that brings the breath in and out. To do this, it is enough simply to remember the existence of that larger presence and then attune yourself to it. Be in it. Explore it. Open into it. A meditator who one day had the insight that she was being breathed later sat for meditation and held the awareness: "The whole force of this universe moves through my every breath." I have practiced for years with the dharana "God is breathing me," which came out of an actual experience I had in meditation.

Each meditation experience suggests new avenues for meditation. When you feel dull, in need of inspiration, or simply adventurous, it is there in your journal for you to explore.

Eventually, you will begin to notice that your practice of staying in touch with your meditation insights is affecting your experience in the waking state. The impressions of unity and love, of mindful attentiveness, of inner Presence, will become more firmly fixed in your awareness. They will often arise when you need them, showing up as natural antidotes to feelings of anger or sadness, helping you when you feel disconnected or scattered. That is when you will begin to see the real transformations inside yourself, real changes in your way of seeing. In fact, that is when many meditators begin to realize that the skills they have learned in meditation are transferable. In other words, you begin applying what you learn in sitting meditation to daily life.

CHAPTER ELEVEN

The Daily Life of a Meditator: Holding Inner Attention

*M*editation practice, most of us discover sooner or later, is not just what happens when you are sitting on the mat. Eventually, it radiates outward until your whole life becomes an ongoing training in living from the center. As the intrinsic alchemy of meditation works its subtle changes in your consciousness and character, it simultaneously challenges you to take action on what you are becoming to bring your meditative skills, insights, and experiences into the rest of your life.

The strength of your practice is tested in every single moment and interaction. Are you able to bring the love you experienced in meditation into your actions? Are you able to stay in touch with Awareness when you are working, when you are moving into a new house, or when someone you care for disappoints you? Are you speaking and moving from that deeper level of being, or are you on automatic pilot, perhaps even doing the right thing but with no sense of contact with your deeper being, no access to its inspiration and love?

While yet you live, practice meditation. Do not meditate only hidden in a dark corner, but meditate always, standing, sitting, moving, and resting. When your meditation continues throughout waking and sleeping, wherever you are is heaven itself.

—HAKUIN [1]

Certainly there will be times when the inner world with its inspiration and broader vision seems to be at your fingertips, moments when love sweeps over you all on its own. You may suddenly find yourself in the state called "flow," acting unerringly without any apparent effort and with a quiet mind. The witness may rise up in the midst of an argument or crisis, holding you steady and poised in a situation where you would ordinarily go off the emotional deep end. You might have mornings when the world shimmers with sacredness, when you find meaning in the blown leaves on the sidewalk, when the newspapers in the gutter seem to pulsate with the overflow of your own happiness. You will experience the ongoing magic of synchronicity, when a conversation overheard on the bus or a message seen on a billboard seems to give subtle spiritual teachings. At such times, work is transmuted into worship, and a walk in the woods turns into a processional up the nave of a cathedral.

Yet there will be other moments, many of them, when the gifts of meditation are there only if you work for them. The mere fact

246

that you meditate will not suddenly make you immune to psychological pain. It won't eliminate mood swings, feelings of inadequacy, or problems with other people. People who meditate can be just as subject to ups and downs as anyone else. The major differences lie in their *attitude* toward their mood and tendencies, and in the resources they have to deal with them. When sadness, anger, and frustration arise, experienced meditators can separate their intrinsic sense of self from their moods and feelings. They know that a core part of them is untouched by the emotional weather. Not only that, they have learned some skills in meditation that can help them through a difficult encounter or a mental traffic jam. They have more choices about how they deal with their feelings, how they work with the desires, fears, and crises that might otherwise derail them.

Living from your own center takes effort, but it is also exciting. When you see life as an ongoing spiritual training, you live inside a view that lends significance to even the most ordinary interactions. You don't think so much in terms of winning or losing, success or failure. Instead, there is only the training, the consistent effort to come back to the love and lucidity you carry inside, and to bring the values of the inner world into your outer actions.

This, then, is the second level of practice: the waking practice of staying in touch with your center, cultivating your character, contemplating and learning from the situations life presents to us, and discovering the techniques, teachings, disciplines, and forms of open-eyed practice that will allow us to live from the developing awareness of the Self.

MAINTAINING INNER ATTENTION

In the Shaiva yogic tradition, an enlightened being is said to live in *shambhavi mudra,* a state in which, even when her eyes are open, her attention is centered in the inner field of unchanging luminous Awareness. This is a powerful depiction of the enlightened state; it is also a key to open-eyed practice. Open-eyed practice is a kind of "as if" game. You are practicing to be an enlightened being by acting and thinking as you would if you were actually in that state.

The true man of God sits in the midst of his fellow-men, and rises and eats and sleeps and marries and buys and sells and gives and takes . . . and yet never forgets God even for a single moment.

—ABU SA'ID IBN ABI'L-KHAYR [2]

A key practice for this is to maintain inner awareness—a steady current of attentiveness to your own Awareness, to the sense of being or Presence that you tune in to when you turn attention back on itself. Like most essential practices, this one is extremely simple without being at all easy. Inner attentiveness has a frustrating way of dissolving at crucial moments, such as when you are worried, excited, or under pressure. Even on ordinary days, you naturally move in and out of it, since that essential Awareness tends to be experienced in flashes, in glimpses that come and go. That is why it is helpful to work with different practices at different moments. At times you will face directly into the light of Awareness. At other times you will approach it sideways, through the breath, a bhavana, or even a physical posture.

To maintain inner attention in a steady way demands a three-fold effort.

First, you need a quiverful of practices for inner focus, or remembering the Self. They should be practices that work for you, and you need to do them regularly.

Second, you need to be doing "character work," examining your motives and attitudes and learning how to express the qualities of the Self—compassion, gentleness, kindness, steady wisdom, truthfulness, and the rest.

Third, you need to develop the habit of checking in with yourself to monitor your state so that you can recognize when you have slipped off-center, and then discover how to return.

OPEN-EYED PRACTICE

Many of the practices described in this book—practices like mantra repetition, awareness of Awareness, focus on the witness, attention to the breath, seeing thoughts as energy—are also meant to be practiced in day-to-day situations. So are the different bhavas, the spiritual attitudes you work with when you meditate.

Just as you begin meditation by offering your practice to God or for the upliftment of humanity, you can also offer your daily actions as service, and see how that simple act shifts you out of self-centeredness and unknots the tendency to grasp at outcomes. Your sitting practice of becoming aware of Awareness, being the witness of your thoughts, or seeing the whole content of your meditation experience as shakti, can become an inner baseline that you return to during the day. It helps you move out of heavy emotions, distractions, or neurotic thinking patterns. Remembering oneness, holding the understanding that the seemingly solid world is essentially energy, will let you act in the world with a sense of openness and fluidity, and with a sense of your kinship with others, with nature, and even with inanimate objects like your computer or your car.

It can be helpful to create set times in your schedule for your practice of mantra repetition, awareness of Awareness, or remembering oneness. You could make a twice-daily ritual of offering your actions, thoughts, and feelings at the beginning and end of the workday. You could make a habit of remembering to place your attention in your heart once every hour, or you could set your wristwatch alarm to ring five minutes before the hour, and then use that five minutes to bring to mind a teaching you are contemplating, or to spend a moment asking yourself "Who am I?" or "Where is my Self in all this?" You might work with a different practice every day until you find the practice or practices that feel like yours, and then spend some time exploring them deeply. When you're waiting in the doctor's office, instead of reading, do a practice. Practice while you're walking. One of my favorite walking practices is to inwardly welcome everything I pass on the way.

As you practice this open-eyed meditation, you will see its effects. First of all, you should feel more integrated. There will be less of a gap between sitting meditation and the rest of your day: it will be easier to go into meditation when you sit, and you should need to spend less time "deprogramming" yourself from the stresses of the day. Then, during your waking, working hours, there should be a certain sweetness to life, a sense of openness and space in your world. You'll find yourself feeling closer to others, less afraid, calmer, and more inspired. During anxious moments, busy days, and periods when life seems to be caving in on you, these practices can become a real refuge. They help you stabilize your state.

RECOGNIZING WHERE YOU NEED WORK

Few of us can practice for long without noticing how life has a way of confronting us with situations that test how steady we have managed to keep our inner state. Perhaps you get sick and have to stay in bed for a few days. One of the first things you may notice is how cranky you feel—and also that you can't seem to step out of your crankiness! Perhaps your teenager says, "Mom, you're screaming at me again!" or a co-worker asks you pointedly if you have meditated recently.

Such a moment of recognition is extremely valuable, especially if you resist the impulse to kick yourself across the room for not being more together. Not only does it show you where you need to work, but your very awareness of an unconstructive mood or behavior is actually the first step in changing it. *In other words, the awareness that allows you to recognize your state is also the source of the energy that can transform it.*

Most of our more disturbing emotions or behaviors come from areas of our psyche where we have chosen to remain unconscious. In Hindi, the word for these unconscious, immature qualities is *kacha,* meaning "unripe" or "unbaked." All of us are partly kacha. We become *pukka* (ripe) through our practice, specifically through tapas, the process of yogic heat that kundalini ignites and that our practice stokes to blazing.

To attend to the moment is to attend to eternity. To attend to the part is to attend to the whole. To attend to Reality is to live constructively.

—PIRKE AVOT [3]

However, the kind of practice that ripens us is not a mechanical accumulation of rituals and focus exercises. It is practice *with* awareness and practice *of* awareness that actually transforms the texture of our consciousness. Awareness itself, with its clarity, its impersonality, its spaciousness, and its capacity to hold everything within itself, is the fire that will cook or ripen our immature feelings and behaviors. Just holding these feelings nonjudgmentally in Awareness—being their witness without either acting on them, trying to suppress them, or getting lost in your stories or beliefs about what is happening—is often enough to change their quality from raw to baked.

This principle holds true for any situation we face, whether internally or externally generated. Because our awareness is a small-scale version of the great Awareness that underlies all that is, when we direct attention nonjudgmentally toward something that causes suffering either to ourselves or to others, we are actually bringing that state or mood or behavior into the light of the great Awareness itself. Awareness not only illumines the dark corners of our psyches, but can also transmute the strange energies and raw feelings that dwell there. Then the energy that has been tied up in them is freed to become available for more creative endeavors.

We are spiritually ripe, baked, when all our knotted energies and feelings have been freed and rechanneled to manifest as wisdom, power, and love. How this happens is one of the mysteries of Consciousness, but our act of turning Awareness toward our inner moods, states, and feelings is the great tactic for setting that alchemy in motion.

SELF-INQUIRY

The sages of Vedanta gave the name *atma vichara,* or self-inquiry, to this act of becoming aware of ourselves. *Vichara* is not just thinking about something, nor is it the same as psychological self-analysis. It is a yogic practice or self-reflection in which we hold our attention on inner phenomena in a steady, focused fashion without going into meditation.

There are two basic types of vichara. One is the contemplation we do to get in touch with our deeper wisdom, to open the space of revelation, to understand a spiritual teaching, or to touch our Self. The classical inner question "Who am I?" (taught by Ramana Maharshi and others) is an example of this type of vichara.

The other type of self-inquiry is contemplation of what blocks our experience of the Self. When we feel out of sorts, instead of giving way to the feelings or getting lost in the story we are telling ourselves about them, we focus our attention on the feelings themselves. We let ourselves fully experience the feelings. We notice the thoughts that accompany them. We observe the state of our energy, the sensations in our body. At times it can be helpful to trace a feeling back to its source, perhaps to discover the frustrated desire or fear or expectation that may have triggered it. But the most important thing is to keep noticing our inner feelings and the state of our energy until it becomes second nature to notice the symptoms of being off-center.

Only when we can recognize and identify the actual inner sensations of being out of alignment with ourselves can we get back in touch. Without that recognition, we only know that we are uncomfortable, and we have little chance of adjusting our state.

Self-Inquiry in Action

Imagine the following scenario: It is early morning, and you have been up late working on a project that is approaching its deadline. You need to get to the office early to meet with your team so you can finalize some important loose ends. As you put the coffee on the stove, your ten-year-old daughter announces that she feels sick. She has a high fever and a bad cough. She needs a day in bed and a trip to the doctor. You realize that there isn't anyone you can have stay with her at such short notice. You will have to stay home and take care of her. Yet if you don't keep your appointment at the office, your project hasn't a chance of being completed in time. The thought of what this will mean sends you into a rapid spiral of panic. "Why do things like this always happen to me?" you hear yourself thinking. "My life is so impossible." Fear, frustration, anger, and despair.

The more awareness one has The closer to God one is.

—RUMI [4]

At this moment, you make a crucial yogic choice. Instead of letting yourself careen into acting out of your panic and anger, you consciously pause. You make up your mind to pay attention to your own state and to deal with it before you try to take action.

You take a couple of deep breaths, and then you check in with yourself. You scan your body and notice the rhythm of your breath. You discover that your breathing is choppy—in fact, you are actually holding your breath. You notice a clenched sensation in your diaphragm and stomach muscles, and a tightness in your chest. You realize that your heart is also feeling tight and closed, and that there are threads of fear shooting through it. Your energy is alternately fluttering and sinking, sometimes rushing through you in waves of panic, sometimes flattening out as depression and a feeling of helplessness. Your thoughts are all about victimization: "It's so unfair. Why can't someone besides me take care of things for a change? Why is this always happening?"

This moment of stopping, turning inside, checking yourself out, noticing how you feel, and observing your thoughts without buying into them is a profoundly significant moment of yoga. It will give you the power to act from a more resourceful, skillful place, rather than simply reacting to the difficulties in the situation. Now instead of blocking your discomfort or trying to distract yourself, instead of overriding your emotions and plunging ahead regardless of how your inner energy feels, instead of letting your strong reactions overwhelm you so that you blow up at your daughter or paralyze yourself with resentment or paranoia, you use these feelings as a signal to stop and return to yourself.

Once you have recognized your own state, you can begin to work with it. For this you have a number of options.

TAKE REFUGE IN THE BREATH

The first thing I do when I find myself getting caught up in anxiety, hurry, or desire is to silently remind myself, in a reassuring, steady, and deliberate voice, to pause and breathe. Sometimes I actually say it to myself like a mantra: "Pause. Pause. *Breeeaaathe. Breeeaaathe.*" The breath automatically connects the ordinary mind to the deeper Self. When we grab hold of the breath and center our minds on it, it will eventually draw our awareness inside to the heart. So when we want to center ourselves, we always begin with the breath.

You can begin by simply following the breath with your attention, taking a natural inhalation and letting the exhalation be long. Breathe to a count: four heartbeats in, eight heartbeats out; or four in, hold for four, eight out. Do this for five minutes, or practice a full three-part breath. Breathe in with the feeling that you are filling your lungs in three sections: the lower third first, then the middle third, then the upper third. Exhale, emptying the top part of the lungs first, then the middle, and then the lower lungs.

PULL YOUR ATTENTION TO THE HEART

For me this is the second step. Once I have recovered my wits through a few rounds of steady, deliberate breathing, I drop a sort of inner plumb line inside to the area of the middle chest, beneath the breastbone, and I let my attention rest there until I feel the inner heart-space relax and expand. When energy is stuck in the head, your thoughts tend to go in circles and you come up with rote, uncreative solutions to your issues. Once your attention moves into the heart, you are automatically in

Exercise: Coming into the Heart

Focus your attention in the heart center. As we've seen, this subtle spiritual center is located inside the body, beneath the breastbone, at a point about four or five inches (or approximately eight finger-widths) below the collarbone. You may want to place your hand there as you begin this exercise in order to help anchor your awareness. Breathe in and out of the heart-space until you feel centered. If you find it easier to center yourself by breathing into the center below the navel, you can breathe into a point in the center of the body, about three finger-widths below the navel.

If the energy in the heart area feels blocked, imagine an opening in the energy block, and let your awareness move through it. Keep moving through openings in the energy until you feel the block begin to disperse.

touch with your intuition. You are in one of the essential centers of spiritual wisdom and awareness. Resting in that seat in the heart, you can do whatever other practice is needed.

Putting your attention in the heart will almost automatically loosen the grip of the superficial mind, with its tendency to worry, fantasize, and feel uncomfortably separate from others and the world around you. When you contact the heart center in your own body, you open the door into the great Heart, the core of being, the Consciousness that is the source of your fundamental love, inspiration, and wisdom. If you are feeling emotionally overwhelmed, you can actually hold your emotions in that heart-space and allow the power of Consciousness to melt them back into their essential energy. Or you can ask your intuition—which for most of us is more easily accessed through the heart center—what is the best thing to do.

But these are just two of your available options. You have others. You might decide that you need to spend some time soothing yourself, perhaps by replacing your agitated thoughts with a more positive thought or a mantra. You would then bring your attention to your mantra, and hold it in the forefront of your awareness until you feel the mantra soothing your inner energy field. You could practice a few moments of mindfulness, "sitting" in the heart and noticing the thoughts, feelings, and inner sensations as they arise. You could ask yourself a question like "Can you let this thought go?" or simply wait for a natural recognition that the thoughts and feelings are simply arising and passing through—and that you can let them go.

You could also choose to work directly with the energy behind your feelings of panic, anger, and frustration. First remind yourself that behind the content of the feelings is pure energy. Fear is simply a particular kind of energy. Anger has its own energy, and so does despair. Let yourself feel the energy *as energy* by letting go of the content of the feeling and focusing on the *sensation* the feeling creates in your psychic space and in your body. Notice the energy within the feeling. As you do, be aware of the background energy, the awareness within which the feeling arises and subsides. Let the feeling be in Awareness and notice how the fearful or angry energy naturally dissolves into the underlying Awareness, the Consciousness that is its base.

TAKE REFUGE IN THE TRUTH

Another thing you can do is remind yourself of the Truth. I mean the great Truth—the Truth of oneness. If your daughter begins to whine or act cranky, try remembering that the same Self, the same energy, the same Consciousness that has become you has also become her; remember that her mood, your frustration, and everything else are simply forms of one energy. Holding this bhavana, even provisionally, can have a global effect on your state—opening you up to your compassion, eliminating the sharpness of fear, and allowing you to act resourcefully— simply because you no longer feel so overwhelmed by the world's seeming refusal to work the way you want it to.

If you don't realize the source, you stumble in confusion and sorrow. When you realize where you come from, you naturally become tolerant, disinterested, amused, kindhearted as a grandmother, dignified as a king.

—LAO-TZU [5]

Certain spiritual teachings will have particular relevance to a situation or will carry a special resonance for you. For example, one woman was having a difficult season while chairing her university department. During meetings, a hostile colleague kept undermining and harassing her. She got through it by reminding herself, "You are in the peaceful mind of God."

259

Similarly, a man with a tendency to lose his temper during moments of frustration works with a famous yogic technique called "Practicing the Opposite" from Patanjali's *Yoga Sutras*.[6] When he notices rage surging up inside him, he takes time to become aware of the thoughts associated with the feelings, and then fills his mind with counter-thoughts, like "I have great tolerance and respect for these people." Even though it isn't always true, holding the positive thought calms his mind enough to make him less reactive.

For me, a line from the *Bhagavad Gita*, "You have a right to the work alone, but not to its fruits,"[7] often comes up when I'm caught in desire for a particular outcome. Contemplating this resonant, mysterious teaching helps me detach myself from my fears, my wants, and my expectations so that I can act more objectively.

So once you have paused, checked yourself out, and recognized the way it feels to be out of your center, you have many options for beginning to come back to yourself. As you keep working with this threefold process of recognition, self-inquiry, and practice, you learn to navigate your own rough waters and to find the harbors that are always there.

At some point, you may recognize that you need to process the emotions more directly or to discover just what the issues are that are creating anxiety or fear. For this you will need to set aside some time to sit quietly. Then you can work with the practice for dealing with intense emotions that we discussed in chapter 7 (pages 157–58), or use the following exercise variation, which also works with a mantra.

Exercise: Processing Emotions in Your Own Heart

Once you have centered yourself in the heart (see page 257 for instruction on this), bring the emotion into the heart-space, holding it there and letting it be surrounded by the heart-energy. Still focusing on the heart, expand your awareness so that you are conscious of the entire field of Awareness in which your experience is taking place. Hold the entire room, including your own body, in your awareness. Simultaneously, keep holding the emotion in your heart-space and maintain your sense of a field of Awareness that surrounds and contains your body.

Feel the energy in the emotion. Become aware that the emotion is actually a bundle of energy. Then imagine an opening in the energy bundle and move through the opening. Keep doing this, noticing how your state shifts.

If you prefer, you can mingle the mantra with the emotion, letting the energy of the mantra begin to break up or dissolve the heavy feelings. It is important here not to create a sense of opposition between the mantra and your emotions—not to use the mantra as a club to beat back intense feelings. Simply bring the mantra into the emotion and let the mantra work its alchemy in whatever way this happens, without trying to force anything.

Some rather miraculous side effects flow from this practice of noticing when we are off-center and then going back into the heart. Everything we do becomes a lot more fun. It seems to take less effort to achieve results. We feel closer to our intuitive wisdom and more likely to trust and follow it. We are not so impatient with ourselves and others. Responsibilities seem less burdensome, and routine not so dull. So naturally, it is easier for other people to be around us.

The mountain is the mountain, And the path unchanged since the old days. Verily what has changed is my own heart.

—KUMAGAI [8]

As we keep turning toward our center and acting from it, we find we can take strength, understanding, and love for granted. We have access to them because we are being fed at the source. That is when meditation truly begins to change our lives.

CHAPTER TWELVE

The Three-Week
Breakthrough Program

*T*he decision to go deeper into meditation is not made just
once. We make it again and again, at deeper and deeper
levels, knowing that no single intention will carry us forward
forever. This month's strong resolution becomes next month's
malaise, unless we keep renewing the resolution, reinventing it,
refocusing ourselves on it. At best, we renew our intention daily
and re-motivate ourselves as necessary—reminding ourselves
of the shortness of human life, of the opportunity it offers
us, of the speed at which everything in this world changes, of
the suffering we experience when we're out of touch with our
center, of the sweetness of the inner world, and of the benefits
of stable awareness.

Yet everyone has periods when practice is strong, as well
as times when it is less focused. And sometimes you will notice that you have simply fallen asleep to yourself, that you

have begun taking your practice for granted, that you are stuck in a routine. This is one good reason to set aside time to invite a breakthrough.

Another reason you might decide you are ready for a breakthrough is that you hear the call of the inner Self, the pull of the inner world. You sense that the walls in your consciousness are ready to come down, that the doors are ready to open. So you commit yourself to making a greater effort. You say, "This week, this month, this year, I'm going to meditate more seriously. I'm going to have a breakthrough."

Everyone who has ever made a successful raid on the forces of inertia knows that the decisive gesture is the gesture of commitment. As soon as you are willing to direct your full intention toward a plan, a project, or a goal, the universe begins to shift in your favor. Pathways open up; events conspire to help you. This is especially obvious in meditation, where you are dealing with the infinitely fluid and expansive inner universe. Because your inner Consciousness is so endlessly creative, a single strong intention can have an almost miraculous effect.

So the first step in breakthrough is your intent, and the more passionate and serious your intention, the more powerful an instrument it will be.

Traditionally, people who want to go deeper into meditation go away on retreat. The program that follows can certainly be done on retreat—and if you are very busy or have small children, you will probably need to set aside time for retreat in order to follow it. In fact, those of you whose days are so packed with responsibilities that it is hard to find more than a few minutes for sitting practice might consider making space for a retreat day once a week or even once a month.

For those who can do it, this program has been designed to fit into your daily life, and there are great advantages to integrating it into your routine. Meditating on retreat is relatively easy. We are outside our ordinary context, away from at least some of our daily commitments, and we may be in a place that is especially quiet and conducive to meditation. Yet any retreat, no matter how deep and quiet, inevitably comes to an end. Then we are faced with integrating our retreat life into our ordinary existence. The further we have taken ourselves from ordinary life, the harder it can be to import our practice into the routine of busy, crowded days.

The pearl is in the oyster. And the oyster is at the bottom of the sea. Dive deep.

—KABIR [1]

When you do your breakthrough program at home, you create a retreat atmosphere inside your ordinary environment. You create a new routine, and the habit of it remains in the atmosphere, spurring you forward even after the program is done.

MAKING THE COMMITMENT

To begin the breakthrough program, you will need to make a commitment to:

1. **Meditate daily—if possible, for one and a half to three hours per day.**

   This can be done in one meditation session or two. If you are simply too busy to sit for an hour or more of meditation at a time or if you have young children or a very demanding job, please feel free to adapt the program to your needs. The principles of it will help you even if you only meditate for twenty minutes to half an hour at a time, and as you establish a continuity of practice, you may start to find that your situation opens up in unexpected ways.

2. **Keep a meditation journal in which you write down whatever happens, and set aside some time each week to read through your experiences and contemplate them.**

3. **Spend at least ten minutes a day reading from a book that induces meditation and inspires love for the inner world.** A list of recommended books appears in the Further Reading section.

It might seem daunting to think about spending that much time in meditation every day, especially if you are very busy. That is why the breakthrough program is set up to last only three weeks. With proper planning, even people with very crowded lives can usually find three weeks in which to commit themselves to meditating strongly.

For breakthrough in meditation, continuity of practice is important. When we meditate twice a day, it bookends our day in meditation and also gives us the opportunity to consolidate states we may have experienced during the previous session. As we have said before, most people need to sit for about an hour to significantly deepen their meditation, simply because it takes time for the outgoing mind to settle, reverse its normal tendency to rove through the universe, and begin to sink back into itself. The more active we normally are, the more time it takes to digest the residue of our day's impressions. But if we sit long enough, Consciousness will naturally begin to emerge from the layers of thoughts that stir up its surface, revealing its own quiet depths.

SETTING ASIDE TIME

All of us have our own best times of day to meditate. This is not always in the early morning. Each period of the day has its own particular energy, which affects your own energy field. Traditionally, the most powerful times of day for meditation are the *sandhyas,* or junction points. The sandhya is a period in the day when there is a shift in the atmospheric energy.

We must, then, . . . even in the midst of occupations, withdraw within ourselves.

—TERESA OF AVILA [2]

There are three sandhyas. The early morning sandhya is the period of dawn, just before and just after sunrise. The midday sandhya marks the switch from morning to afternoon and lasts from about eleven-thirty until approximately twelve-thirty. And the late-afternoon sandhya begins just before sunset and lasts until darkness falls.

Just as the space between the in-breath and the out-breath is an open doorway to the madhya, the center of Consciousness, these spaces between one part of the day and another are like cracks between the worlds, times when our inner energy shifts in rhythm with the energy of the day and creates a natural opening into the inner world.

This doesn't mean that we can't get into meditation at other times. However, many people find that their energy naturally turns inward during the sandhyas. Observing your own daily rhythms, you may have already noticed a tendency to get "sleepy" during these times. It is not low blood sugar; it is actually the power of the sandhyas drawing you inside.

So it is very good to experiment with meditating at different times of day. You may have been assuming that early morning is the best time for you, when actually you meditate as well or better in the late afternoon or even at lunchtime.

Once you have discovered the best period of the day for meditation, make sure to set aside enough time during that period to let yourself go deep. In general, have at least one time during the day when you meditate for at least an hour, with perhaps some open space at the end in case you want to sit longer. Your second period, if necessary, can be as short as a half hour.

YOUR BREAKTHROUGH PROGRAM LIFESTYLE

When you are seeing a breakthrough in meditation, your lifestyle matters. Of course, it is not necessary to follow a monastic schedule, to become vegetarian or celibate, or to overwhelm yourself with yogic discipline. However, certain core disciplines will make a distinct difference in your experience of meditation. Here are some of them:

1. **If you meditate in the early morning, go to bed early enough to comfortably get up in time. Before you go to bed, read something uplifting or repeat mantras.**

   A friend of mine always says that the decision to meditate is made the night before. If you are going to get up for meditation, you will need to be in bed at a reasonable hour and with your mind clear. This is one of the great secrets of early morning meditation. If you watch television or read the newspaper or a stimulating novel before bed, it not only affects your sleeping patterns, but also programs the way you wake up in the morning.

You can experiment with this. Notice what you are thinking about when you go to sleep. Then notice the first thoughts that come into your mind when you wake up the next morning. Unless you have had a strong dream that stays with you on waking, the thought you wake up with will almost always be the thought you went to sleep with. If, in the moments before sleep, you are thinking about your problems at the office or the project you are working on or the Lakers' chances of making it to the play-offs, there is a fair guarantee that you will wake up with the same issue on your mind.

However, if before you go to sleep you have been reading the poetry of Rumi, a book by your teacher, or some other spiritual book, that is what will come into mind when you wake up. Even better, if you go to sleep doing a practice, you should find that the practice is with you when you wake up.

2. **Repeat a mantra or focus on the breath before you go to sleep and when you wake up.**

3. **In the morning, get up immediately.**
   If you lie in bed, you give the inner dialogue time to start, and you risk going back to sleep.

4. **Shower or wash your hands, face, and feet immediately before meditation.**

   Washing before meditation does more than cleanse the body and wake you up. It is also a way of cleansing the mind. As the water pours over your body, you can mentally repeat your mantra or imagine the water as a shower of light that is washing your inner body of its accumulated thought-dust.

5. **Observe moderation in eating.**

   The real key to a yogic diet is not to overeat. This doesn't mean you should fast. The ideal is to get up from the table before you feel full. Eating to fullness strains the digestive system and uses up energy that you could use for meditation.

   Many meditators prefer a vegetarian or mostly vegetarian diet. Still, make sure you get enough protein. Lack of protein makes many people spacey, and even though this might feel like a pleasant state for a while, ultimately it makes it harder both to function and to integrate your experiences.

   Try to eat at regular times and create a pleasant ritual around your meals. If possible, eat at least one of your meals in silence. It is better not to read or watch television when you eat, but to focus fully on the act of eating.

   Chew your food well—at least fifty times per mouthful. Not only does this make the food easier to digest, it also

> *For one who is moderate in food and diversion, whose actions are disciplined, who is moderate in sleep and waking, yoga destroys all sorrow.*
>
> —BHAGAVAD GITA [3]

helps you to focus on the eating process. You become more conscious, more mindful, and more centered as you eat. And you eat less.

Repeat a mantra or keep your awareness focused on the breath while you are eating and, if you cook for yourself, while cooking. The energy of the mantra will mingle with the food and will give you subtle as well as physical nourishment.

6. **Regulate your social life.**

Ask yourself now, "Without abandoning my family or depriving myself of normal human interaction and appropriate social nourishment, what unnecessary engagements can I eliminate during my meditation breakthrough program?"

It is partly a matter of time. When there are only so many hours in the day and you want to devote some of them to spiritual practice, the easiest way to make that time available is to take it out of your social or leisure-time schedule.

But there are other reasons why you might want to scrutinize your engagement calendar at this point. The people you spend time with influence your inner state profoundly. Though it may not be possible to surround yourself entirely with uplifting people who support your meditation practice, you can certainly stay away from the people and events that will unnecessarily draw you into states of mind that agitate you or make it harder to go inside.

Of course, this presents certain challenges if the people who distract you are the people with whom you live! Perhaps your housemates, spouse, or children make quiet time difficult to find. Or maybe the people close to you—your spouse, partner, roommate, or children—feel threatened by your practice. Maybe they think it is taking you away from them. Maybe they feel jealous. Maybe they think meditation is stupid. Or perhaps they give you support but find it hard to help create a meditation-friendly atmosphere.

One weekend when I was first practicing meditation, I went to stay with a friend. This was during the seventies, when meditation seemed a strange practice to many. Every morning halfway through my practice, my friend would begin loudly rattling dishes in the next room. "Are you through meditating yet?" she would call periodically. My annoyed reaction to her was just as distracting as the interruption itself.

Even if your dear ones are enthusiastic about supporting your practice, it is still a good idea to take time to discuss it with them. Tell them what you are trying to do and why. Tell them what you require in terms of time and privacy. Ask for their support. Then give them a chance to state how *they* feel about it and what they need from you in order to be comfortable and supportive. Be willing to engage, within reason, in whatever process you need to go through to make it all right with them.

7. **Regulate your reading, television-watching, and film-going during this period.**

The images, ideas, and impressions in your mind determine your mood, your inner state, and your feelings. You already have a huge bank of images, ideas, and impressions boiling around inside your unconscious, thickening your consciousness, and creating subtle barriers between yourself and the inner world. The clearer you can keep your mind during your breakthrough program, the easier it will be to meditate more deeply.

Many serious meditators when on retreat give up all reading matter that isn't related to meditation. If you can do that during your breakthrough program, so much the better. It may be professionally impractical for you to ignore the morning paper or the evening news. In that case, decide on the minimum amount you need in order to keep well informed, and try to cut down on unnecessary reading.

All this talk and turmoil and noise and movement and desire is outside the veil; inside the veil is silence and calm and peace.

—ABU YAZID AL-BISTAMI [4]

You might find that your information/entertainment "fast" creates such a welcome space in your mental atmosphere that you want to keep it up after the three-week program. Many of us live with an addiction to information—to movies, novels, and magazines. Sometimes we unconsciously use reading or television-watching to barricade ourselves against feeling an underlying depression or looking at life questions we want to avoid. We may even associate quiet with boredom.

But the price of such avoidance is steep. When we fill our inner space with noise and color, with story and

273

distraction, we also cut ourselves off from the natural joy and insight that arise from simply being with ourselves. So take advantage of this opportunity to experience the power of quiet, even if it means you have to listen to the mental static you have avoided, or experience the buried feelings you have hidden from yourself.

8. **Inject practices such as mantra repetition, contemplation, or yogic breathing into the spaces in your day.**
   Whenever your mind is unoccupied with work or other essential interactions—for example, when you are walking, during drives or bus rides, or while cooking or cleaning—turn your awareness toward the inner world. Do the mantra with a feeling that you are calling out to your inner Self. Perform your tasks in rhythm with the breath. Do an exercise in awareness—imagine that you are surrounded by a blanket of divine love, or look into someone's eyes with the awareness that the same Consciousness is looking out of their eyes as from yours. Walk with the feeling that you are walking into the Vastness. Offer your actions to God, for the benefit of others or the healing of the earth, or to the ever-present inner Self. Become aware of the witnessing Awareness at different points during the day.

THE BREAKTHROUGH PROGRAM SCHEDULE
The Day Before You Begin

Set aside some time to be alone and do the following process of inner examination.

Exercise: Inquiry into Your Meditation Practice

Ask yourself:

> What are the strengths of my meditation practice?
>
> Where do I think there could be improvement?
>
> Why do I meditate? What do I hope to gain from it?
>
> What are my short-term goals in meditation?
>
> What are my long-term goals?
>
> When have I most enjoyed meditation?
>
> What was going on in my life at those times?

Still looking at the times you have most enjoyed in meditation, ask yourself whether there were any practices or attitudes that contributed to your enjoyment.

Which practices have helped you most in getting into meditation?

Spend as much time as you need contemplating all these questions and write down your conclusions.

Now write in your journal the following promise to yourself (which you may reword if the language does not suit you):

> I, (name), promise myself that I will make my meditation practice a priority during the next three weeks. I will arrange my schedule to give myself time to meditate

regularly for (number) hours a day. I will also live my life during this time so that my diet, my sleeping schedule, and my social life support meditation. I offer this promise to my own inner Self and for the benefit of all beings, and I ask that the supreme Self, living within me and within all things, give me the grace to carry out my promise.

THE MEDITATION PROGRAM

During each meditation session of your three-week program, it is suggested that you follow the same sequence of preliminary steps. These are given below. The sequence is designed to help move you out of ordinary, mundane awareness and into the subtler state of awareness that leads to meditation.

Preliminary Practices

1. **Set Your Timer for One Hour.**

   Or for however long you have agreed with yourself to meditate each day.

2. **Offer Salutations.**

   Light a candle. If you have an altar, focus on it for a few minutes. Bow to the altar or simply to the space in front of you. As you do, have the feeling that you are bowing to your inner Consciousness, the supreme spirit within yourself and within the universe. Now bow to each of the four directions—north, east, south, and west—moving in a clockwise direction. As you make each bow, have the feeling that you are offering your salutations to the divine Consciousness that resides in every corner of the universe.

3. **Take a Posture.**

Sit in an erect and relaxed posture, making sure that you are physically comfortable. (See pages 75–77 for the basic points of meditation posture and the method of relaxing the body in the posture.)

God must act and pour himself into you the moment he finds you ready.

—MEISTER ECKHART [5]

4. **State Your Intention.**

Formulate to yourself a clear, strong intention. For example: "I am meditating on my inner Self. I regard whatever arises in meditation as a form of Consciousness. I let go of distracting thoughts or emotions, and immerse myself in my own pure Awareness (or 'in the energy of the mantra' or 'in the heart')."

5. **Invoke the Grace of the Guru.**

Imagine that your guru, or a great teacher or saint to whom you feel deeply connected, is sitting before you. Feel that a ray of energy, or a current of love, connects your heart to the teacher's heart. Imagine that streams of grace and blessings are coming from the guru's heart to yours.

Feeling that heart connection, speak to the teacher in your own words, offering your salutations and asking for blessings to enter deeply into meditation. You might ask for blessings to meditate with focus, or to immerse yourself in the Self, or to enter the heart. You might simply offer the meditation to the guru. Feel that the guru hears and grants your request. Allow yourself to receive the blessings that flow from the great teacher's heart.

Once you have done the preliminary steps, you can practice any of the techniques in chapter 4 or follow the instructions given in the following section, which are somewhat more advanced versions of practices in chapter 4. Feel free to try them out or to use whatever practice opens up the inner space and helps you go deeper. It is important to remember that we use these techniques to quiet our mental energy, to calm our thoughts, and to help our attention move inside and stabilize itself. They are doorways into meditation, not ends in themselves.

Once your thought-stream has calmed and slowed down, you can begin sensing where the inner energy wants to take you. At that point, you might want to let the technique go and follow the inner pathways that your own shakti suggests. If thoughts arise, if you become distracted, or if you lose touch with the feeling of the shakti, come back to the technique.

Once you have decided how long you intend to meditate during a given session, it is important to stay with your meditation until the session is over. No matter what your mind does, keep your body on the mat. (It is fine to move in your posture or to stretch if you are uncomfortable.) Your steadiness in staying on the mat is essential for going deeper. It creates the container, the framework, within which a state of meditation can arise.

Of course, it may happen that you come out of meditation once, twice, or several times during the course of a session. This is normal. Simply sit, tune in to the energy in your body, and return to whatever technique or centering practice you have been using until you feel your attention turning inward once again.

A Three-Week Meditation Practice Schedule

For each week, two to four practices are offered. You might choose one and work with it all week, or you might experiment with different sets of instructions. I would also suggest that you work with the practice described on pages 177–79, "Invoking the Shakti's Guidance," at least once or twice each week.

You might like to record your own audio of some of these instructions to play before meditation.

WEEK ONE

Suggested Focus: Meditation on Entering the Inner Pulsation

Meditation Instructions 1: Meditate on the Pulsation of the Mantra

Perform the five preliminary practices (pages 276–77).

Begin to repeat your mantra, coordinating it with your breathing. Focus on the energy, the pulsation within the syllables—not the meaning of the syllables themselves, but the pulsation inside them.

Now imagine yourself surrounded by the mantra. You are inside the mantra. You might imagine a door inside the mantra pulsation and enter the doorway. Or imagine the mantra as a cloud that surrounds you and holds you within itself.

When you feel truly immersed in the mantra, let go of the syllables and focus on the pulsation of energy they have created in your mind. Understand that the pulsation is the mantra. That pulsation of energy is the shakti of the mantra. It is filled with grace, with divine Awareness, with insight, and with love.

Allow yourself to rest in the pulsation of energy. Imagine an opening or a doorway inside the pulsation, and feel yourself gliding through this opening. It is not your body that enters the pulsation. It is you as energy, as a point of awareness. As you enter the pulsation, you are entering deeper into your own consciousness, your own inner energy field.

Rest there. If thoughts arise, understand that they are energy, shakti.

At any point in this meditation process, the shakti of your own inner consciousness may shift your state, or guide your meditation in some way. Remember, inner experiences that arise in meditation—subtle feelings, lights, sounds—are all expressions of shakti. Let yourself open to the process, allowing the energy to carry you deeper inside. If thoughts arise, remember to regard the thoughts as pulsations of shakti. If you should become distracted, return to focusing on the pulsation within the mantra.

Variation
Once you've centered your awareness on the inner pulsation, you may want to ask the shakti for guidance in meditation, as in the practice described in chapter 8, pages 177–79. Focusing on the pulsation inside your awareness, honor it, recognizing it as a pulsation of the kundalini. Then ask the kundalini to guide your meditation, to show you how it wants you to meditate, or simply to give you whatever experience of meditation is right for you today.

Meditation Instructions 2: Meditation in the Heart-Space

Begin with the five preliminary steps (pages 276–77).

Follow the rhythm of the breathing, focusing on the space where the inhalation dissolves in the heart region and where the exhalation dissolves outside. Have the understanding that the thoughts that arise and subside are made of Consciousness, and let them dissolve into the breath.

Become aware of the inner heart-space. It is located at a point four to five inches below the collarbone, inside. (This is not, of course, the physical heart, but a subtle center of Consciousness, a center where we can directly experience the inner Self.)

Let your awareness, with the breath, center itself in the inner heart-space. Be aware of the energy in that space, the energy inside your heart. How does it feel? What do you sense there? Let yourself explore the space of the heart. See if you can feel the subtle pulsation, the throbbing energy within the heart-space. The heartbeat is there, but there's a subtler throb, the throb of your deeper energy, the throb of the heart.

As your awareness explores the heart-space, have the feeling that there is an opening, a doorway, within the energy of the heart. It's leading inward. You may imagine the opening visually, or simply feel the presence of an opening. Allow your attention to move inward through that opening, deeper into the heart-space. It's not your body that moves through the heart-space, it's your attention. As you rest in this deeper heart-space, let your attention merge with the energy there.

When you are ready, imagine another opening within the heart-space. Let your attention move through it, entering deeper into the heart until you come to the place where your attention wants to rest. Rest there, in your spacious heart. As you breathe in, feel that you breathe in pure conscious energy. As you breathe out, allow the pure conscious energy to expand the energy in your heart. Your breath is pure conscious energy. Your thoughts are pure conscious energy.

It may happen during this exercise that the energy draws your attention to another spiritual center such as the space between the eyebrows or the crown of the head. If this happens, let yourself go with it.

Meditation Instructions 3: Entering the Space Between Breaths

Begin with the five preliminary practices (pages 276–77).

Focus your attention on the movement of the breath. As you breathe in, feel that you are breathing pure, subtle Consciousness. With each exhalation, feel that you are breathing out your thoughts.

At the end of the in-breath, notice the place where the breath dissolves in the region of the heart. Focus gently in that space, not straining or forcing yourself to hold your breath, but simply noticing the space when it occurs. In the same way, focus on the place at the end of the exhalation where the breath dissolves outside the body.

God is much closer to us than our own soul, for he is the ground in which our soul stands.

—JULIAN OF NORWICH [6]

Sometimes as you practice this dharana, you will find that the inner and outer space become one. You realize that your body is no longer a barrier between inside and outside. You can simply rest in that space.

As you become more and more centered in the space between breaths, imagine an opening at the end of the exhalation. You may visualize it as a doorway, or simply feel it as an open space. Enter that opening. It is not your body that enters it, but yourself as awareness, as attention. Hold your awareness in the space you sense there, even as the breath continues to flow in and out naturally. You are not holding your breath. You are simply letting yourself rest in the space at the end of the exhalation.

Keep moving deeper into the space at the end of the exhalation. Meditate on that inner space. If thoughts arise, remember that they are made of Consciousness, of energy, of shakti.

After Meditation

Take some time to come out of meditation, and let yourself sit long enough to savor the subtle feeling that remains. If you have space, you can lie on your back in the corpse pose (as described on page 237) for a few minutes. Sometimes those few moments of rest after meditation bring you all the fruits of meditation. The shift into the Self that may have eluded you during your sitting meditation practice may come all on its own when you relax in the moments after meditation.

As soon as your meditation is finished, record what you experienced. If the experiences are very subtle, you may have to contemplate them for a while to find language to describe them. It is important to do this, no matter how imprecise you feel the language to be.

Offer your meditation for the benefit and upliftment of all beings.

See how long you can keep the sense of connection to your inner spaciousness. You can do this by bringing your attention into the heart, by focusing on the breath, or by repeating the mantra with awareness of the pulsation in the syllables.

Continue to practice these exercises each morning and evening for the rest of Week One.

WEEK TWO

Suggested Focus: Meditation on Consciousness

Meditation Instructions 1: Become the Knower

The following meditation is based on one of the classical Self-knowledge practices of Vedanta, often called the practice of *neti neti,* or "not this, not this." In this profoundly liberating process, we detach ourselves from identifying with the body, mind, and ego so that pure Awareness can reveal itself.

Begin with the five preliminary practices (pages 276–77).

Sitting comfortably, become aware of your experience of being where you are at this moment. Notice the sounds around you, the sensation of the air against your face, the clothes against your skin. Notice the sensations that go with sitting—your thighs meeting the floor or chair, the way your muscles grip to hold you in position. Be aware of the back muscles—how they contract to hold up the spine or relax against the back of the chair.

Now become aware of the internal sensations in your body. How is your stomach feeling? Are your cheeks and forehead relaxed or tight? Does some part of your body feel warm or cool?

Say to yourself, "I observe this body. If I can know my body, it must be outside me." Tell yourself, "I am aware of my body, but I am not my body."

Become aware of the breath, noticing how it flows in and out of your nostrils, how it moves downward to expand your lungs. As you follow the breath, tell yourself, "I am observing my breath. Since I can observe the breath, it must be outside me. I am not my breath."

Become aware now of the experience of your own energy. How is your energy? Do you feel alert? Dull or sleepy? Fresh? Wired?

As you observe your energy, tell yourself, "I witness the state of my energy. Since I can observe my energy, it must be outside me. It must be other than me. I am not my energy."

Become aware of the flow of thought and images in your mind, the running commentary, the mental static. Be aware, too, of any emotions that arise, of the underlying mood that prevails. Observe the flow of thoughts and feelings. Observe your mood.

Indeed, it is the Infinite, beginningless and endless, which exists as the pure experiencing Consciousness.

—YOGA VASISHTHA [7]

Now tell yourself, "I know my thoughts. I am aware of my feelings. I witness my moods. Therefore, they are external to me. I am not my thoughts and feelings. I am not my moods."

Become aware of your feeling of "I-ness," your ego. Notice how there's a part of you that feels like a particular "me," that identifies itself as someone. Say to yourself, "I am the knower of this feeling of 'I-ness.' Since I am observing it, it must be outside me. I am not my ego."

Now ask yourself, "Who is the knower, the witness, of the body, the mind, the ego? Who is the knower?"

Just ask the question, "Who is the knower?" and wait to see what arises. If you are moved to do so, keep asking the question, waiting in silence, then asking again. You are not looking for an answer in words or for a particular experience. You are inviting the Self, the witnessing Consciousness, to reveal itself.

Finally rest in the knower. Meditate *as* the knower.

(As you experiment with this practice, you may find that you prefer to ask a different question, such as "Who is the witness?" or "Who am I?")

When you let yourself become quiet, when you settle into the breath, you find yourself in the heart . . . . As you become accustomed to this practice, you can simply sit on your meditation mat and walk into your own heart, the subtle heart, the innermost core of your being.

—SWAMI
CHIDVILASANANDA [8]

Meditation Instructions 2: Meditate on Your Own Awareness

Begin with the five preliminary practices (pages 276–77).

Focus your attention on the breath, following each breath as it comes in and goes out. With each exhalation, have the feeling that you are letting go of any tension in your body, any fear, any feeling of limitation. As thoughts arise, breathe them out. If emotions arise, breathe them out as well. Notice the inner space that remains each time you breathe out thoughts or emotions or limitations. Continue breathing out your thoughts, tension, fear, and limitations until your mind begins to become quiet.

Allow yourself to notice the Awareness through which you know your body, your breath, and your thoughts. Keep your attention on Awareness. As thoughts come up, as your attention moves to different objects, let the thoughts and objects go with the breath and focus on Awareness.

After Meditation

Follow the instructions given in Week One.

WEEK THREE

Suggested Focus: Devotional Meditation
Follow the five preliminary practices (pages 276–77), then practice one of the techniques below.

Meditation Instructions 1: Breathing In Love

Begin by becoming aware of the presence of a fundamental tenderness, a softness, a loving-kindness in the atmosphere around you. (You might do this by asking, "Is love present?") The love you are tuned in to here is not an emotion. You are attuning to the tenderness of life for life, the natural, loving quality of Presence, the benign, affectionate intention that flows through the universe and gives life.

Allow your attention to center on the breath as it flows in and out. Feel that you are breathing in love as a tender, sweet sensation that flows from the air itself. Inhaling, feel that loving tenderness suffusing your body, and as you exhale, allow it to flow through your body and out into the atmosphere.

Meditation Instructions 2: Devotional Mantra Repetition

Repeat your mantra with one of the following bhavanas:

1. Have the feeling that you are offering the mantra to the Beloved inside your heart or dropping it into the heart of God.

2. Imagine each repetition of the mantra as a flower being offered to the Beloved in your heart.

3. As you repeat the mantra, feel that it is God, your own divine Self, who is repeating it.

Meditation Instructions 3: Resting in the Divine Heart

Focusing your attention on the breath, allow each in-breath to bring you to the awareness of the inner space of the heart. It is not the physical heart you are touching here, but the subtle center in the chest region, at the place where the inhalation naturally comes to rest.

> *What is the body? That shadow of a shadow of your love, that somehow contains the entire universe.*
>
> —RUMI [9]

Say very gently to yourself, as if you were saying a mantra, "My heart is God's heart" or "My heart is the heart of the universe." Each time you repeat the words, pause and rest in the space created inside you by the thought that your heart is God's heart, the heart of the universe. Feel that you rest in the divine heart. If thoughts arise, let them dissolve into the space of the divine heart.

288

CHAPTER THIRTEEN

The *Process* of Ripening

*M*uch of the work of meditation takes place underground, and much of it is imperceptible. That is one reason we measure our progress in meditation not so much by what happens during a particular session of meditation, as by the subtle ways in which a regular meditation practice changes our feelings about ourselves and the world. Otherwise our day-to-day experience in meditation often seems to follow no discernible progression. More often it is rather like moving through different weather patterns.

If you look at a weather map, you will see that it is marked with colors and swirls. In the blue zone, there is rain; in the red zone, sunshine. The green zone is facing tropical storms, and the yellow zone shows an unseasonable snowfall. It often feels like that in meditation. Different weather patterns seem to succeed each other. A period of profound, quiet meditation might be followed by a stormy period of agitation when the mind just won't get quiet, and then by a sort of gray period when meditation feels rather shallow, or by a period when you feel resistance to meditating.

You might go through a day or a week of great lightness and bliss. Then the next day, you are stuck in some heavy emotion. Your heart feels dry; your mind, thick and opaque. One day you have a full experience of the witness, and the next, your mind refuses to let go of thinking. On Tuesday you come out of meditation feeling brilliant, attuned to your world. You think, "Meditation is so great—it makes my mind sharp as a tack." On Wednesday you walk around feeling so dull or spacey that you can't help wondering, "Maybe meditation is making me lose my memory."

Do you remember how your life yearned out of childhood toward the "great thing"? I see that it is now yearning forth beyond the great thing toward the greater one. That is why it does not cease to be difficult, but that is also why it will not cease to grow.

—RAINER MARIA RILKE [1]

Why is it like this? It isn't because meditation changes. It is simply because, as we have seen, our journey inward is always taking us through different layers or terrains of our inner Consciousness. My guru used to astonish me sometimes by his insistence on seeing whatever you brought him in a positive light. You would tell him, "I'm ecstatic," and he would say, "Very good." You would say, "I'm feeling so much sadness," and he would say, "Very good." You'd report a vision, or an avalanche of thoughts, or the feeling that nothing was happening at all, and he would say, "Very good." Impatient for analysis or distrustful of the process, I would sometimes wonder whether he understood how boring the nothingness was, or how special the vision.

As the years passed, and we, his students, passed through different phases of the inner universe, we began to understand what he meant—in other words, to recognize that it really was all very good. The more we internalized the tantric recognition that human consciousness is dyed irrevocably with the hue of divinity, the more we would experience how all these bubbles and waves of feeling, thought, and image eventually dissolved back into the underlying fabric of Awareness, whose essence is love. Where else can thoughts and images of feelings and emotions go if not back into the Consciousness of which they are made? And—here, for me, was the miracle—as they arose in meditation and were allowed to subside, the inner fabric of my consciousness lightened, became freer, more playful, less volatile. More pure.

Over time, I came to see that the most important thing was to keep meditating, because the very process of meditation itself would take me through whatever I needed to go through and out the other side. One of the great principles of spiritual life is "Keep moving." Our belief structures and fears—the ones that are always hanging about in the recesses of the personal mind—can start to jam us if we spend too much time thinking and worrying about our experiences. Contemplation is necessary. But trying to figure out the whys and wherefores of what we are experiencing, or letting ourselves be frightened or discouraged by a strange sensation or mood (or alternatively, letting ourselves get overexcited by a "high" experience), can lock us right into one of our limiting concepts. The only solution is to keep on going. Consciousness itself will correct any imbalances that you feel.

Meditation itself will show you what you need to know. It's a process, and it evolves.

In this practice, no effort is ever lost. Even a little of this practice protects one from great fear.

—BHAGAVAD GITA [2]

When a pilot flies from New York to Paris, he is never exactly on course. He is always adjusting, always correcting slight deviations. So his flight pattern can be described as a process of error-correction, error-correction—until he finally arrives at his destination. Our inner process is much like this: a constant process of balance. Spiritual progress is not, as we sometimes imagine, a straight line. It is more like a zigzag, two steps forward and one step back. Yet if we keep at it with a strong intention, we do arrive at the destination.

RIPENING

Inner unfolding takes its own time. That's simply one of the great universal truths of spiritual life. We can't rush the process of awakening, no matter how much we may want to do so. On the other hand, once it's started, we can trust that our inner process will unfold.

Sometimes we want to storm the inner world, like Ramakrishna's first disciples who would wake up and say, "Another day gone, and still no vision of God!" Filled with aspiration and longing, we can't understand why the inner universe won't open up to us immediately.

At other times, we wonder if we will ever learn how to hold the mind still for longer than five minutes. We become discouraged because "bad" feelings that we think we should be rid of by now are still with us. We forget how much the process of meditation is about self-confrontation, self-recognition, and the humbling daily encounter with the gap between who we want to be and who we actually are.

When you plant a peach tree, it has its season of sprouting. It grows through several seasons, bearing leaves and then flowering. When it reaches a certain point of maturity, it bears fruit. How long this takes depends on many things—the soil, the weather, the type of tree, the quality of the water—but eventually the tree will bear fruit, and once it does, it gives fruit year after year. Spiritual growth is exactly like that. It is for most people a slow and gradual process, a matter of ripening. It happens in its own time. We don't know when fruition will happen. All we can know is that it will.

Let me give you one more personal example. I wrote in chapter 1 about one of the milestone experiences in what I would call the opening of my heart. In fact, this was a stage in a process that took years. After the intense sweetness of my early, post-awakening experiences, I entered a phase where whenever I sat for meditation, I would feel a hard and almost painful energy around my heart. Occasionally, the shell over my heart would seem to dissolve, and I would find myself in an inner field of sweetness. Mostly, though, I spent my hours of meditation face to face with the wall around my heart. I came to take it for granted, to accept this prickly sensation of intense energy pushing up against the heart region. I would repeat the mantra, focus on the breath, and often go quite deep into a state of wide, expansive quiet. But the shell around my heart remained firmly in place.

During this time, I used to pray intensely to feel more love and for my heart to open fully. But it never happened for more than a few hours or, at most, days. It was terribly frustrating.

Then after nearly ten years of steady practice, I realized one day that, without my having noticed what had happened, my heart had become softer. The energy was no longer hard and painful. Gradually during the next few years, the feeling of softening and opening in the heart kept growing. Nowadays my normal daily experience is of a silky and tender sweetness around the heart that deepens during meditation into what I can only describe as a sensation of golden love.

In hindsight, of course, I understand why it took so long. Opening the knot of the heart is not a simple matter, not for anyone. I had many, many layers of armor around my heart, layers that had to be removed one by one—layers that are still being removed, since we often tend to replace one form of armor with another. So much goes into these deep inner transformations, including a tremendous configuration of grace, personal effort, and the sheer work of time. That particular transformation involved years of inner practice, steady daily meditation, and chanting. It also included acts of service, much prayer, and the process of life itself—the inner work of relationships, of the demands of living in a community, of doing work I liked and didn't like, of getting what I wanted and failing to get it.

Running through all of this, powering it, and making it possible was the great imponderable, unquantifiable, undercover work of grace. Working through my practice and the situations that rubbed against my heart, grace gradually cleansed and made subtle my inner energy field. Layers came off so that I could feel the sweetness of what lay behind them. The subtle will got strengthened so that my body could hold more energy. More than that, during this time that loving inner energy, the energy of grace, soothed and healed many of my emotional wounds, the raw places that we all hold in our hearts, so that finally I could let go of the carapace that I had built up to guard the wounded place inside. Then the love that was there could be felt and expressed.

The whole process becomes even more mysterious when I realize that even though I say "I" let go, the truth is that I didn't let go. I *couldn't* let go. Letting go simply happened. It happened in its own time, and it took as long as it took.

The process of ripening is like this. Our practice creates the arena that allows it to happen. But the shifts, the inner changes, and the openings—how do they happen? So naturally, so subtly, that when the process is done, we often feel that our efforts had nothing to do with the change. Yet it is the interaction of our efforts with grace that makes change possible.

I salute the Self! Salutations to myself—the undivided Consciousness, the jewel of all the seen and unseen worlds!

—YOGA VASISHTHA [3]

Perhaps that is why it is a good idea to ask yourself periodically, "How have I been transformed since I started meditating?"

You might look at the shifts in the way you feel about yourself, the changes in your character and in the way you relate to other people, the difference in the way you work. Look, too, at the more subtle shifts in your inner atmosphere, in the clarity of your mind, and in the flow of your energy. Write down what you discover, and also take some time to honor your own process and the power that plays through your meditation.

Let the Inner *Dance* Unfold

*T*he purpose of this book and of the whole experience of meditation is to help you enter into a deeper relationship with yourself. The principles and disciplines in these pages—the commitment to daily meditation, to keeping a journal, and to entering meditation with conscious intention and respect—are offered not as rites you must follow but as clues to speed up your own process. They are designed to create a structure within which you can soar. All the instructions should be taken as launching platforms for your inner exploration, vehicles through which kundalini can direct your meditation. The more you invest them—and any practice—with your own feeling, intention, and inspiration, the more the energy that unfolds will leap up and dance through your being and the more she will inspire you.

So when inspiration arises, when new ways of meditating suggest themselves, think of them as gifts of the shakti. If you feel drawn to sit for meditation in a different place than usual or at an odd time, give in to the impulse and contemplate its effect. Let the thread of meditation weave its way through your life, and see how it makes you feel.

These practices can set a pattern for the rest of your life as a meditator, especially if you remember that what you seek in meditation is your own Beloved, your own inner intelligence, your own Awareness, your own Truth. The one who lives inside you reveals herself in so many ways. She dances as the subtle energy that gathers in your body when you close your eyes. She pulses in the breath and surges forth as the understanding that your breath is being moved by a greater force. She is there as the feeling of love or softness that sneaks in when you relax your tense muscles, as the pressure in your forehead, and as the awareness of Awareness. She comes as the peaceful feeling in inner quiet, as the insight into your own magnificence, as the highest thought you are capable of holding about yourself, and as the ease you feel when you breathe out tension.

Even when your energy feels tense, ragged, opaque, or painful, even when thoughts and emotions whirl like dust devils through your inner space or when dullness lies like sludge in your heart, she is there at the bottom of your agitation and behind the feelings, memories, and sensations. She is in every moment of your meditation; she is your inner friend, your lover, and your Self.

Keep looking for her, for him, for That—always knowing that what you are looking for is what you already are. As you sense that presence, let yourself be with it. Moreover, let yourself *be* it. Meditate on your own Self, the one who is always there for you, the one who contains you in its stillness, the one who is always meditating on you.

May your practice of meditation unfold joyfully in all its seasons and bring you again and again to your own heart, the Heart of the universe, the great Self.

APPENDIX ONE

*K*undalini

*Y*our life alone, great Mother, is the breath of every creature,"[1] wrote the nineteenth-century Bengali poet Ramprasad. His lines touch the mystery of kundalini shakti, the inner power that many yogic texts describe as the force behind spiritual growth. Kundalini is a mystery, a source of both fascination and confusion, and the subject of one of the most esoteric branches of spiritual literature. It is also a very palpable—though subtle—energy that you will begin to recognize as your meditation unfolds.

Mentioned in Indian yogic texts dating at least as far back as the sixth century CE, kundalini is also described in the Taoist yoga manual *The Secret of the Golden Flower* and in many key texts of Tibetan yoga. In our time, traditional texts on kundalini yoga like the *Shiva Samhita* and the *Hatha Yoga Pradipika* are available through online booksellers, along with contemporary scholarly and popular books on the subject. Many longtime meditators, especially those who have been initiated by teachers of certain Indian and Tibetan Guru lineages, have experienced kundalini in the course of their practice. Even so, kundalini is often discussed—at least, on the face of it—in many classical yogic texts as if it were an almost mechanical energy, an energy that can be manipulated, an energy that one can learn to control or that can go awry.

In fact, kundalini is much more than that, and here is the heart of both its fascination and its mystery. As French scholar Jean Varenne says in *Yoga and the Hindu Tradition,* "The kundalini is shakti, the divine power incarnated in the body and inextricably involved in its destiny."[2] The sages who compiled the Hindu Tantras, yogic texts in which kundalini is invoked and celebrated, regarded it as an inner form of the divine feminine, the Goddess, whose special gift to us is spiritual awareness.[3] As a verse in the *Niruttara Tantra* states, "Without knowledge of shakti, liberation is unattainable."[4]

In the Tantric tradition, the name *kundalini*—which means "coiled"—is one of the names for the cosmic creative energy, the shakti or power aspect of the divine, and to understand how she works within the human body, we need to understand this basic fact about her nature. This tradition, which includes the texts of Kashmir Shaivism, describes the ultimate reality as an inseparable dyad known as Shiva/Shakti. Often personified in mythology as a divine couple, Shiva and Shakti represent the two complementary poles of a single unbroken divine reality. Shiva is the still ground, the pure witnessing Consciousness that contains all that is. Shakti is the dynamic creative power inherent in reality, the power that, according to the tradition, manifests universes in blissful freedom. As the *Pratyabhijna Hridayam* puts it, "Supremely independent Chiti [a name for shakti] is the cause of the manifestation, maintenance, and reabsorption of the universe. She manifests it upon her own screen."[5] Shakti, then, is the energy that becomes everything in the universe—and everything beyond the universe. She is Becoming itself, the primordial creative ground within which all becoming manifests. There is nothing in this universe or beyond it that is *not* shakti, and thus nothing which is without consciousness, since shakti is above all conscious, alive, sentient. This is a radical notion, though easier to grasp when you have some understanding of quantum physics.

Shakti, the Kashmir Shaivite texts tell us, becomes the universe by a process of contraction—vast, formless, infinitely subtle energy becoming solidified into matter, rather as vapor condenses to form water and then ice. As the cosmic energy contracts, she veils her real nature, concealing herself behind the screen of forms—and identifying herself as particular forms, bodies, and egos. When shakti is contracted, a human being—who is in essence pure, free Consciousness—identifies with his own body, mind, and personal history. So he cannot really know the truth about himself.

This is an essential point of the tantric worldview: the very power that has manifested the forms of this world works inside us to turn our senses outward and create the illusion that we are a particular individual, separate from all else. Therefore, there can be no experience of oneness unless the power consents, as it were, to turn the mind within and reveal the essence behind forms.

When we are in this state of contraction and limitation, kundalini is said to be "asleep." In this state, our energy is bound up in identification with the limitations of the body, mind, and personal history—the condition called "ego" or self-contraction. What is called "the awakening of kundalini" is actually the reversal of the energy's contracting tendency, so that instead of concealing the truth that we are pure energy, light, and bliss, the awakened kundalini begins to *reveal* it. But first the human body has to be prepared to experience itself as pure Consciousness. Otherwise, our physical density, our physical and psychological blockages, and our emotional blockages, distortions, and fears make it impossible for us to contain the level of energy that the expanded kundalini would let loose in our system.

So typically, when the awakening takes place, the energy that has been turning the mind and senses outward and giving us the experience of separation and difference, now begins to facilitate the movement toward inwardness and unity. The energy moves through the physical body, as well as the subtle system, purifying them, removing toxins from the system, dispelling emotional blocks, making the mind subtle, and giving it the power to focus inward.

Kundalini works through the prana, the vital force in the body, and through the pranic channels called nadis. Most yogic traditions describe the action of kundalini as a rising movement, where the energy flows upward through a subtle channel called the sushumna nadi, which runs from the base of the spine to the crown of the head within our subtle, or energetic, system. But it also flows with the vital force *throughout* the body, removing blockages from the physical nervous system as well as from the energy channels. When kundalini is working within the body, it will create a variety of physical and psychological effects. Some of the physical effects have been described in chapter 9. Others can be found in the literature mentioned in the Notes and Further Reading sections.

Psychologically, the activity of kundalini gives enormous power to any practice or discipline we have been doing—whether meditation, yoga, psychotherapy, art, or self-help work. This power may be felt as a direct sense of being blessed, inspired, or transformed from within, as fears fall away, and higher emotions like courage and love arise. Kundalini can dramatically increase your spiritual aspiration and capacity for practice. On another front, it may bring up buried emotions or memories, allowing you to face them directly. Moreover, the awakened energy supports any practice you use to clear your psychological blocks, beliefs, and personal traumas, so that every form of self-help work, as well as spiritual practice, gives results more quickly.

For me, like many others, the most dramatic shift I noticed when my kundalini awoke was a measurable deepening of my meditation practice. Practices I had been doing for some time with very little result began to open realms within my heart and mind that I'd never experienced before. States of meditation began to arise spontaneously, along with spiritual insights and a new level of philosophical understanding, creativity, and open-heartedness. At the same time, there would be periods of emotional upheaval, when long-buried emotional wounds would surface—and I had to learn how to work with them without, say, acting out a burst of anger, or getting lost in sadness, or believing that a feeling of romantic infatuation necessarily heralded a soul-mate connection.

If you are what the texts call an average "worldly" aspirant—that is, a practitioner who has not gone through the rigorous disciplines of the traditional yogic schools—it is normal for the kundalini to work initially on the physical and psychological levels. Many Western writers, following Carl Jung, associate these psychological shifts with the movement of kundalini through the chakras. But most traditional texts consider the opening of the chakras to be a separate movement of kundalini, one that may take place simultaneously with the physical and psychological purification process, but which often occurs only after a certain amount of purification has already taken place.

In this process, called *vedha mayi,* or the piercing of the centers, kundalini moves through the chakras, or spiritual centers that lie along the sushumna nadi; it opens them, thus opening the doors to the mystical dimensions of experience. Eventually, as kundalini becomes stable in the topmost chakra in the crown of the head, the practitioner experiences union—oneness with all things. Over time, this experience begins to permeate the activity of the outgoing senses, allowing the experience of uninterrupted unity consciousness.

KUNDALINI AND THE TRADITIONS

Since kundalini is a universal power, its effects have been felt—and recorded—by mystics of every tradition and also by many who would not call themselves mystics. The visions, raptures, insights, and mystical realizations described by Christian mystics like Teresa of Avila or Hildegard of Bingen, by Jewish mystics like Baal Shem Tov, and by Sufi, Taoist, and Buddhist practitioners, correspond to experiences of awakened kundalini described in Indian yogic texts. Vajrayana Buddhist writings, as well as some of the writings in Western hermetic and Kabbalistic traditions, closely resemble descriptions of kundalini found in the Hindu Tantras. Elaine Pagels, in *The Gnostic Gospels,* quotes an early text of Gnostic Christianity that says, "In every human being dwells an infinite power, the root of the universe. That infinite power exists in a latent condition in everyone."[6]

Christian writers speak of this spiritual energy as the Holy Spirit. In Chinese yoga, it is called inner *chi;* and in Japanese, inner *ki,* to distinguish it from the external physical energy. The !Kung bushmen of Africa speak of a powerful subtle energy called *n/um,*[7] while the Hopi of the American Southwest describe the human spinal column as an axis containing vibratory centers.[8] These centers correspond to the chakra system of kundalini yoga.

In the Indian yogic texts, kundalini is often depicted as a serpent. Sir John Woodroffe, the first Western scholar to write extensively about the Indian tradition of kundalini yoga, referred to kundalini as the serpent power. Revered texts from Egypt and the Celtic traditions associate the image of the serpent with the ancient goddess religions. Some contemporary writers in the Kabbalistic tradition have pointed out that the serpent in the Garden of Eden might be associated with kundalini and the initiation into higher knowledge. Carlos Suarès, in *The Cipher of Genesis,* describes how Kabbalah refers to the serpent that appeared to Adam and Esha (Eve) in the Garden of Eden as the resurrection of Aleph, the principle of all that is and all that is not, from its entombment in earth.[9] According to this tradition, when the serpent appears, Adam and Eve are just emerging from a state of deep oblivion. The task of the serpent is to awaken them and begin their journey of evolution. One Kabbalistic text states that when the voice of God questions Eve about this event, what she actually says is not, "The serpent beguiled me." Instead, she explains that the serpent has blended his earthly fire with her lost heavenly fire, which has come to life again.

Explore the life that is the life of your present form. One day you will discover It is not different From the life of the Secret One, And your heart will sing triumphant songs Of being at home everywhere.

—THE RADIANCE SUTRAS [10]

AWAKENING KUNDALINI

How then is kundalini awakened? The Eastern texts tell us that it can happen in one of four ways: spontaneously, perhaps as a result of previous practices; through certain hatha yoga postures and breathing exercises;* through concentrated meditation, worship, and prayer; or through the transmission of energy from a guru. Traditional texts say that the most natural and safe means of awakening kundalini is through the transmission of energy

---

*Traditional teachers sometimes warn students that when forceful hatha yoga and pranayama are practiced to activate kundalini, it can create a sudden or partial awakening that can be harmful to the practitioner. For that reason, it's important to do such practices only with an experienced guide.

from a guru whose own kundalini is fully unfolded. This process, called shaktipat in the Shaiva yoga tradition of India, is rare but extremely effective. When the guru activates the energy, a connection is formed between the guru and the student through which the energy is automatically regulated and guided.

When the kundalini is awakened through other means—through practice, or as a spontaneous arising—it is still important to have guidance and advice from qualified teachers. A knowledgeable teacher can help you work with the awakened energy, and can help you understand what the spontaneous movements and experiences actually mean. In most people, the energy works according to the individual's preparedness and needs, yet if the awakening has been strong and the person is unprepared or ignorant about the process, fear and misunderstanding can create problems unless there is proper guidance. Of course, this is particularly true for anyone who is psychologically unstable. While the awakened kundalini can help cure psychological imbalances, it can also exacerbate them. A person who has such an imbalance should continue with their therapeutic regime, taking medication if appropriate, and receiving counseling.

For the average practitioner, however, kundalini is a powerful aid to practice. The awakened energy gives impetus to any practice they might be doing, so that even very simple practices can bring profound insights and openings in their wake. This is especially true when the practitioner understands the nature of the energy. However, it is important for the practitioner to have a practical, experimental attitude and sense of how their own system responds to it.

Below, I offer some tips on how to work with an unfolding kundalini.

Attitudes That Support Kundalini Unfolding

First, understand that kundalini is your own vital energy—not something imposed from outside. Therefore, when it works within you, it is working through your system, and under normal circumstances will process and purify at the rate suited for your constitution and inner preparation.

Second, recognize that kundalini is not just a personal or physical energy. It is our personal portion, as it were, of the divine creative energy of the universe. The more we are able to see this, and to appreciate and respect the cosmic quality in kundalini, the more loving will be our experience of it. In chapter 8, I describe how, when we take a respectful attitude toward kundalini, the energy itself will begin to guide and teach us from within. Everyone needs to develop their own relationship with the energy, and to learn how to distinguish the guidance of the kundalini from the various voices of the egoic mind. Over time, with appropriate feedback and attention, we do begin to recognize how kundalini works within us, and to know how to partner with it.

Third, an important aspect of working with kundalini is diet and exercise. Traditionally, a diet rich in protein, fruits, and vegetables will help nourish the energy. When it is working intensely, sweet cooling fragrances like sandalwood can help settle it. So can vigorous physical exercise. It's important to eat regularly—three light meals a day—when kundalini is working strongly, because the energy can eat up nutrients if not fed. When this happens, we may lose weight, and feel weak or off-kilter. Tonic herbs, either Chinese or Ayurvedic, can help with this, as can remembering to eat more protein. On the other hand, disciplined food intake allows the energy to work dynamically—if you overeat, it will dampen the energy.

Nourished with discipline and understanding, kundalini will spiritualize your life in myriad ways. The ultimate effect of practice with an awakened kundalini is the experience of union: the union of the human consciousness with the vast Consciousness of which it is a part, or as the yogic texts put it, the recognition that there is no separation between ourselves and the whole. In this state, the Self recognizes herself, and we realize our own true identity as limitless Consciousness—while rejoicing in our unique particularity, our own place in the cosmic dance. This is the state called nondual—literally, not-two—in which we can simultaneously experience the diversity of the multiverse and recognize that none of it is different from Awareness itself.

APPENDIX TWO

Troubleshooting Guide

*O*bstacles are important. B. K. S. Iyengar, the hatha yoga master and author of the classic *Light on Yoga*, has written that most of his innovations in therapeutic hatha yoga practice came from working with his own injuries and obstacles. His own obstacles taught him how the body works. Obstacles are our teachers, and meditation is a perfect laboratory for learning from them. Most inner blocks that come up when we meditate are versions of quite familiar obstacles. Fear, frustration, dullness, and distraction plague us not only in meditation but also at work, in love, and in our family lives. This is because much of the time we have learned to override these feelings, to distract ourselves, or in some other way to keep ourselves from confronting them. When we sit on the meditation mat, though, our tendencies and obstructions sit right in front of us, challenging us to look them in the eye and move through them.

Fortunately, there is no block, obstruction, or challenge you can face in meditation that hasn't been faced by the sages. We are deeply fortunate that so many determined men and women have traveled before us on the inner path and left us records of what they did when they came up against the problems that we face. The questions below come from the students in my meditation classes. The answers are based on the advice of my own teachers, as well as on my own experiences in practice.

How can I keep myself from sleeping in meditation?

First of all, make sure you are getting enough sleep at night. If your body is tired, it will use your meditation time to snooze.

Next, you need to determine whether you are really sleeping. There are levels of deep meditation that seem like sleep but are actually yogic states. As we saw in chapter 9, when your meditation enters the causal body, you go into a dark and apparently unconscious state. Here you rest while the energy of meditation clears out your deepest limiting samskaras, or buried impressions. This process is a significant part of the inner journey.

> *Whenever the unsteady mind wanders away, He should bring it back to control in the Self.*
> —BHAGAVAD GITA [1]

However, meditation in the causal body leaves you refreshed and energized. If you come out of meditation feeling groggy and dull, you have probably been snoozing and not meditating.

Sometimes we simply can't help falling asleep. As kundalini becomes active during a meditation session, your mind begins to turn inward. At this point, you will be drawn out of the waking state and into a subtler state—which, depending on the strength of your focus, will be either sleep or meditation. If your inner will isn't trained to stay alert when the force of meditation is very strong, you will fall asleep.

Most of us, when we first begin meditation, are in that situation. We aren't used to surfing the inner world, so we don't know how to stay afloat in it. That is why there is so much emphasis in the meditation texts on learning how to focus the mind.

Focusing, as we have said before, develops a kind of subtle will, so that the mind can hold steady and enter meditation instead of sleep. This subtle will can be developed in different ways. One is to practice keeping your attention focused during those moments in the day when you tend to space out or fantasize. While in the car, on the bus, walking, or washing dishes, notice where your attention is wandering and keep bringing it back to the situation at hand. Keep focusing on your actual tasks—the act of walking or the movement of your hands over the dishes.

Another way to develop strength of focus is to work with a mantra. Keep repeating your mantra even when the energy of meditation is pushing you into sleep. At first, you will feel that you are fighting sleep. After a while, though, you will find that you are able to keep the mantra going even when you are "out." Eventually, it becomes automatic for you to keep a part of yourself alert and focused. Then as the mind turns inside, it will move into samadhi rather than into sleep.

Other Solutions

Certain practices can help you conquer your tendency to fall asleep. Most of those listed below are explained in more detail throughout the book.

- **Sit in a strong posture.** Keep your sitting bones grounded and steady, your spine elongating, your shoulderblades down and back, and your heart lifting upward. Refresh the posture periodically during meditation.

- **Do a few hatha yoga postures before meditating.** Besides helping you become more flexible, hatha yoga shifts the energy in the body so that you become simultaneously calmer and more alert.

- **Ask for grace.** When you invoke grace before meditation, ask, "Please allow me to focus deeply and to remain conscious during my meditation today."

- **Have a strong intention to stay awake.** Make a bargain with yourself: "Today, for just this hour, I'm going to stay conscious." Then keep your focus on the object of meditation very strong and sharp. Try doing each repetition of the mantra as if it were going to be your last thought on earth.

- **Reread chapter 4 and choose a new focal point or doorway to bring you into meditation.**

What does it mean when I feel sick or nauseated during deep meditation?

Unless you have the flu or some other acute physical disorder, nausea during meditation is often a sign that the meditation current is working more strongly than your body can handle right now. Meditation can be a powerful force, and in order to integrate it, we need to have strong, stable bodies. When the body isn't strong enough, it signals us with feelings of weakness, spaciness, and nausea. If your sickness or nausea happens only during meditation and disappears when you get up, this is probably your problem.

The immediate solution here is to reduce your meditation time for a while. This may mean not meditating for a few days or a week, or meditating for only a few minutes at a time, while you build up your strength (read on!).

When we meditate deeply, we tap into our vital energy reserves. In Sanskrit this energy reserve is called *ojas*. According to Ayurveda, the traditional system of Indian medicine, ojas is a subtle fluid located in the bone marrow. Intense activity, especially sexual activity, depletes it. So do irregular eating and sleeping habits, or too much talking, thinking, and worrying. Many modern people have depleted ojas reserves.

The traditional way to replenish ojas is to eat foods that nourish it, especially protein. Protein drinks such as milk or almond milk are helpful here. So is a moderate amount of fruit and natural sweets, like raw honey. Check to see if you are protein-deficient; some vegetarians suffer from ojas deficiency, especially when they have been on an extremely low-protein diet. There are also certain Ayurvedic and Chinese herbal tonics that specifically address ojas deficiency, known in Chinese medicine as *jing* deficiency.

Moderate physical exercise, especially hatha yoga and walking, is good for building up strength.

Sometimes symptoms like nausea or sickness are signs of yogic purification, signs that a latent illness is coming up to be expelled from your system. When this happens, you might feel sick or very hot, or you might feel flulike symptoms for a brief while. If your symptoms are the result of yogic purification, they will be short-lived. They will arise intensely and be gone within a few hours or a day.

Yoga is not eating too much, nor is it absolutely not eating, and not the habit of sleeping too much, and not keeping awake either.

—BHAGAVAD GITA [2]

When I was first meditating, I used to get high fevers from time to time. The fever would rise to 102 or 103 degrees Fahrenheit, last for an afternoon, then drop to normal. No one could ever find anything organically wrong with me. When the fever left, I would feel refreshed and light, as if something had been lifted. That is one of the classic signs that purification has occurred: a feeling of release, of lightness, that follows the episode.

What can I do about the fact that I don't seem able to stay in deep meditation? I will be deep inside when suddenly I shoot back up to an ordinary waking state.

This is quite normal. In the course of an hour, we may go in and out of meditation over and over again. We go deep for some time. Then our consciousness might rise again to the surface, only to turn inward and sink again. A quite advanced meditator once counted the number of times he came out of meditation in the course of a single session, and discovered that it happened nearly ten times.

The secret is to accept the rhythm of your meditation experience and allow it to be what it is. When you feel yourself pop out of meditation, remain sitting in your posture. If you need to shift your legs or stretch, do it slowly and gently. Relax and let yourself experience how it feels to sit in this posture. Be aware of how your body feels. Be aware of the breath. Repeat your mantra, or practice the technique you were using at the beginning of meditation. Gradually you will sink inside again—and often go deeper.

I have been meditating for two years, and I never seem to stop thinking or to get into meditation. What should I do?

Even experienced meditators go through periods when meditation is nothing but hard work. It is like rowing against the current. You field the thoughts and you try to focus, but there is no release into your deeper Self, no experience of your state shifting from "waking consciousness" to "meditation consciousness," no feeling that the shakti is embracing you and bringing you inside. Even though you have heard again and again that a meditator is supposed to let go of expectations, still you wonder, "Why is it like this? What's the matter with me that I don't have any palpable experiences?"

The short answer is, "Nothing." If you were learning tennis, you wouldn't expect to have an effortless serve after three weeks of lessons. You would surrender to practicing your serve for hours, to making bad shots, and to trying again. You would train until the technique became second nature and you began to feel tennis playing you.

Meditation is also a skill. It takes time to develop your inner "muscles" of focus and to learn how to let go into the inner world.

It takes practice to discover how to let yourself move along the pathways of the inner shakti, to stay aware without thinking, and to hold an inner state when it arises.

If you have a hard time getting into meditation, the best solution is to set aside a longer period of time for each meditation session. Each of us has a natural point when thoughts automatically slow down and a meditative state emerges. You just have to be willing to sit long enough for that point to arrive. For most people, that automatic entry point occurs between forty-five minutes and one hour into meditation. If you have a very busy mind, it might take longer. Most people will have their best meditations if they allow an hour to seventy-five minutes for any given session.

Can you coax your mind from its wandering and keep to the original oneness? . . . Can you cleanse your inner vision until you see nothing but the light? . . . Can you step back from your own mind and thus understand all things?

—LAO-TZU [3]

I know a man who complained for years that all he did in meditation was sit and think. To make matters worse, he was married to a woman whose meditation had caught fire immediately and who used to swim ecstatically through realms of light every morning or sit peacefully in the velvety blackness of the void, emerging with a starry and beatific light in her eyes. Her husband felt like a spiritual deadbeat by comparison.

He persisted. Like many other mentally active people, he discovered that sitting for more than an hour worked magic. He began entering a state of soft, blissful energy during meditation. His mind became calmer, and after a while he noticed that meditation was beginning to affect his outer life. The feeling of frustration over his unsatisfied ambitions cooled down, and paradoxically the professional recognition he had been missing began to come to him.

Ten years went by—ten years of daily meditation and steady inner growth. Then one day during a meditation workshop, he had a vision of a temple half-buried in the earth. He saw that the temple had once been completely buried. He realized that this is what his inner work had done. It had cleared away enough of the layers of "dirt" around his inner being so that he could now begin to see it.

This man had a deep interest in meditation, and so he stayed with it. He experimented with different techniques, attitudes, and disciplines. It was his continued steady effort that brought breakthrough for him—and when the breakthrough came, he had earned it. He owned it, so to speak. His inner experiences are his earnings, as well as gifts of grace. So he was able to hold them and to incorporate them into his days.

What can I do to keep the mind from commenting on my meditation? It's driving me crazy.

This is one of the mind's tricks. When your mind realizes that you aren't going to pay attention to its mundane chitchat, it starts commenting on your meditation. "Am I doing this right? Wow, I'm having an experience!" You can treat spiritual chitchat like any other chitchat. In other words, try to avoid getting seduced by the message. Remember that all thoughts are made of Consciousness, of energy, and let them go.

If the comments bring you out of meditative awareness, refocus yourself on the practice you were doing or simply breathe out with the thought "Let go." Let yourself flow back into meditation.

I keep getting to a point where I really feel that I'm going to merge into a sort of inner sky. Then I get terrified and I bring myself back. I'm furious with myself because I feel that I could have made a huge shift, but I was too scared. What can I do about the fear that comes up in meditation?

There is probably no one in the world who, at some point, hasn't fearfully pulled back from what could have been a profound experience. Part of this is inevitable. We all have pockets of fear inside us, and just as we pass through other states in meditation, we also pass through fear. We also tend to become frightened when we don't understand what is happening to us.

An example: Sometimes the breath stops in meditation. If you don't know that this is a profound yogic kriya that can lead into the state of samadhi, you will be afraid that the breath won't come back. In the same way, when your consciousness expands for the first time, you may not realize that you are experiencing the original state of your own Awareness, which actually encompasses all things. Understanding the meaning of a particular experience can sometimes eliminate the fear.

Another reason we become frightened is because the ego—the part of us that identifies "me" as the psychological self—is out of its depth and is trying to bring us back to a state in which it feels comfortable.

Let's look at the relationship of the ego to meditation. The ego performs an important psychic function. Its job is to make sure that we don't forget our identity as an individual being. If we are going to function in the world, remembering our name and where we are supposed to be at ten o'clock, we need the ego to keep reminding us of small details of our personal identity, like "You look good in beige" and "Remember there's milk in that, and you're lactose-intolerant."

Unfortunately, the ego tends to extend its portfolio until it feels as though it is the sole protector of our life. That's one reason why it gets into trouble in meditation. Initially, the ego enjoys spiritual practice. It likes the idea of self-improvement, which of course it defines in its own fashion. The ego wants to get better at its game—faster, smarter, humbler, purer, or whatever our particular ego seeks. It hopes that meditation will help it carry out its agenda.

The problem for the ego occurs when meditation begins dissolving its boundaries. If we were to truly experience God, the ego wouldn't be able to come along. There is no room for the feeling of being a small, limited person in the ocean of Consciousness. And the ego knows that. So whenever our boundaries of body, mind, feelings of doership, and so forth look as though they are losing their grip, whenever it looks as if our identity is about to expand a bit, the ego recognizes that its territory is being threatened and throws up its first line of defense. The fear you experience is actually the ego's terror that you will turn out to be bigger than it, bigger than the carefully delimited territory of memories and opinions and affections and aversions that the ego thinks of as "me."

Rather than being afraid of your fear, you might see it as a signal that you need to take care of and reassure your small self. Then it will have an easier time integrating your expansion experiences. And it will let you move forward.

The first thing to do with the fear is to name it. Sometimes I say to my fear, "Hello, fear. I know you are just my ego talking." This alone might be enough to dispel it. If it isn't, here are some antidotes.

You could remember that whatever is frightening you and the fear itself are all aspects of your own Consciousness. There is nobody in there but you. As you may have noticed, the understanding "All that I experience in meditation is a manifestation of my own Consciousness" solves many meditation difficulties. Why? Because it returns everything to its source. This understanding puts us back in touch with our true Self, which is ever-present and which is the fabric of our whole life, as well as of our meditation. When we are in touch with our truth, we are also in touch with our natural courage.

Another thing you can do is face your fear and become its witness. This is the warrior's method. Here is how it works: You start to move deep inside. You feel fear

> *How could we forget those ancient myths, . . . the myths about dragons that at the last moment are transformed into princesses? Perhaps all the dragons in our lives are princesses who are only waiting to see us act, just once, with beauty and courage. Perhaps everything that frightens us is, in its deepest essence, something helpless that wants our love.*
>
> —RAINER MARIA RILKE [4]

come up. You notice your tendency to move away from the fear—to run before it, so to speak, and to let it chase you right out of meditation. Instead of giving in, you linger on the edge of your fear and look right at the fear. Notice how it feels. Where is it in your body? Do you feel it in your heart? What words is it saying to you? Does it have a color? A shape? Stay close to the fear, but at the edge of it, observing. Notice that as long as you are observing your fear, there is a part of you that is not affected by it. The observer is untouched by the fear. Keep watching the fear, remembering to identify yourself with the observer rather than with the fear.

An alternative to this is to enter your fear and feel its energy. Fear is nothing but an energy. You can actually ride that energy to a deeper state.

A man who did this exercise said: "As I entered the fear, I felt almost overpowered by it. Then I noticed that it wasn't just fear I was feeling. There was also resistance, a feeling of holding back. I stayed with it, letting myself feel those feelings. For a moment, I was just filled with fear energy. Then I sort of dropped deeper into it, and it was just pure, strong energy. A knot of energy. I stayed with the energy, and at a certain point, the hard knot began to soften. Then it expanded, and I could feel a soft pulsation, expanding outward from my heart."

In the *Spanda Karikas,* one of the advanced yogic texts of Kashmir Shaivism, a verse refers to the state of fear as a state filled with potential for high Awareness. It says that the pure experience of the spanda, the pure creative energy of the universe, is particularly present "when one is in the state of terror or running for one's life."[5] Fear is a condition of intense, focused energy. As we enter the energy, it takes us to its source.

Finally, you can take refuge in your guru—in the image of the enlightened being that you most resonate with—or in God. The guru-energy is fully present in your inner universe. When you call out, you will discover how firmly that protective presence can support you. This is one reason why we invoke grace in meditation, so that when we feel scared or out of our depth, we can pray for help and guidance.

Here is a prayer I have used when I have felt my inner process moving too quickly for comfort: "This is too much for me. Please cool my meditation down; make it a little gentler."

Notice the wording. You are not asking for the experience to go away. After all, you don't want these expansion experiences shut down. You just want them to be a bit less intense.

Sometimes we wonder what is really happening when we call out to a guru or to a personal form of spirit. In what sense does the guru hear us? Is it really a personal intervention from the guru that we are asking for? Or is it a kind of trick we play on our unconscious to access our inner source of strength and courage? My experience is that when we call on spirit as a "thou," we are actually accessing the guru-shakti, the protective, grace-bestowing force of the universe that is in us as much as it is in everything else. It is not a personal energy, but neither is it "other." Though it is called forth through our connection to a particular teacher or personal divine form, it is actually an aspect of our own shakti, or awakened kundalini energy.

Something in me just resists sitting to meditate. Even when I do it, as soon as I start to go deep, the resistance becomes so strong it actually pulls me out.

Like fear, resistance is a normal manifestation of the ego. When fear of going deeper doesn't work, the limiting mind comes up with other strategies to keep you under control. It reminds you of all the other things you could be doing. It points out that you never have interesting experiences in meditation. It tells you that one hour is too long and that if you stopped a half-hour earlier, you could make some of the phone calls you need to make. There is nothing arcane about these voices. They are simply signals from your mundane mind. After a while, if you pay attention, you should get to know them well.

Resistance often arises just at the moment when you are about to go deeper. It arises as an impulse, almost a need to retreat back to the familiar and the known. That membrane of resistance, that deep, conservative desire not to go forward, is extremely tenacious and persuasive. It can hurl you right out of meditation. George Gurdjieff, the twentieth-century master, used to say that there are two forces in the universe: one that says "Yes" to spiritual growth, and another that says "No." These two forces play in us continually, and we constantly make choices about which one we'll follow. Resistance is the expression of the "No" force.

Fighting and peacefulness both take place within God.

—RUMI [6]

The best thing to do when resistance arises is to stay put. Just sit. Keep your body on the mat, no matter how much you want to get up, and keep your awareness focused, without judgment or aversion or fear, on the feeling of resistance. You don't have to do anything else. If you can sit with awareness of your resistance, your awareness itself will eventually dissolve it. Then:

- **Ask yourself, "What is behind my resistance to going deeper?"** Write down what comes up. Then ask the question, "Is there anything more?" Keep asking until you feel you have gone as deeply into the question as you can go. Look at the answers you get, then ask yourself, "Is there anything behind this?"

- **Sit quietly and summon the feeling of resistance.** Let yourself be with it for a few minutes. Then ask your resistance, "What do you have to tell me? What are you resisting?" Write down whatever response arises in your mind, no matter how odd or irrelevant it may initially seem to you.

A woman who asked herself this question came up with "People who meditate are weird." Going deeper with it, she came up with "I'm afraid that if I let myself go, I won't be able to function." Going even deeper, it was "Suppose I lose my personality?"

A young man came up with "I need to hold on to my thoughts because they're important." Deeper than that, he found the feeling "I need to be doing something. Meditation is a waste of time compared to the work I have to do."

When you have discovered your specific resistances, then you can address them. You can answer them. You can reassure yourself.

For example, "Rather than making me less able to function, meditation gives me a base to function from." "Look at X, X, and X (insert the names of any great teachers or long-term meditators you've met or read about). They have very strong and definite personalities." An even more powerful answer to the fear of being weird is the stance of global self-acceptance: "It is all right for me to be weird."

Another way of inquiring into your resistance is to speak to the feeling directly as if it were a person, and ask your resistance how to work with it. One young woman summoned the feeling of resistance and asked, "How can I learn to let go of you?" From inside she heard, "Just keep turning back to your mantra. The mantra will dissolve me."

Even if you examine and understand and answer the content of your resistance, you may also need to work on an energetic level (as on page 157) with the feeling of resistance itself—to hold the feeling in Awareness until you feel it dissolving into pure, contentless energy. Nothing is more powerful at dispelling blocks in your consciousness than pure Awareness.

Nothing ever happens in my meditation. What can I do?

I can't tell you how many times I have heard people ask this. Usually, their meditation is much richer than they think. Their problem is that they have concepts about what constitutes a proper "meditation experience," and their actual experience doesn't match their ideas.

This is something that meditators need to contemplate carefully. It may be that the type of meditation experiences normally spoken of in your spiritual tradition actually represent only a part of the spectrum of inner experience. Every path has its own language for describing spiritual experience, and no matter how universal that path may be, most spiritual communities tend to emphasize certain kinds of experience over others. Usually, these are the ones that the teacher encountered on their own journey. The teacher describes these experiences for the benefit of their disciples, to inspire them or to show them some of the landmarks on the path. Ramana Maharshi woke up to the ultimate truth by asking the question "Who am I?" until the I-sense revealed itself to be a fiction—and that is the path that he and his contemporary followers have taught. Buddhists privilege experiences of emptiness, while Christian mystics like Teresa of Avila or meditators on the Indian devotional paths will often describe extraordinary visions and inner "gifts." Yet most great teachers have said that their path and their experience is just that—their personal experience—and that another meditator might have a very different journey.

Still, no matter how many times the teacher reminds us that the inner world is limitless, and that each individual has their own trajectory in meditation, disciples tend to assume that their teacher's descriptions encompass the whole range of "acceptable" spiritual experience. If their own experience is different, they conclude (if they are the self-deprecating type) that they are failing at meditation, or going the wrong route, or (if they are the arrogant type) that their teacher is wrong.

Many people suffer these conclusions because their experience isn't described in the texts of their particular tradition. In her book *How to Grow a Lotus Blossom,* Jiyu-Kennett Roshi described how she experienced doubts about the authenticity of her visions because in her school of Zen, visions are neither admired nor encouraged. When a Catholic contemplative experienced a state of inner emptiness in which her personal self disappeared, her Catholic spiritual director was unfamiliar with the experience and doubted its authenticity. One student of mine was drawn to focus on an inner field of energy with the feeling that God was present in that energy field. The only exact description he could find for this experience was in a Christian mystical text called *The Cloud of Unknowing.* Yet this did not make him a Christian meditator any more than the Catholic meditator was a Buddhist just because her experience was described in Buddhist texts.

*I have a feeling
that my boat
has stuck, down
there in the depths,
against a great thing.
And nothing happens!
Nothing . . .
Silence . . . Waves . . .
—Nothing happens?
Or has everything
happened,
and are we standing
now, quietly, in
the new life?*

—JUAN RAMÓN JIMÉNEZ [7]

The truth is that we have no idea what samskaras we have, what spiritual practices we did in the past that are now bearing fruit, or what country of the inner universe we have entered into. We also have no way of knowing how much inner purification needs to be done before we begin having obvious "experiences." The *Pratyabhijna Hridayam* says that from the point of view of the ultimate Reality, every philosophical position and every type of spiritual experience is simply a stage on the ladder to ultimate oneness.[8] The Splendor, in short, can appear any way it wants to—and does. It often appears in the form of life changes that become apparent only after you have arisen from your meditation cushion.

If you feel that nothing is happening in your meditation, the first thing to do is to examine the quality of that "nothing." Before you write off your meditation as dull and static, investigate your inner state, both during and after meditation. The state of blankness and dullness, or the experience of thoughts lingering, does not necessarily mean that something is wrong. It may simply be an invitation to enter your own inner field and to work with it, as described in chapters 1 and 4. Maybe now it is time to explore your own bare Awareness or to see thoughts as shakti. If you go into the inner emptiness that you think you are experiencing, you may discover that what seems like "nothing" is actually immensely full, pregnant with Awareness and creativity.

Think of the empty space enclosed by a jar. When the jar is broken into pieces, the jar alone breaks, not the space. Life is like the jar. All forms are like the jar. They constantly break into pieces. When gone, they are unaware. Yet He is aware, eternally.

—BRAHMABINDU
UPANISHAD[9]

Here is another clue to look for in evaluating subtle meditation. Pay attention to the perceptual shifts that come when you get up after meditation. Even if you never stopped thinking during your time of practice, you might notice when you get up that you feel lighter, as if something has been lifted. Perhaps your mind, which might

Exercise: Investigating Nothingness

Close your eyes. Focus on the empty "space" that appears in front of your eyes. Look at the emptiness, the field in front of you. How does it look? Perhaps you see a field of gray shot with little streaks or points of light. Perhaps it is black. Perhaps it is blue with streaks of gold.

This field is the field of your consciousness. It is the background consciousness within which all your experience rises and falls. Let yourself be with it. If thoughts come up, allow the thoughts to be there within the field of your own consciousness. Keep your awareness focused on the space itself, on the inner "nothingness" that you see when you close your eyes.

When you are ready, have the feeling that you are moving through this inner field of nothingness. It is not your body, of course, that moves through it, but you as attention, as Awareness. Allow your awareness to float, swim, or sail through the field of emptiness. Notice what you encounter. Notice the different energy fields that rise and fall within your field of consciousness. Explore your consciousness—all the while understanding that this emptiness, this space within you, is Consciousness itself. This very field of emptiness is the Self, the ultimate reality. In time it will reveal itself to you.

have seemed so busy when your eyes were closed, is noticeably clearer. Maybe you feel calm and happy. Maybe something you were worried about has been resolved.

Perhaps your vision has shifted and enlarged, so that you can see the world with deeper, more wonder-filled eyes. Maybe your dreams are becoming more lucid—or perhaps the glimpses of deeper states, the heightened awareness, and the numinous feelings and visions that you seek in meditation are happening in your dreams. Many meditators have such dreams. Often we can recognize them by their light and their colors, by the fact that they are pervaded by a numinous brightness that is clearly a glimpse of another world. These, too, are meditation experiences—it is just that they are coming in the dream state.

When you meditate sincerely, it will always create shifts in your life. It will always, ultimately, transform you.

NOTES

INTRODUCTION: AWAKENING TO MEDITATION

1 "In meditation, the Self . . ." *Bhagavad Gita* 13.25.

2 "The spirit is so near . . ." Robert Bly, ed., *When Grapes Turn to Wine: Versions of Rumi* (Cambridge, MA: Yellow Moon Press, 1986).

CHAPTER ONE: THE LURE OF MEDITATION

1 "The true practice . . ." Shunryu Suzuki, *Zen Mind, Beginner's Mind* (New York: Weatherhill, 1970).

2 "Set fire to the Self . . ." *Shvetashvatara Upanishad.*

3 "The Infinite Goodness . . ." Frank Mead, ed., *12,000 Religious Quotations* (Grand Rapids, MI: Baker, 1989).

4 "There is a secret . . ." Robert Bly, ed., *The Kabir Book: Forty-Four of the Ecstatic Poems of Kabir* (Boston: Beacon Press, 1977).

5 "Use your own light . . ." Stephen Mitchell, ed., *Tao Te Ching: A New English Version* (New York: HarperCollins, 1988), verse 52.

6 "The world of qualities . . ." Bly, ed., *The Kabir Book.*

CHAPTER TWO: HOW DO WE EXPERIENCE THE INNER SELF?

1 "The one you are looking for . . ." Attributed to Francis of Assisi.

2 "Knowing the Self . . ." David Godman, ed., *Be As You Are: The Teachings of Sri Ramana Maharshi* (London: Penguin, 1985).

3 "The eye through which . . ." Stephen Mitchell, ed., *The Enlightened Mind: An Anthology of Sacred Prose* (New York: HarperCollins, 1991).

4 "Be as you are . . ." Godman, ed., *Be As You Are,* 69.

5 "Even when a person . . ." *Vijnana Bhairava,* 131.

6 "Who is it . . ." Swami Muktananda, *The Self Is Already Attained* (South Fallsburg, NY: SYDA Foundation, 1993).

7 "The naked, stark, elemental awareness . . ." William Johnston, ed., *The Cloud of Unknowing and The Book of Privy Counseling* (New York: Doubleday, 1973).

8 "No words are necessary . . ." Coleman Barks, trans., *Feeling the Shoulder of the Lion: Poetry and Teaching Stories of Rumi* (Putney, VT: Threshold Books, 1991).

9 "There is something . . ." *Kena Upanishad* 1.6.

10 "No, my soul is . . ." Robert Bly, ed., *The Soul Is Here for Its Own Joy: Sacred Poems from Many Cultures* (Hopewell, NJ: Ecco Press, 1995).

11 "That which cannot . . ." *Kena Upanishad* 1.5–6.

12 "All things are born . . ." Swami Prabhavananda, adapted from *The Upanishads: Breath of the Eternal* (Hollywood, CA: Vedanta Press, 1975): *Tattiriya Upanishad* 3.6.1.

13 "Who could live . . ." Ibid., 2.7.1.

14 "It is my nature . . ." Fiona Bowie, ed., and Oliver Davies, trans., *Beguine Spirituality: Mystical Writings of Mechthild of Magdeburg, Beatrice of Nazareth, and Hadewijch of Brabant* (New York: Crossroad Publishing, 1990).

15 "He who goes . . ." Douglas Bloch, ed., *I Am With You Always: A Treasury of Inspirational Quotations, Poems, and Prayers* (New York: Bantam, 1992).

16 "The Self reveals itself . . ." *Katha Upanishad* 1.2.23.

CHAPTER THREE: PREPARING FOR PRACTICE

1 "There is an unseen presence . . ." Coleman Barks, trans., *The Essential Rumi* (New York: HarperCollins, 1995).

2 "The Friend has such . . ." Daniel Ladinsky, trans., *The Subject Tonight Is Love: Sixty Wild and Sweet Poems of Hafiz* (North Myrtle Beach, SC: Pumpkin House Press, 1996).

3 "O grace of the Guru . . ." Attributed to Jnaneshwar Maharaj.

4 "Unless taught by a teacher . . ." *Katha Upanishad* 1.2.8–9.

5 "Think this over . . ." Quoted in Swami Muktananda, *The Perfect Relationship: The Guru and the Disciple* (South Fallsburg: NY: SYDA Foundation, 1999), 71.

6 "Affix to the bow . . ." Swami Prabhavananda, adapted from *The Upanishads: Breath of the Eternal* (Hollywood, CA: Vedanta Press, 1975).

7   "The guru is not different . . ." *Nectar of Chanting* (South Fallsburg, NY: SYDA Foundation, 1983): *Guru Gita* 9.

8   "I am the same Self . . ." *Bhagavad Gita* 9.29.

9   "From the blossoming . . ." Sogyal Rinpoche, *The Tibetan Book of Living and Dying* (New York: HarperCollins, 1992).

10 "Give up to grace . . ." Barks, trans., *The Essential Rumi.*

CHAPTER FOUR: CHOOSING THE RIGHT DOORWAY

1   "The mind is truly fickle . . ." Attributed to Jnaneshwar Maharaj.

2   "Concentrate wherever . . ." *Yoga Sutras* 1.39.

3   "This alone is obligatory . . ." *Malini Vijaya Tantra.*

4   "A yogi . . ." *Shiva Sutras* 3.16.

5   "God is at the midpoint . . ." Attributed to Julian of Norwich.

6   "When a man meditates . . ." Attributed to Baal Shem Tov.

7   "God is in your bhava . . ." Attributed to Tukaram Maharaj.

8   "The Word . . ." T. S. Eliot, "Ash Wednesday," *The Waste Land* (New York: Harcourt Brace, 1958).

9   "The one truth . . ." M. P. Pandit, *Kularnava Tantra* (Pondicherry: All India Press, 1973).

10 "According to the . . ." *Shiva Sutras* 2.3.

11 "During worship . . ." Swami Muktananda, *Lalleshwari* (Ganeshpuri, India: SYDA Foundation, 1981), verse 117.

12 "If you want the truth . . ." Bly, ed., *The Kabir Book.*

13 "Mantra is our real nature . . ." Godman, ed., *Be As You Are.*

14 "Try to gain one moment . . ." Mitchell, ed., *The Enlightened Mind.*

15 "The Kashmiri sage . . ." *Pratyabhijna Hridayam* 17.

16 "God is at the midpoint . . ." Attributed to Julian of Norwich.

17 "At the still point . . ." T. S. Eliot, "Burnt Norton," *Four Quartets* (New York: Harcourt Brace, 1971).

18 "Fleeting samadhis . . ." *Tripura Rahasya* 17.2–3.

19 "The Props assist . . ." Thomas H. Johnson, ed., *Final Harvest: Emily Dickinson's Poems* (Boston: Little, Brown, 1961).

20   "Thinking of the magnitude . . ." Garma C. C. Chang, trans., *The Hundred Thousand Songs of Milarepa,* Vol. 1 (Boston: Shambhala, 1962).

21   "The one that follows . . ." *Vijnana Bhairava* 46–47.

22   "The mind, turned outwards . . ." Godman, ed., *Be As You Are.*

CHAPTER FIVE: MOVING INWARD: THE PRACTICE OF ONENESS

1   "The knowledge . . ." Adapted from Swami Jagadananda, *Upadeshasahasri: A Thousand Teachings* (Mylapore, Madras: Sri Ramakrishna Math, 1949), verse 2.4.5.

2   "Take a pitcher . . ." Bly, ed., *The Kabir Book.*

3   "Can you coax . . ." Mitchell, ed., *Tao Te Ching.*

4   "You who want knowledge . . ." Bowie, ed., *Beguine Spirituality.*

5   "Whether through immense joy . . ." Constantina Rhodes Bailly, trans., *Meditations on Shiva: The Shivastotravalai of Utpaladeva* (Albany: State University of New York Press, 1995), stotra 5.

6   "When, with a . . ." *Vijnana Bhairava* 63, quoted in Swami Muktananda, *Secret of the Siddhas* (South Fallsburg, NY: SYDA Foundation, 1994), 198.

CHAPTER SIX: WORKING WITH THE MIND, PART 1— NAVIGATING THE THOUGHT-STREAM

1   "The Mind . . ." Daniel Ladinsky, trans., *The Gift: Poems by Hafiz* (New York: Penguin Putnam, 1999).

2   "The second part . . ." *Yoga Sutras* 1.12.

3   "Our desires . . ." Hari Prasad Shastri, *World within the Mind (Yoga Vasishtha)* (London: Shanti Sadan, 1975).

4   "In this nakedness . . ." Kieran Kavanaugh, ed., *John of the Cross: Selected Writings* (Mahway, NJ: Paulist Press, 1987).

5   "Pure Consciousness . . ." Godman, ed., *Be As You Are.*

CHAPTER SEVEN: WORKING WITH THE MIND, PART 2— LIBERATING YOUR THOUGHTS

1   "You lose sight . . ." Trevor P. Leggett, trans., *A First Zen Reader* (Boston: Tuttle, 1991).

2   "The Essence of Mind . . ." Chang, trans., *The Hundred Thousand Songs of Milarepa.*

3   "O wavering mind . . ." Lex Hixon, *Mother of the Universe: Visions of the Goddess and Tantric Hymns of Enlightenment* (Wheaton, IL: Quest Books, 1994).

4   "One deluded thought . . ." Timothy Freke, *Zen Wisdom: Daily Teachings from the Zen Masters* (New York: Sterling, 1997).

5   "Wherever the mind goes . . ." *Vijnana Bhairava* 116.

6   "When you are . . ." *Spanda Karikas* 1.22.

7   "Your own mind . . ." Mitchell, ed., *The Enlightened Mind.*

CHAPTER EIGHT: LETTING THE SHAKTI LEAD

1   "Although kundalini . . ." Adapted from Arthur Avalon (Sir John Woodroffe), *The Serpent Power* (New York: Dover, 1974).

2   "I have realized . . ." Hixon, *Mother of the Universe.*

3   "The most exalted . . ." Ibid.

4   "Often when I step . . ." Grace Turnbull, ed., *The Essence of Plotinus* (New York: Oxford University Press, 1934).

5   "You are no longer . . ." Hixon, *Mother of the Universe.*

6   "Please show me . . ." Attributed to Ramakrishna Paramahamsa.

7   "Holy Spirit . . ." Stephen Mitchell, ed., *The Enlightened Heart: An Anthology of Sacred Poetry* (New York: HarperCollins, 1989).

8   "Trust the divine . . ." Aurobindo Ghose, *The Mother* (Twin Lakes, WI: Lotus Press, 1998).

9   "Emerging into . . ." Hixon, *Mother of the Universe.*

CHAPTER NINE: WHERE DO YOU FIND YOURSELF? A ROAD MAP OF THE MEDITATION JOURNEY

1   "Be strong . . ." Bly, ed., *The Kabir Book.*

2   "In this body . . ." *Shiva Samhita.*

3   "The unpracticed one . . ." *Yogashikha Upanishad* 1.26–30.

4   "According to the . . ." *Brihadaranyaka Upanishad* 4.4.3–6.

5   "Student, tell me . . ." Bly, ed., *The Kabir Book.*

6   "Light devoured darkness . . ." A. K. Ramanujan, *Speaking of Siva* (London: Penguin, 1973).

7   "During the period . . ." *Shvetashvatara Upanishad* 2.11.

8   "Our Lord opened . . ." Grace Warrack, ed., *Revelations of Divine Love: Recorded by Julian, Anchoress at Norwich* (London: Methuen, 1952).

9   "Last night . . ." Bly, *The Soul Is Here for Its Own Joy*.

10 "In that moment . . ." Attributed to Tevekkul-Beg.

11 "The soul is not . . ." Turnbull, ed., *The Essence of Plotinus*.

12 "Darkness within darkness . . ." Mitchell, ed., *Tao Te Ching*, verse 1.

13 "Everything depends . . ." Evelyn Underhill, ed., *The Adornment of Spiritual Marriage* (London: John M. Watkins, 1951).

14 "Gaze intently . . ." Hixon, *Mother of the Universe*.

15 "Eye cannot see it . . ." Mitchell, ed., *The Enlightened Heart*.

16 "Nirvipalka is chit . . ." Godman, ed., *Be As You Are*.

17 "The divine flashes forth" *Shiva Sutras* 1.5.

18 "Again the light . . ." Attributed to Simeon, the New Theologian.

19 "My mind melted . . ." *Viveka Chudamani* 482.

20 "The light . . ." E. Allison Peers, trans., *The Life of Teresa of Jesus: The Autobiography of Teresa of Avila* (New York: Doubleday, 1991).

21 "God alone reveals . . ." Attributed to Meister Eckhart.

22 "My I is God . . ." Catherine of Genoa, *Life and Doctrine of Saint Catherine of Genoa* (Christian Classics Ethereal Library: ccel.org/ccel/ catherine_g/life.toc.html).

23 "I do not know . . ." Ibid.

24 "For a while . . ." Jnaneshwar Maharaj, *The Nectar of Self-Awareness* (South Fallsburg, NY: SYDA Foundation, 1979), verse 7.174–75.

25 "He who without hesitation . . ." Bailly, trans., *Meditations on Shiva*, stotra 13.

26 "Ever immersed . . ." Rabindranath Tagore, *Songs of Kabir: Mystical and Devotional Poetry* (York Beach, ME: Samuel Weiser, 1991).

27 "It is told . . ." Attributed to Martin Buber.

CHAPTER TEN: COMING OUT OF MEDITATION—
CONTEMPLATION, RECOLLECTION, AND
JOURNAL WRITING

1 "A person looks . . ." Jane Hirschfield, ed., *Women in Praise of the Sacred: 43 Centuries of Spiritual Poetry by Women* (New York: HarperCollins, 1994).

2 "A great yogin . . ." Commentary on *Pratyabhijna Hridayam* 19.

3 "Be—and yet know . . ." Stephen Mitchell, ed. and trans., *The Selected Poetry of Raine Maria Rilke.*

4 "The beloved heart . . ." Godman, ed., *Be As You Are.*

5 "Learn to listen . . ." Mitchell, ed., *The Enlightened Mind.*

CHAPTER ELEVEN: THE DAILY LIFE OF A MEDITATOR—
HOLDING INNER ATTENTION

1 "While yet you live . . ." Leggett, trans., *A First Zen Reader.*

2 "The true man of God . . ." Mitchell, ed., *The Enlightened Mind.*

3 "To attend . . ." Rabbi Rami M. Shapiro, *Wisdom of the Jewish Sages: A Modern Reading of Pirke Avot* (New York: Bell Tower, 1993).

4 "The more awareness . . ." Coleman Barks, trans., *Rumi: One-Handed Basket Weaving: Poems on the Theme of Work* (Athens, GA: Maypop Books, 1991).

5 "If you don't realize . . ." Mitchell, ed., *Tao Te Ching,* verse 16.

6 "Similarly, a man . . ." *Yoga Sutras* 2.33.

7 "You have a right . . ." *Bhagavad Gita* 2.47.

8 "The mountain . . ." Leggett, trans., *A First Zen Reader.*

CHAPTER TWELVE: THE THREE-WEEK BREAK-
THROUGH PROGRAM

1 "The pearl . . ." Hari Prasad Shastri, trans., *Indian Mystic Verse* (London: Shanti Sadan, 1984).

2 "We must, then . . ." Kiernan Kavanaugh and Otilio Rodriguez, trans., *The Collected Works of St. Teresa of Avila,* Vol. 2 (Washington, DC: ICS Publications, 1980).

3 "For one who is moderate . . ." *Bhagavad Gita* 6.17.

4 "All this talk . . ." Mitchell, ed., *The Enlightened Mind.*

5   "God must act . . ." Ibid.

6   "God is much closer . . ." Warrack, ed., *Revelations of Divine Love.*

7   "Indeed, it is the Infinite . . ." Adapted from Swami Venkatesananda, *Vasishtha's Yoga* (Albany: State University of New York Press, 1993).

8   "When you let yourself . . ." Gurumayi Chidvilasananda, *Courage and Contentment: A Collection of Talks on Spiritual Life* (South Fallsburg, NY: SYDA Foundation, 1999), 117.

9   "What is the body . . ." Barks, trans., *The Essential Rumi.*

CHAPTER THIRTEEN: THE PROCESS OF RIPENING

1   "Do you remember . . ." Rainer Maria Rilke, *Letters to a Young Poet,* translated by Stephen Mitchell (New York: Vintage, 1986).

2   "In this practice . . ." *Bhagavad Gita* 2.40.

3   "I Salute the Self! . . ." Swami Venkatesananda, *Concise Yoga Vasishtha* (Albany: State University of New York Press, 1984).

APPENDIX ONE: KUNDALINI

1   "Your life alone . . ." Hixon, ed., *Mother of the Universe.*

2   "The kundalini is shakti . . ." Jean Varenne, *Yoga and the Hindu Tradition,* translated by Derek Coltman (Chicago: University of Chicago Press, 1976).

3   "Hindu Tantras . . ." Tantra (literally, "weaving") is a yogic tradition that was first written down in the early Middle Ages; it is notable for dealing extensively with shakti and kundalini. Though in the West, tantricism has been associated with sex, it is in fact a broad-based and highly diverse tradition of practical yoga, which deals with the internal transmutation of energy and includes some of the loftiest philosophical texts in the Hindu tradition, including Kashmir Shaivism.

4   "Without knowledge . . ." Quoted in Sir John Woodroffe, *Principles of Tantra* (Madras: Ganesh and Company, 1986).

5   "Supremely independent Chiti . . ." Adapted from Jaideva Singh, trans., *Pratyabhijna Hridayam* (Delhi: Motilal Banarsidass, 1977), sutras 1–2.

6   "In every human being . . ." Elaine Pagels, *The Gnostic Gospels* (New York: Random House, 1979).

7   "The !Kung bushmen . . ." John Marshall, *N/um Tchai: The Ceremonial Dance of the !Kung Bushmen* (Somerville, MA: Documentary Educational Resources, Inc., 1957).

8   "The Hopi . . ." Frank Waters, *The Book of the Hopi* (New York: Penguin, 1977).

9   "Carlos Suarès, in . . ." Carlos Suarès, *The Cipher of Genesis: The Original Code of the Qabala as Applied to the Scriptures* (Boston: Shambhala, 1981).

10 "Explore the life . . ." Lorin Roche, *The Radiance Sutras: A New Version of the Vijnana Bhairava Tantra* (Marina del Ray, CA: Syzygy Creations, 2008), 77.

APPENDIX TWO: TROUBLESHOOTING GUIDE

1   "Whenever the unsteady mind . . ." *Bhagavad Gita* 6.26.

2   "Yoga is not . . ." Ibid., 6.16.

3   "Can you coax . . ." Mitchell, *Tao Te Ching*, verse 10.

4   "How could we forget . . ." Rilke, *Letters to a Young Poet.*

5   "When one is in the state . . ." *Spanda Karikas* 22.

6   "Fighting and peacefulness . . ." Barks, trans., *The Essential Rumi.*

7   "I have a feeling . . ." Bly, ed., *The Soul Is Here for Its Own Joy.*

8   "The *Pratyabhijna Hridayam* says . . ." *Pratyabhijna Hridayam* 8.

9   "Think of the empty space . . ." William K. Mahony, *The Artful Universe: An Introduction to the Vedic Religious Imagination* (Albany: State University of New York Press, 1998): *Brahmabindu Upanishad* 13–14.

GLOSSARY

Abhinavagupta *(c. 975–1025 CE)* An important Kashmir sage and guru, whose Sanskrit texts, *Tantraloka* and *Tantrasara,* are considered the authoritative works on the Shaiva and Shakta tantras. His treatise on aesthetics is a basic text on Indian dramatic theory.

Ajna Chakra A spiritual center located in the center of the head, sometimes known as the third eye.

Amrita Anubhava (lit., Nectar of Self-Awareness) A poetic text in which the thirteenth-century saint-poet Jnaneshwar Maharaj describes his experience of nondual reality.

Arjuna A hero of the Indian epic, the *Mahabharata.* The *Bhagavad Gita* is a dialogue between Arjuna and his friend and guru, Krishna.

Asana *(lit., seat)* A posture used to strengthen and purify the body and acquire stability in meditation.

Ashram A monastery or spiritual retreat center.

Atman The true Self, pure awareness without an object, residing as the inner core of all living beings.

Avadhuta Gita A Sanskrit text of nondual Vedanta, describing the state of total freedom.

Bhagavad Gita (lit., Song of God) An essential text of Indian religion and a key work of yoga and spiritual practice. It contains the instructions on yoga and life offered to Arjuna by his guru, Krishna.

Bhava *(lit., becoming; being)* An attitude or emotional state in which one becomes fully absorbed or identified. Often used in spiritual life as a way to reorient one's consciousness toward a state of enlightenment or devotion.

Bindu A point; a point of light sometimes seen in higher stages of meditation. In tantric metaphysics, the bindu is considered to contain the concentrated power of the Absolute reality.

Brahman A member of the priestly caste in Hinduism.

Brihadaranyaka Upanishad One of the ten major Upanishads, significant philosophical texts of India. It contains teachings on the universal Self, and explores the Indian teachings on the after-death experience.

Chakra *(lit., wheel)* An energy center, lying within the subtle body. According to the tantric map of the subtle body, there are seven major chakras as well as a number of minor ones. The major chakras form plexuses of nerve currents in the body, and are sometimes said to be related to the endocrine system. *See* ajna chakra, kundalini, nadi, sushumna nadi

Chit; chiti *(lit., supreme consciousness)* The creative power of the universal Consciousness, embodying the absolute freedom of knowledge, action, and will.

Chitta 1. Mind-stuff—the energy within which thoughts manifest. 2. Human consciousness, with its capacities for cognition, sensation, and volition.

Consciousness 1. The all-knowing, blissful transcendent and immanent absolute awareness, described in Vedanta and Kashmir Shaiva philosophy as the divine source and ground of all. 2. The human capacity for awareness, a limited form of the absolute consciousness, which in meditation can be experienced as the absolute consciousness itself.

Dharana 1. Meditative focus, or concentration. 2. A practice for centering the mind and expanding consciousness.

Eckhart, Meister (Johannes) *(c. 1260–1327)* A Dominican friar and great nondual mystic.

Ego In yoga, the individual's I-sense that identifies with the body, mind, and senses.

Eknath Maharaj *(1528–1609)* An important saint of western India, author of many devotional poems and songs.

Guru *(lit., heavy)* A spiritual master able to initiate and guide students into the highest states of awareness.

Guru Gita A sacred Sanskrit song describing the mystical relationship between a guru and disciple.

Hatha Yoga Disciplines for purifying and strengthening the body, arousing kundalini, and stabilizing the prana.

Hildegard of Bingen *(1098–1179)* Benedictine abbess and mystic, she was an artist and composer as well as a poet.

Jnaneshwar Maharaj *(1275–1296)* A child yogi, nondual realizer, and mystical poet. His commentary on the *Bhagavad Gita, Jnaneshwari,* written in the Marathi language, is considered one of the most important commentaries on that text.

Kabir *(1440–1518)* An enlightened mystic and poet, whose songs are still sung throughout India. He was a weaver whose teachings brought together Muslims and Hindus.

Kashmir Shaivism A monistic and nondual philosophical system originating in the vale of Kashmir. Also known as the Trika system, because it purports to explain the nature of the divine, the world, and the individual, Kashmir Shaivism describes reality as a display of God's energy, and teaches that the divine exists in every particle of the universe.

Krishna The playful hero-god of Hindu mythology, considered to be an incarnation of Vishnu, the sustaining energy of the universe. His spiritual teachings are contained in the *Shrimad Bhagavat Purana* and the *Bhagavad Gita.*

Kriya *(lit., action or activity)* 1. The power of action, described in the tantras as intrinsic both to the Absolute and to human consciousness. 2. A subtle or physical manifestation of awakened kundalini, through which kundalini purifies and strengthens the human organism.

Kshemaraja *(10th century CE)* A disciple of Abhinavagupta and prolific author of many texts, including the *Pratyabhijna Hridayam.*

Kumbhaka Retention of breath, a yogic practice that stabilizes the mind and is a precursor to samadhi.

Kundalini *(lit., coiled one)* A form of the universal energy, existing in the human body for the purpose of evolving human consciousness so that it can recognize its oneness with the supreme Consciousness. (See appendix 1 for details.)

Maharashtra *(lit., great country)* A state in western India.

Malini Vijaya Tantra A key text of north Indian tantra.

Mantra *(lit., mind-tool)* A sacred word or syllable, used as a means of focusing the mind, communing with higher powers, accessing devotional states, and acquiring powers of various kinds.

Maya The power that divides the One into many, and veils reality so that consciousness experiences separation and multiplicity.

Mudra *(lit., seal)* 1. A gesture that both expresses and invokes an inner state of awareness. 2. A gesture that seals energy within the body for meditative purposes.

Nada *(lit., sound)* 1. Inner sounds that can be heard in meditation. 2. Primordial vibration, said to be the vibration that gives rise to the universe.

Nadi *(lit., channel or nerve)* An extremely subtle channel in the energy system of a human being, through which life force flows. A network of nadis flows through the subtle body, but three are considered significant in yoga. These are the ida and pingala, which regulate the flow of breath, and the sushumna, or central nadi, which, as the pathway of the awakened kundalini, unfolds higher states of consciousness.

Nanak, Guru *(1469–1539)* Original Sikh guru and founder of the Sikh religion; an enlightened teacher who spread liberal religious ideas in India.

Nityananda *(d. 1961)* A powerful and eccentric yogi and guru of western India, considered a siddha, or fully enlightened master.

Om The primordial sound form, the vibratory essence from which the universe emanates, according to Indian philosophy.

Patanjali *(2nd century BCE)* Sage and author of the *Yoga Sutras,* a Sanskrit text that is considered the authoritative treatise on *raja yoga,* the path to enlightenment through meditation.

Prana The vital force within the human body and the universe.

Pratyabhijna Hridayam (lit., the heart of the doctrine of recognition) A short text, written in the eleventh century, that gives a condensed explication of the teachings of the Self-Recognition School of Kashmir Shaivism. It describes how the universal consciousness manifests as the world, and the path through which a human being can recognize their own awareness as identical with the supreme Awareness.

Ramakrishna Paramahamsa *(1836–1886)* A revered saint and guru of Bengal, whose inspiration helped to revolutionize modern Hinduism through his disciples Swami Vivekananda and others.

Ramana Maharshi *(1879–1950)* A highly influential enlightened master, and leading modern exponent of the path of Advaita (nondual) Vedantic Self-inquiry.

Rumi, Jalalludin *(1207–1273)* Important Sufi guru and founder of the Mevlavi order of dervishes. His ecstatic wisdom poetry is among the most popular poetry in the world today.

Sadhaka An aspirant on the spiritual path.

Sadhana A spiritual discipline, practice, or path.

Sahaja Samadhi *(lit., natural state of union)* The ultimate state of oneness with the Absolute, considered the culminating stage of realization in many mystical traditions of India. It is called "natural" because in it one's absorption in the Absolute remains unbroken and requires no special practice.

Samadhi Meditative state of complete absorption.

Samskara Latent impression of past actions and thoughts remaining in the unconscious as well as in the physical and energy bodies.

Self The atman, or consciousness-without-an-object of a human being. It is often described as the pure I-awareness, or as the witness of the mind.

Shaivism *See* Kashmir Shaivism.

Shakti *(lit., power)* 1. The divine feminine. 2. Dynamic aspect of the supreme reality, the cosmic energy that manifests as the universe and carries out all its functions.

Shaktipat *(lit., descent of power)* A cosmic process that awakens the capacity for spiritual evolution in a human being.

Shankaracharya; Shankara *(788–820)* Celebrated Indian philosopher and sage, who expounded the philosophy of Advaita Vedanta, and founded an order of renunciant *(sannyasi)* monks that continues in India as the Dasnami Order of Sannyasa.

Shiva *(lit., that which underlies)* 1. A name for the absolute reality, or supreme Consciousness. 2. One of the Hindu trinity of deities, representing God as the destroyer. 3. The original yogi and guru of the Indian yogic tradition. In this role, he is the destroyer of the illusion of multiplicity and separation. He is considered the source of many of the texts of yoga and tantra.

Shiva Sutra A Sanskrit text consisting of seventy-seven aphorisms, which describes the nature of reality from the point of view of a fully enlightened yogi, and reveals a path to realization. Said to have been revealed to the sage Vasugupta by Shiva himself, this is one of the authoritative texts of the Kashmir Shaiva tradition.

Siddha *(lit., accomplished)* An enlightened yogi or fully Self-realized master possessing powers that allow them to transmit their own state to others.

Spanda *(lit., throb or pulsation)* The primordial vibration at the root of all manifestation; a form of shakti.

Spanda Karikas A ninth-century work consisting of forty-five verses that describes the universe as the play of spanda, divine vibration, and offers a set of radical practices for attaining Self-realization.

Sushumna Nadi Central energy-channel that extends from the base of the spine to the crown of the head. When the mind and breath are merged in the sushumna nadi, internal states of samadhi arise naturally.

Sutra *(lit., thread)* An aphoristic phrase that carries a philosophical teaching in a brief, nuggetlike form.

Tantra *(lit., weaving)* 1. A series of esoteric practices in which one harnesses the life force for the purpose of Self-realization. 2. One of a number of texts that unfolds these practices and the philosophy behind them.

Tukaram Maharaj *(1608–1650)* A saint of western India, singer of devotional songs celebrating his path and his evolving relationship with the divine.

Turiya *(lit., the fourth)* The transcendental state of awareness, beyond the waking, dream, and deep sleep states. In turiya, one directly perceives pure consciousness as one's own Self. The turiya state runs through all other states.

Upanishads *(lit., sitting near)* The teachings of forest sages of India, which teach the oneness of the individual soul and the divine soul. The fundamental teachings of the Upanishads are carried in such statements as "Thou art that" and "I am Brahman."

Vairagya Dispassion.

Vedanta *(lit., end of the Vedas)* One of the great world traditions of nonduality, Vedanta teaches the oneness of the soul with the Absolute. The core of the Vedantic teachings maintains that consciousness is the true reality, and that the manifest world is an illusion superimposed on consciousness.

Vedas The foundational texts of Indian spirituality, regarded as the basis of all Indian philosophy. The *Rg Veda, Atharva Veda, Sama Veda,* and *Yajur Veda* are collections of hymns, ceremonies, and teachings about the nature of the divine and the ways that human beings can relate to a divine source.

Vijnana Bhairava A foundational text of tantra, consisting of 112 centering practices for accessing divine consciousness.

Yoga *(lit., yoke or union)* Spiritual disciplines leading to oneness with the Self. There are a number of yogic paths, including hatha yoga, bhakti yoga, karma yoga, raja yoga, which develop and balance different aspects of the human being, with the object being the union with the Absolute as an inner experience.

SOME FURTHER READING

On Practice and Yoga

The Bhagavad Gita
Translated by Winthrop Sargeant

The Concise Yoga Vasistha
Swami Venkateshananda

How to Know God: The Yoga Aphorisms of Patanjali
Swami Prabhavananda and Christopher Isherwood

I Am That: Talks with Sri Nisargadatta Maharaj
Nisargadatta Maharaj

Jnaneshwar's Gita: A Rendering of the Jnaneshwari
Swami Kripananda

My Lord Loves a Pure Heart: The Yoga of Divine Virtues
Swami Chidvilasananda

Paths to God: Living the Bhagavad Gita
Ram Dass

Poised for Grace: Annotations on the Bhagavad Gita from a Tantric View
Douglas Brooks

The Upanishads: Breath of the Eternal
Translated by Swami Prabhavananda and Frederick Manchester

The Wisdom of Yoga: A Seeker's Guide to Extraordinary Living
Stephen Cope

The Yoga of Discipline
Swami Chidvilasananda

Yoga Philosophy of Patanjali
Swami Hariharananda Aranya

The Yoga-Sutra of Patanjali
Chip Hartranft

The Yoga Tradition: Its History, Literature, Philosophy, and Practice
Georg Feuerstein

On Kashmir Shaivism

Primary Texts

The Doctrine of Recognition: A Translation of Pratyabhijnahrydayam
Kshemeraja, translated by Jaideva Singh

The Radiance Sutras: A New Version of the Bhairava Tantra
Lorin Roche

Shiva Sutras: The Yoga of Supreme Identity
Commentary by Kshemeraja, translated by Jaideva Singh

The Stanzas on Vibration
Translated by Mark S. G. Dyczkowski

Vijnana Bhairava, or Divine Consciousness
Translated by Jaideva Singh

Vijnana Bhairava: The Practice of Centering Awareness
Commentary by Swami Lakshman Joo

The Yoga of Vibration and Divine Pulsation: A Translation of the Spanda Karikas, with Kshemaraja's commentary, the *Spanda Nirnaya,*
Translated by Jaideva Singh

Contemporary Scholarly and Interpretive Sources

Consciousness Is Everything
Swami Shankarananda

The Doctrine of Vibration: An Analysis of the Doctrines and Practices of Kashmir Shaivism
Mark S. G. Dyczkowski

Nothing Exists That Is Not Shiva: Commentaries on the Shiva Sutra, Vijnanabhairava, Gurugita, and Other Sacred Texts
Swami Muktananda

The Philosophy of Sadhana: With Special Reference to the Trika Philosophy of Kashmir
D. B. Sen Sharma

The Splendour of Recognition: An Exploration of the Pratyabhijinahrdayam, A Text on the Ancient Science of Soul
Swami Shantananda with Peggy Bendet

Tantra: The Path of Ecstasy
Georg Feuerstein

*The Triadic Heart of Shiva: Kaula Tantricism of Abhinavagupta in the
Non-Dual Shaivism of Kashmir*
Paul Eduardo Muller-Ortega

On Kundalini

Devatma Shakti: Divine Power
Swami Vishnu Tirtha Maharaj

*Eastern Body, Western Mind: Psychology and the Chakra System as a Path to
the Self*
Anodea Judith

Kundalini Rising
Various authors, edited by Sounds True

Kundalini: The Arousal of the Inner Energy
Ajit Mookerjee

Kundalini: The Secret of Life
Swami Muktananda

Play of Consciousness: A Spiritual Autobiography
Swami Muktananda

The Sacred Power: A Seeker's Guide to Kundalini
Swami Kripananda

The Serpent Power: The Secrets of Tantric and Shaktic Yoga
Arthur Avalon (Sir John Woodruffe)

The Soul's Journey: Guidance from the Divine Within
Lawrence Edwards

PERMISSIONS CREDITS

Excerpt from *When Grapes Turn to Wine: Versions of Rumi,* translated by Robert Bly. ©1986 Robert Bly. Used with author's permission.

Excerpt from *The Essential Rumi,* translated by Coleman Barks. ©1995 Coleman Barks. Used with author's permission.

Excerpt from the Penguin publication *The Subject Tonight Is Love, 60 Wild and Sweet Poems of Hafiz,* ©1996 & 2003 Daniel Ladinsky. Used with author's permission.

Excerpt from the Penguin publication *The Gift, Poems by Hafiz,* ©1999 Daniel Ladinsky. Used with author's permission.

Excerpt from *Rumi: One-Handed Basket Weaving,* translated by Coleman Barks. ©1991 Coleman Barks. Used with author's permission.

Excerpt from *Indian Mystic Verse,* translated by Hari Prasad Shastri. ©1984 HP Shastri. Reprinted with permission from Shanti Sadan, London, www.shantisadan.org.

Excerpt from *The Radiance Sutras: A New Version of the Vijana Bhairava Tantra* by Lorin Roche, PhD. © Lorin Roche, Syzygy Creations, Inc, www.LorinRoche.com.

Excerpt from *The Kabir Book,* by Robert Bly. ©1971, 1977 Robert Bly, ©1977 the Seventies Press. Reprinted by permission of Beacon Press, Boston.

Excerpt from *Wisdom of the Jewish Sages: A Modern Reading of Pirke Avot,* by Rabbi Rami M. Shapiro. ©1993 Rami M. Shapiro. Used with author's permission.

Excerpts from *The Hundred Thousand Songs of Milarepa,* by Garma C.C. Chang. Copyright © 1962, by the Oriental Studies Foundation. All rights reserved. Reprinted by arrangement with Kensington Publishing Corp. www.kensingtonbooks.com.

Excerpt from *The Soul Is Here for Its Own Joy,* edited by Robert Bly. ©1995 Robert Bly. Used with author's permission.

Excerpts from *A First Zen Reader,* translated by Trevor P. Legget. ©The Trevor Leggett Adhyatma Yoga Trust. Used with the permission of the Trevor Leggett Adhyatma Yoga Trust.

INDEX

Abhinavagupta, 32, 43, 114
abhangas, 227
abhyasa, 133
the Absolute, 40, 44, 220, 227, 230
accidental meditation, xii
ahamkara, 35
Al'Bastami, Abu Yazid, 90, 273
altars (for meditation practice),
   51–52
ananda, 36, 42
atman, 6, 33, 34, 35
attention, 248–49
Aurobindo, Sri, 180
Avot, Pirke, 252
Awareness, 1, 6, 30–31, 120–21,
   129, 155–57, 252, 311
   and awareness (small a), 30
   exercises, 30–31, 41, 121–22, 225
   see also Consciousness; the Self
Ayurveda, 317

Baal Shem Tov, 80
the Beloved, 20, 22, 288, 298
Bhagavad Gita, 6, 65, 260, 270,
   292, 314
bhakti, 66
bhastrika pranayama, 202–3
bhavas, 80–82, 210
bindu, 219
the body
   exercises, 58

cleansing, 52
the four states and the four
   bodies, 189–232; causal body,
   211–16; physical body, 191–
   98; subtle body, 198–211;
   supracausal body, 217–32
   invoking spirit of, 57
   kriyas, 195–98
   posture, 74–77
   and *vairagya,* 135
The Book of Privy Counseling, 29
Brahmabindu Upanishad, 332
Brahman, 32
breakthrough program, 263–88
   lifestyle of the program, 268–74
   making the commitment,
      265–67
   preliminary practices, 276–79
   schedule of the program, 274–76
   setting aside time, 267–68,
      274–76
   week 1, 279–84
   week 2, 284–87
   week 3, 287–88
breathing, 95–100, 256
   bellows breathing (*bhastrika
      pranayama*), 202–3
Brihadaranyaka Upanishad, 198
Buber, Martin, 231
Buddhist traditions and quotes,
   26, 32, 34, 126, 142, 152, 168,
   262, 330
   Vajrayana Buddhism, 58, 307

Catherine of Genoa, 226, 227
causal body, 211–16
chakras, 187–88, 193, 195, 306, 307
   ajna chakra, 196
(Swami) Chidvilasananda, 286
chit, 36, 143
chiti, 32, 115, 143, 144
chitta, 32, 143, 144
cleansing (as meditation preparation), 52
Consciousness, 4, 6, 26, 32, 127, 139, 158–61, 311
   and consciousness (small c), 30
   exercises, 102–3, 105
   field of your consciousness, 18–20, 100
   pure Consciousness meditation, 101–5
   see also Awareness; the Self

daily life and meditation, 245–62
Dame Ragnell story, 148–50
Dante, 16
deliberate meditation, xii
desire, 135–38
dharana, 87, 242, 282
Dharmakaya, 32
Dickinson, Emily, 101–2
distractions, 27, 141
duality/non- or anti-duality, 110, 111–12, 113, 116, 141, 147, 175, 218, 230, 311

Eckhart, Meister, 27, 110, 226
ego, 35, 36, 134, 199, 285–86, 304, 322, 323, 327

Eliot, T. S., 83, 96
emotions, 18–19, 154–58, 260
   exercises, 157–58, 261
   fear, 322–26
emptiness, 221, 228, 330, 332, 333
exercises
   aware of your awareness, 30–31
   body, mind, and heart helping you turn inside, 58
   breathing out thoughts, desires, and emotions, 137–38
   coming into the heart, 257
   connecting to Spirit in the universe, 56–57
   consciousness dissolving intense emotions, 157–58
   experience of love, 45–46
   exploring the inner heart, 18
   God at the end of the exhalation, 100
   God is in everything, 229
   invoking the guru, 67–68
   invoking the *shakti's* guidance, 177–79
   light of Awareness, 225
   mantra as light, 94–95
   mantra practice with *So'ham,* 91–92
   meditation practice inquiry, 275
   nothingness, 333
   open ocean of space, 105
   processing emotions, 261
   pulsation in your consciousness, 102–3
   pulsation of energy, 173–75
   seeing the mind as *shakti,* 151
   space between breaths, 97–98
   space between one thought and another, 39

360-Degree Awareness, 41
watch your thoughts move like
clouds, 139–40

fear, 322–26
the four states and the four bodies,
189–232
causal body, 211–16
physical body, 191–98
subtle body, 198–211
supracausal body, 217–32
Francis of Assisi, 25

goddess concepts, 146–152
see also shakti
grace, 54–69
basic forms of, 55–56
of body, mind, and heart, 57
and enlightened masters, 62–68
and a personal deity, 58–62
of the universe itself, 56–57
gurus, 58–68
definitions of, 61
enlightened masters gurus,
62–68
"Invoking the Guru" (exercise),
67–68
personal deity gurus, 58–62
sadguru, 62

Hadewijch II, 115
Hafiz, 52–53, 126
Hakuin, 246
heart, 18, 19, 26, 37, 58, 78, 79,
157–58, 288
the Heart, 97
heart rate and heart focus, 256–59
exercise, 257

heart-space, 19, 78, 79, 157–58
Hildegard of Bingen, 179, 207, 219
Hindu traditions, xvi, 45
see also yoga and yogic traditions/
practices
Hridaya, 32
Hui-Neng, 152

"I am," 227
inner attention, 248–49
the inner Beloved, 20–22
see also the Beloved
inner dialogue, 129–30

Janaka, 110–11
Jiménez, Juan Ramón, 331
jiva, 220
Jnaneshwar Maharaj, 59, 72,
218–19, 228
John of the Cross, 44, 138, 228
joy (of the Self), 42–46
journaling, 238–41
Julian of Norwich, 79, 96

Kabir, 20, 24, 37, 60, 89, 112, 185,
200, 230–31, 265
Kashmir Shaivism. See Shaivism
Katha Upanishad, 48, 50, 60
karma yoga, 13
kriyas, 195–98
Krishnamurti, U. G., 231
Kshemaraja, 95, 223, 236
Kularnava Tantra, 84
Kumagai, 262

kundalini, xvi, 129, 164–67,
214–16, 301–11
awakening of, 3–4
bhastrika pranayama, 202–3
kundalini shakti, 3, 176
literal meaning, 3
see also shakti

Lalla Ded, 87
Lao-Tzu, 23, 114, 212, 259, 320
letting go, 133–39
Lingpa, Jikme, 66

Machado, Antonio, 35, 206–7
madhya, 37, 95, 98
mahamudra, 195
Maharshi, Ramana, 17, 26, 28, 89,
107, 139, 221, 239
Malini Vijaya Tantra, 74
manas, 124
mantras, 38, 79, 82–100, 131–32,
258
breaths, 95–100
exercises, 91–92, 94–95, 97–98,
100
levels of, 85–86
practicing with, 84–85
So'ham, 90–92, 94–95, 110–11
syllables, 92–95
maya, 213
Mechthild of Magdeburg, 45
meditation
author's journey to, 1–4, 16–17
accidental, xii
altars, 51–52
awakening to, 1–7
benefits, 22–24

cleansing, 52
contemplation/recollection,
234–44
and daily life, 245–62
deliberate, xii
desire for, 9
distractions, 27, 141
as a duty, 11
and emotions, 18–19, 154–58,
260; fear, 322–26
as an experiment, 17
and fear, 322–26
goals, 25–26
"good" and "bad" meditation,
12, 17
and grace, 54–69
honeymoon metaphor, 6–7
honoring your practice of, 51–54
the inner Beloved, 20–22
journal, 238–41
lure of, 9–24
"meditation current," xvi
physical place for, 51
as play, 12–18
preparation, 49–62; altars,
51–52; cleansing of the body,
52; relaxation, 53–54
questions to ask yourself, 12, 14,
15–18
as a relationship, 5–7
ripening, 289–96
a roadmap of the meditation
journey, 183–232
as routine, 10–11
visions, 203–10
"we meditate to know ourselves," 5
meditation practices and techniques,
71–74
basic practices, 77–79
bhavas, 80–82

breathing, 95–100, 256
closing/ending ceremonies, 105–6; moments after meditation, 236–38
concentrative practices, 77–78
contemplative or analytical practices, 78
essence of a practice, 79–82
improving practice of, 251–55
mantras, 38, 79, 82 100, 131–32, 258; breaths, 95–100; exercises, 91–92, 94–95, 97–98, 100; levels of, 85–86; practicing with, 84–85; *So'ham,* 90–92, 94–95, 110–11; syllables, 92–95
mindfulness practice, 78
oneness practice, 109–24
posture, 74–77
pure Consciousness meditation, 101–5; exercises, 102–3, 105
resistance to meditation, 327–29
self-inquiry, 253–55
sleeping when meditating, 314–18
thought-stream navigation, 125–40
three-week breakthrough program, 263–88
see also exercises; the mind
Mencius, 47
Milarepa, 104, 145
the mind
exercises, 137–38, 139–40, 151
as Goddess manifestation, 146–51
inner dialogue, 129–30
liberating your thoughts, 141–61
purification, 130–31, 132

thought-stream navigation, 125–40
see also thoughts
(Swami) Muktananda, 29
mumukshutva, 9
Mundaka Upanishad, 64, 220
The Mystique of Enlightenment (Krishnamurti), 231

The Nectar of Self-Awareness (Jnaneshwar Maharaj), 218–19, 228
negative thoughts, 151–54

om, 219
oneness practice, 109–24, 259

Padmasambhava, 159
panditas, 112
Parama Chaitanya, 32
Paramahamsa, Ramakrishna, 227, 230
Paramashiva, 32
Paramatma, 32
Parasurama Kalpa Sutra, 85
Patanjali, 73, 87, 133, 260
physical body, 191–98
see also the body
play (role in meditation), 12–15, 16–17
Plotinus, 173, 209
posture and postures, 74–77, 191, 194, 195, 197, 198, 316
Prabhu, Allama, 201
prana, 198, 199–203

Index

Pratyabhijna Hridayam, 115–16, 236, 331–32
Presence, 20–22
pure Consciousness meditation, 101–5
purification (of the mind), 130–31, 132
purno'ham vimarsha, 29–30

questions to ask about your meditation practice, 12, 14, 15–18
quotations from
Al'Bastami, Abu Yazid, 90, 273
Aurobindo, Sri, 180
Avot, Pirke, 252
Baal Shem Tov, 80
Bhagavad Gita, 65, 270, 292, 314
Brahmabindu Upanishad, 332
Buber, Martin, 231
Catherine of Genoa, 226, 227
(Swami) Chidvilasananda, 286
Dante, 16
Eckhart, Meister, 27, 226
Eliot, T. S., 83
Francis of Assisi, 25
Hadewijch II, 115
Hafiz, 126
Hakuin, 246
Hildegard of Bingen, 179
Hui-Neng, 152
Jiménez, Juan Ramón, 331
John of the Cross, 138
Jnaneshwar Maharaj, 59, 72
Julian of Norwich, 79
Kena Upanishad, 31, 40
Kabir, 20, 24, 89, 112, 185, 200, 265

Kularnava Tantra, 84
Kshemaraja, 236
Kumagai, 262
Lalla Ded, 87
Lao-Tzu, 23, 114, 212, 259, 320
Lingpa, Jikme, 66
Machado, Antonio, 35
Maharshi, Ramana, 107, 139, 239
Malini Vijaya Tantra, 74
Mechthild of Magdeburg, 45
Mencius, 47
Milarepa, 104, 145
(Swami) Muktananda, 29
Mundaka Upanishad, 64, 220
Padmasambhava, 159
Plotinus, 173, 209
Prabhu, Allama, 201
Ramprasad, 147, 167, 169, 175, 181, 218
Rilke, Rainer Maria, 237, 290, 324
Rumi, 6, 50, 68, 254, 288, 327
Shankaracharya, 111
Shiva Samhita, 188
Shiva Sutras, 75
Shvetashvatara Upanishad, 15, 202
Simeon, the New Theologian, 223
Spanda Karikas, 156
Sun Bu-Er, 233
Suzuki, Shunryu, 13
Tauler, Johannes, 215
Teresa of Avila, 267
Tevekkul-Beg, 208
Utpaladeva, 118, 230
Vijnana Bhairava, 28, 123, 153
Yogashikha Upanishad, 191
Yoga Vasishtha, 135, 285, 295
Zenji, Dogen, 242

rahasya, 85
rasas, 210
Ramprasad, 147, 167, 169, 175, 181, 218
relaxation, 53–54
reverie, 27
Rilke, Rainer Maria, 237, 290, 324
ripening, 289–96
Roshi, Jiyu-Kennett, 331
rudra granthi, 196
Rumi, 6, 31, 50, 68, 254, 288, 327

samadhi, 90, 220, 221, 230, 236
samskaras, 129, 215
samavesha, 220–21
sat, 36
the Self, 6, 25–48, 50–51, 72
    as aware, 38–42
    and the causal body, 212
    and the ego, 35, 36
    as ever-present, 36–38
    identifying, 28–33
    as joyful, 42–46
    and meditation goals, 26–27
    and Maharshi, Ramana, 17, 26, 28
    Vedanta sages' three basic qualities of, 36
    what is the Self?, 33–48; as aware, 38–42; as ever-present, 36–38; as joyful, 42–46
    see also Awareness
self-inquiry, 253–55
Shaivism, 29–30, 32, 43, 55, 112–16, 119, 169, 302, 303
    and moments after meditation, 236–37

Self-realization, 230
Spanda Karikas, 89, 104
tattvas, 188
shakti, xv, xvi, 147–51, 303
    exercises, 167, 173–75, 177–79
    kundalini shakti, 3, 176
    letting the *shakti* lead, 163–82
    pathways, 169–71
    see also kundalini
shambhavi mudra, 248
Shankaracharya, 111
Shiva, 220
Shiva Drishti (Somananda), 110
Shiva Sutras, 75, 83, 85
Shiva Samhita, 188
Shvetashvatara Upanishad, 15, 185, 202
Simeon, the New Theologian, 223
sleeping when meditating, 314–18
So'ham (*mantra*), 90–92, 94–95, 110–11
Somananda, 93, 110
Spanda Karikas, 89, 156
the Spirit, 56–57
subtle body, 198 211
Sufi traditions, 20, 44
    Hafiz, 52–53
Sun Bu-Er, 233
supracausal body, 217–32
surrendering, 180–82
sushumna nadi, 195
Suzuki, Shunryu, 13

Taittiriya Upanishad, 43
tandra, 206–10

tanmatras, 199

tantra and *tantric* traditions, xv–xvii,
78, 160–61, 187, 302, 342n3
  bindu, 219
  Kularnava Tantra, 84
  the mind, 141–42
  om, 219
  pulsation, 104
  Shiva Sutras, 75, 83, 85, 226
  Vijnana Bhairava, 28, 45, 78

tapas, 131–32

tat, 34

Tauler, Johannes, 215

Teresa of Avila, 224–25, 267, 330

tetragrammaton, 86

Tevekkul-Beg, 208

thoughts
  as consciousness, 144–45
  inner dialogue, 129–30
  liberating your thoughts, 141–61
  negative thoughts, 151–54
  purification (of the mind),
    130–31, 132
  thought-stream navigation,
    125–40

three-week breakthrough program,
263–88
  lifestyle of the program, 268–74
  making the commitment,
    265–67
  preliminary practices, 276–79
  schedule of the program, 274–76
  setting aside time, 267–68,
    274–76
  week 1, 279–84
  week 2, 284–87
  week 3, 287–88

Tripura Rahasya, 96, 222

the Truth, 259–60

Tukaram, 81–82

turiya, 218, 224, 226

Upanishads, 34
  Brahmabindu, 332
  Brihadaranyaka, 198
  Mundaka, 64, 220
  Katha, 48, 50, 60
  Kena, 31, 40
  Shvetashvatara, 15, 185, 202
  Taittiriya, 43
  Yogashikha, 191

Utpaladeva, 118, 230

vairagya, 133–39

Vedanta, 36, 110, 113, 160, 218,
253
  Tripura Rahasya, 96

Vijnana Bhairava, 28, 45, 78, 105,
123, 153

visions, 203–10

vital energy, 199–203
  Viveka Chudamani, 223

YHWH, 86

yoga and yogic traditions/practices
  bhastrika pranayama, 202–3
  chakras, 187–88
  karma yoga, 13
  kriyas, 195–98
  laya yoga, 227
  Parasurama Kalpa Sutra, 85
  prana, 198, 199–203
  shambhavi mudra, 248
  tapas, 131–32
  yoga nidra, 206–9

Yoga Sutras (Patanjali), 73, 87,
133, 260
Yoga Vasishtha, 127, 135, 285,
295
see also kundalini; tantra and
tantric traditions
Yogashikha Upanishad, 191

Zenji, Dogen, 242
zen traditions and quotes, 34, 142,
152, 168, 262
see also Buddhist traditions and
quotes

ABOUT THE AUTHOR

Sally Kempton has spent more than forty years practicing, studying, and teaching meditation and spiritual philosophy, including two decades as a swami, or monk, in one of the Saraswati orders. A former New York journalist and chronicler of the downtown culture of the 1960s and 1970s, she lived and studied for many years with her guru, an enlightened Indian master. She received an extended training in the texts of Indian yogic philosophy, including Kashmir Shaivism, and has been teaching since the early 1980s. Sally writes a regular column, "Wisdom," for *Yoga Journal,* and teaches workshops, teleclasses, retreats, and spiritual trainings around the United States and in Europe. She is known both for her ability to lead students into deep states of meditation and for her gift for making yogic wisdom applicable to the situations of daily life. Her website is sallykempton.com.

ABOUT SOUNDS TRUE

*S*ounds True is a multimedia publisher whose mission is to inspire and support personal transformation and spiritual awakening. Founded in 1985 and located in Boulder, Colorado, we work with many of the leading spiritual teachers, thinkers, healers, and visionary artists of our time. We strive with every title to preserve the essential "living wisdom" of the author or artist. It is our goal to create products that not only provide information to a reader or listener, but that also embody the quality of a wisdom transmission.

For those seeking genuine transformation, Sounds True is your trusted partner. At SoundsTrue.com you will find a wealth of free resources to support your journey, including exclusive weekly audio interviews, free downloads, interactive learning tools, and other special savings on all our titles.

For a free guided meditation with Sally Kempton plus two free downloads and our latest catalog, please visit SoundsTrue.com/bonus/Sally_Kempton_meditation.